i

The California
Employee Survival Handbook

By David Hurd
Attorney at Law

Introduction by Mark Strom
Attorney at Law

Illustrations by Tim Sinnwell
(916) 729-5535

The Chapter on Workers' Compensation by
Ronald Bremen
Attorney at Law

Third Edition
First Printing
Pro Per Publications, Placerville, California

The California
Employee Survival Handbook

Published by:
Pro Per Publishing
3172 Airport Road
Placerville, California 95667
Voice (530) 626-9518
Fax (530) 626-6727

First edition 1994
Second edition 1995
Third edition 1998
ISBN 0-9639232-2-6

http://www.hspan.com/employmentlaw

Disclaimer

This book is intended for educational purposes only. This book is not meant to provide legal advice, nor does this book recommend that the reader take any particular course of action with regards to the topics discussed herein. For legal advice on a particular matter the author advises the reader to consult a licensed attorney.

In most instances all references to women is meant to include men and all references to men is meant to include women. I have taken best efforts to be gender neutral, where appropriate.

I have deliberately omitted references to specific code sections and court decisions in my efforts to make this handbook easy to understand and use. I have made best efforts to ensure that the rules as set forth are current and correct. However, each individual's situation is unique and the reader is urged to use this book only as a general guide and to further investigate all matters that may pertain to him or her personally.

The reader is further advised to always bear in mind that the laws protecting you are not perfect, are sometimes unenforceable in the "real world," and that care and discretion must be utilized in any situation where your source of income may be placed at risk.

Lastly, the reader is advised that the law changes unexpectedly, frequently and sometimes, substantially. If the reader has any questions regarding potential changes in the law, the reader should contact the publisher to determine whether or not the reader's edition is current. Updated editions will be published as necessary. See our special update offer for our readers on the next page.

A Special Note to Our Readers

It is our goal to make **The Employee Survival Handbook** as useful to you as we possibly can. We welcome comments, ideas or suggestions from you, our readers.

Do you have questions that haven't been answered?
What else would you like to know?
Do you have work experiences that you would like to share to help other readers?
Please jot down your ideas or questions and mail to:

The Employee Survival Handbook
Pro Per Publications
3172 Airport Road
Placerville, CA 95667
(530) 626-9518

UPDATE DISCOUNT:

If you purchased the first or second edition of *The California Employee Survival Handbook* and you would like to be updated to this third edition, enclose the original order page or title page (not a copy) from the first edition with $13 and I will ship you this new third edition.

This edition will also be eligible to be updated to future editions at a discount off the retail price.

Acknowledgements

This book is dedicated to the working men and women of California.

I also dedicate my efforts to my father, Josh Hurd, a most wonderful man, to my mother, Margaret Hurd, and my wife Kelee.

I would like to express my sincere thanks to Mr. Simon D. Reyes, former Assistant Chief of the Division of Labor Standards Enforcement (DLSE) for the State of California for his input in the preparation of the first edition of this book.

I would also like to thank Mr. Dale Louton, former Senior Deputy Labor Commissioner of the Division of Labor Standards Enforcement, Sacramento, California for his help and suggestions in the preparation of the first edition of this book.

...To my few but good ol' friends Ray, Paul, Tom and...

"...and last, all you have to do to qualify for the job is pass this simple physical agility test..."

See PHYSICAL OR MEDICAL EXAMS on page 98.

Table of Contents

Chapter Five 269
Employee Rights on the Job 269

Introduction

OUR OBJECTIVE

This book is written to inform you of your legal rights as an employee and most importantly, it is intended as a practical guide to recovering your money, whether by yourself or with the help of an attorney.

This book is dedicated to helping you obtain what is yours. Nothing more. For most of us, all we have to sell to make our living are our skills, both mental and physical. If you are not fully and fairly paid for your labors you have simply lost out, and your life that remains is shorter and poorer than it should otherwise be. This book is the tool you will use to ensure that you receive all that is due you, no more, and perhaps, if it is not too late, that which is past due. This book tells you about the laws that affect you, and suggests how to present your wage case before the Office of the Labor Commissioner. This book is your legal guide, your coach and your advisor.

This introduction is critical for one reason—to teach you how to improve your chances of winning an employment lawsuit before you ever contact a lawyer. Preparation of your "case" before you are terminated can be critical. Read on.

You have been treated unfairly by your boss, and maybe even fired for an improper or false reason, and now you want to sue.

We will begin by telling you that your ability to sue your employer is more complicated than you probably realize. The purpose of this section is to give you a better understanding of this legal relationship, and begin to answer the question: can I sue?

Probably the most important thing to remember when thinking about suing your employer is that you usually cannot sue your employer for just being a jerk. The second thing to keep in mind is if you quit your job, you will probably not be able to sue. (and win) This is discussed in detail in the section titled "constructive discharge" on page 81.

A lawsuit for wrongful termination or discrimination or harassment has very specific legal requirements, so the unfairness you must have experienced needs to fit into one or more specific legal areas. Most all employment disputes may be broken down into three legal areas: contract, statutory, and "other" (what lawyers call common law claims).

"Contract" means that you have rights provided to you by the nature of the contract or employment agreement that you and your employer voluntarily entered into when you were hired.

"Statutory" refers to employment rights provided you by the government in the form of laws passed to protect you, without regard to any agreement you may have made with your employer.

You may have rights to sue based on what is called the "common law." This refers to law that has evolved from decisions handed down in earlier cases.

Contract Cases and the "At-Will" Employee

The courts recognize the employment relationship as basically a contract between you and your company. If you are either treated unfairly or fired unfairly, the question is whether the unfairness was a breach of the employment contract you have with your employer. This rule of employment as a contract, oddly, does not apply to anyone who works for the government or who works in a private job as a member of a union. These employees cannot sue for a breach or violation of contract. These exceptions are discussed below.

The first question to answer is, what do we mean by a contract of employment? A contract is simply a legal requirement to keep a promise. For example, your employer promises to pay you a certain wage or salary —that's a part of everyone's employment contract.

Since your employment is basically a contract, you know what the terms are, right? Wrong. Most people have no clear idea of the terms of their employment contract. Unlike buying a car or a house, where you actually sign a sales document understood by everyone to be a contract, most employment contracts are not written down and signed by the parties.

Most employees do not sign a written employment agreement when they are hired. The kind of contract most employees have with their employer is what is called an oral contract. Oral contracts are made between people verbally, and usually nothing is written down and actually signed by the parties. Oral contracts are enforceable in court. The problem is, of course, by the time you get to court, you and your employer have a much different memory of what the oral contract was between you. You say you were promised work so long as you did a good job, your employer says, "We never agreed to that." Your problem now becomes proving the terms of your verbal or spoken agreement.

There are a number of ways to prove the terms of an oral employment contract, depending on your particular situation. If you believe that you were fired or demoted in violation of company policies, for example, you may have a case for breach of your employment agreement. You should seek legal advise about your specific situation. The advice should be free.

Another concept that we will introduce now is the concept of the "at will" employee. What is an "at-will" employee? An "at-will" employee is any employee that can be fired or demoted at any time for any reason, or no reason at all, as long as the reason given is not against the law, such as, discrimination (discussed below). If you are like most people, when you are being hired you don't want to discuss the reasons where you might be fired. But unless you have an understanding with your employer at some point that you can only be fired or demoted for a good reason, or according to company guidelines, you are probably an "at-will" employee and can be fired at any time. So most people who don't talk about termination at the time they are hired are basically permitting themselves to be fired for no reason at all later on.

Lawyers for California employers have been educating companies in recent years on how to make sure their employees are "at-will" employees. Lately, many California employees have been required by their employers to sign documents which say something like "I understand that my employment is "at-will," and can be terminated at any time for any reason." Very often nowadays you will find this type of language in an employment application. This may or may not make you an "at-will" employee, depending on several other factors. If you feel your employer has fired or demoted you, and it was in violation of a promise or understanding you had with the company, you should seek legal advise without delay.

Supposedly, you can always refuse to sign documents which say that you are an "at-will" employee, but then you may not get the job, or you may be fired. The courts assume that since an employment relationship is a contract, you as the employee have the right to bargain for whatever terms you want. If a company is trying to hire you, and really wants you, you should discuss with them the reasons for which you could be fired, and get a clear understanding that if you are hired, you would not be an "at-will" employee.

As we all know, most people do not have the economic power to bargain for equal terms in an employment agreement —you either accept the job with all the company's policies and rules, or you don't get the job. It usually doesn't hurt to at least ask if you can cross out the "at-will" language in the employment application, or ask if you can add that you will have a job so long as you do good work.

If you feel you have been fired or demoted because you refused to sign an "at-will" document at work, you should seek legal advise about your specific situation.

No Contract Protection for Government and Union Employees

If you work for the federal, state or local government, your

employment is controlled by statute, not contract, and so government employees never have a contract right to their job. If you work
in a job where you are represented by a union, you too have no
contract rights to your job, but your union does! It is strange, but
true. If you are in a job where you are represented by a union, whether
it is in private business or in government, you have fewer rights in
court to sue your employer than a non-union employee, because
you have no contractual right to your job. The union has a contract
called a "collective bargaining agreement" with the employer, which
the union can decide to enforce with such things as grievances and
arbitration. But you, as an individual employee, have no right to sue
your employer because your employer has broken the contract with
the union—not you. Suing your union is possible under certain serious circumstances, and you should seek specific legal advise, or
contact the U.S. National Labor Relations Board to file a complaint
(in the case on non government employees).

**Statutory Cases: Discrimination, Harassment, Retaliation,
Public Policy, and "Whistleblowers"**
        In addition to the right to sue under "contract," the law gives
employees rights through various statutes —the laws that are made
by the Legislature or through ballot initiatives. These claims can be
made by any employee, and in most cases, any applicant for a job.
We will provide a brief introduction to your rights to sue for discrimination, harassment, termination in violation of public policy,
and retaliation for "whistleblowing." Each of these topics will be
discussed again in detail later in this book.

Discrimination
        Both California and federal law prohibit discrimination in
employment. Generally, California law provides the employee with
more protection than the federal laws. The primary California law
prohibiting employment discrimination is called the Fair Employment and Housing Act ("FEHA").
        Legally, discrimination means something very specific. It
means that as an employee or as an applicant for a job, no employer
can make a negative decision about your right to work for them

because of your race, religious creed, color, national origin, ancestry, physical disability, mental disability, medical condition, martial status, sex (gender), or sexual orientation so long as you qualified for the job.

So, if you feel that you were fired, not promoted, denied a job, or paid less because of your race, religious creed, color, etc., you may be a victim of employment discrimination.

Harassment

Harassment, like sexual harassment, is a little different from discrimination. Discrimination is about the employer making some decision about your job based on things like race, religious creed, color, etc. But harassment is more about being criticized, ridiculed or singled out because of your race, religious creed, color, national origin, ancestry, physical disability, mental disability, medical condition, martial status, sex (gender) or sexual orientation. Harassment includes, for example, the African-American employee who finds racially insulting cartoons in his locker, or the foreign-born employee who is called racially insulting names by his supervisor.

Sexual harassment seems to be the most common form of harassment in the courts. There are two types of sexual harassment: (1) where you are actually touched in a sexual way, treated, or spoken to in a way that puts you into a sexually hostile environment, and (2) where your boss says he, or she, will do something for you if you provide a sexual favor for him, or her, in exchange. To be illegal, the harassment usually must be directed at you. In other words, you usually can't sue unless you are the one being harassed, and not just a witness to someone else being harassed. You do not have to be fired to sue. In 1997, in Sacramento, an African-American woman received nearly $900,000 from a jury for racial harassment she suffered as a state employee. She had never been terminated.

To this day, the courts still don't have a very clear idea how bad the harassment has to be before you can sue. It's pretty clear that one act of harassment is not enough to be illegal, unless it is extremely serious, like a rape in the case of sexual harassment. The courts usually require a pattern of harassing conduct before it will say that the harassment is illegal. You also usually need to prove to the court that the harassment has somehow affected your ability to do your job properly.

Retaliation

Retaliation is connected to discrimination and harassment. As an employee, you have the right to complain if you feel you have been discriminated against or harassed on the job. The law prohibits employers from retaliating or punishing employees for complaining about discrimination or harassment. The protection against retaliation applies if you complain to someone in the company, such as human resources, or a public authority or government agency outside the company, such as the California Department of Fair Employment and Housing.

So, if you feel that you have been discriminated against or harassed on the job, and you complain about it, you cannot be fired or demoted because of your complaint. This is true even if you cannot prove that you were, in fact, discriminated against or harassed, so long as you reasonably believed that you were being harassed, etc.

Public Policy

It is illegal to terminate you, even as an "at-will" employee, if the termination is in violation of "public policy." Wrongful termination in violation of public policy is where an employee is fired in one of four situations: (1) for refusing to do something that is illegal; (2) for doing something that is legally required; (3) for doing something that the employee has a legal right to do; or (4) for reporting that the employer has done something illegal.

(1) An example of an employee fired for refusing to do something illegal is where, for instance, an accountant is fired by her employer for refusing to "cook the books" to make the business look better. If you are an accountant and you believe that "cooking the books" is unethical, your employer cannot make you choose between your professional ethical duty and your job.

(2) An example of an employee fired for doing something that is legally required is where, for instance, you are an employee at a meat packing plant and you are fired for cleaning plant equipment. Your plant manager wants to save money, and does not permit you to take the time to properly clean the equipment in compliance with USDA laws. You insist on cleaning the equipment, and you are fired for being "insubordinate."

(3) An example of an employee fired for doing something that he has a legal right to do is where, for instance, you are fired for taking time off to attend a school conference for your son or daughter.

(4) The forth type of wrongful termination in violation of public policy is also known as "whistleblowers."

A "whistleblower" is an employee who has reasonable cause to believe that his employer is violating federal or state law, and reports the employer to the proper authorities. "Whistleblowers" are protected by several state and federal laws, which are outlined below.

Labor Code section 1102.5 says that no employer can prevent an employee from reporting the employer to a law enforcement agency where the employee has reasonable cause to believe that the employer is in violation of federal or state law. Labor Code sections 6310 and 6311 protect employees who report the employer for to OSHA for workplace safety violations.

Government Code section 12653, protects all employees from being fired or demoted for reporting to authorities information about a false claim being made to the State of California.

Government Code section 8547 protects employees of the State of California who, as part of their official duties reports, "improper government activity," such as, corruption, bribery, theft or misuse of government property, gross misconduct, incompetency or inefficiency.

False Claims Act 31 USC sec. 3730(h) (referred to as "qui tam" actions), allows any employee to sue his employer for being discharged or demoted for reporting a false claim to the federal government. The classic example is the person working for a defense contractor, who discovers that his employer is overcharging the government for its products, and is fired for reporting it. Under the "qui tam" statutes, the whistleblower is normally entitled to receive 15-18% of the money saved by the government as a result of the "whistleblowing" activity. A word of advice, consult a lawyer before disclosing the information to the government because the government may try to avoid paying you your 15% later on. (It figures)

"Other" Cases —(Major Common Law Claims)—Defamation

More commonly known as "slander" or "'libel," defamation of character is the law that protects your reputation from being damaged by lies that could hurt you financially. The most common occurrence in employment law is in connection with job references. For example, if you were terminated from a job because your employer thought you were stealing, but the employer has no evidence, and your employer tells people who call to check your references that you are a thief, then you may have been defamed. You could sue, even though you were an "at-will" employee.

Another example of defamation is if you are looking for a job, and you have a have some evidence that a former employer is saying untrue and negative things about you. To soften the blow of the negative reference, you tell employers you are interviewing with that your former employer is going to give you a negative reference, but the former employer's statements are not true. You have been defamed if you do not get the job even though you are the one who actually tells your prospective employer about the negative reference. This topic is discussed in detail later in this book.

WHAT TO DO WHILE YOU ARE STILL WORKING

Many people who are wrongfully terminated know that they are going to be fired before it actually happens. There are things you can do to help prepare your case before you are fired.

File with the Department of Fair Employment and Housing (FEHA) — If you feel that you have been discriminated against or harassed based on your race, religious creed, or any of the other factors discussed above, you should consider filing a "charge of discrimination" with the California Department of Fair Employment and Housing. You do not have to wait and be fired. And if you are fired after you have filed a charge of discrimination, you may have a retaliation case in addition to a discrimination or harassment case.

If you decide to file a complaint with FEHA, I recommend that you obtain the help of an employment lawyer to fill out the complaint form. Believe it or not, if you fail to check the right box, or fail to check a box that you do not regard as important, or necessary, you have a good chance of ruining your case. You may lose a lawsuit for that missed box. Be careful, and get some help from an employment lawyer.

Diary — A diary can be very helpful. Just writing down in a calendar book specific events or incidents will help you remember what happened and when. This is especially important in harassment cases. A court case for harassment or wrongful termination may take several years to get to a trial. You want to have a record of what happened to you as it is happening. What happens and what is said at meetings, for example, is very often where important things occurs. You should always try and make notes of a meeting immediately after the meeting is concluded. In a termination meeting, you may even want to take notes during the meeting.

Dear Diary; Today I was told by...

Documents — Gather or copy documents that may relate to your case- Important documents are those written or printed materials which have to do with the terms of your employment, and anything that will verify what happened to you. Do not make any marks or notes on your documents, use a post-it if you want to note something about a particular document on the document itself. Important documents may include:

1.   Any employee handbooks, personnel regulations, grievances, evaluations, and letter of termination;

2. Your personnel file. Although you employer is not obligated by law to give you a copy of your personnel file, you do have a right to "inspect" your personnel file. While you do not have a right to a copy of the whole personnel file, you do have a right to any document in the file which you signed. If your employer will only a l - low you to inspect your personnel file, you can take notes of what you see. Your notes should include the name of the documents you find in the file, the date of the document, and a brief summary of what the document says. Resumes on file with your employer;

3. Any and all memos, letters, notes, concerning the events which lead to your termination;

You should not try to get confidential documents or documents that you know you are not supposed to see without the assistance an attorney.

WHAT TO DO AFTER YOU HAVE BEEN FIRED

A Chronology — A chronology is a tightly knit and comprehensive list of events in the order they happened, listed by the date of each event or occurrence. It includes the names of persons involved, your thoughts and feelings about the events and termination. The chronology should begin with the events which eventually led to your termination, and include your period of unemployment, efforts to find a new job, and your present employment status, and whether you are making mare or less money in a new job.

It is best not to do the chronology in one sitting. A good technique is to make an outline of the major events, and then after a couple of days, go back to the outline, and fill in the details. After doing a first draft, put the chronology aside again for a couple of days, and go back to add and revise it as necessary. The chronology is a narrative of facts, and words like "harassment," and "stress," are meaningless without a factual description of what actually occurred. Try to refer in your chronology to important documents that you have seen or have in your possession.

Documents —Even after you have been fired you can obtain the important documents discussed above. Ask friends at work to get you documents you need. In addition to the documents already listed, you should also gather the following documents: have had to pay out after termination, especially for items which had been provided by your former employer, such as, medical and dental insurance.

Unemployment Insurance —If you have been wrongfully terminated, you should file a claim for unemployment insurance benefits. If your benefits are denied, go to the unemployment office immediately, in person, and file and appeal. Keep a copy of the appeal application. You should cooperate with representatives from the unemployment office, and if asked why you were terminated, give the unemployment office the real reason why you believe you were terminated, and not necessarily what the company has given as the reason.

Talking To Others About Your Case —In some instances, you may be contacted by other governmental agencies, such as, the Department of Fair Employment and Housing or the EEOC. You may cooperate with these governmental investigators. However, please keep me informed of any such contacts.

It is important that you do not discuss your lawsuit with anyone except your lawyers. While everything said between you and your lawyers is strictly confidential, you may lose your right to confidentiality if you discuss this matter with friends and family. Even if you contact certain persons such as your former co-workers to obtain information or documents for your use, you should avoid telling them that you plan to sue, and never answer questions about your case without your lawyer's knowledge.

Your Doctors and Therapists —You may want to see a health care provider, such as, a psychologist or licensed therapist, in connection with any emotional distress because of your harassment or termination. If you do, remember that the. Doctor's records will be part of any court case -- you lose any confidentiality you have in those records when you sue.

State Court or Federal Court?

I won't go into detail about what determines whether your lawsuit goes to federal court or state court. You should know that there are differences between federal and state courts. Federal jury trials are decided by six jurors, and the decision must be unanimous by all six people for you to win. In state courts, the jury is comprised of twelve people, but you only need to have nine of the twelve agree with you to win the case.

Federal judges use different rules to decide whether to throw a case out without permitting you to have your lawsuit decided by a jury. Most people do not realize, that in civil law, unlike criminal law, you do not have an automatic right to have your "day in court," heard by a jury. In nearly all civil cases, you must first convince a judge that your case has enough merit, (is good enough) that you should be permitted to take your case before a jury to let them determine if you win or lose. If the judge decides that your case is legally defective, he or she can throw it out and you lose, before you even get to a jury. This is what is called a summary judgment motion. If you are the plaintiff, and you defeat the defendant's motion to have your case thrown out in a summary judgment proceeding, you are then entitled to have a trial in front of a jury.

Now that we have provided you with these tips about how to gather information, and prepare in advance, we will begin our discussion of the laws that affect you in your job.

"What, you mean I have rights?!!..."

Chapter One

SUING YOUR EMPLOYER IF YOU ARE FIRED OR DEMOTED

DISCRIMINATION AND HARASSMENT

Federal and state laws prohibit all forms of employment related discrimination based on such characteristics as race, national origin, sex, sexual orientation, pregnancy, color, religious beliefs, political beliefs, arrests not leading to a conviction, physical or mental disabilities, or age. California prohibits discrimination based on marital status.

In California, discrimination based on race, religious beliefs, creed, color, national origin, ancestry, physical handicap, medical condition, marital status, age, or sex, is prohibited by the Fair Employment and Housing Act (FEHA). FEHA applies to most employers with at least five full or part-time employees. For purposes of sexual harassment or other forms of harassment, all employers are covered. In other words, all employers are subject to liability for employees that suffer harassment of any kind, even if the employer has only one employee.

You should understand that the FEHA provides a broader scope of protection in some areas than under the federal ADA law. If you think that you might be facing discrimination or harassment, consult with an employment attorney.

AMERICANS WITH DISABILITIES ACT (ADA)

The ADA is a federal law designed to end discrimination in employment, housing, public accommodations, education, transportation, and communications for Americans who suffer from physical, or mental disabilities. Our analysis will be limited to employment-related provisions of the ADA. We will begin our discussion of this very broad based act with a listing of definitions.

EMPLOYERS COVERED

The ADA applies to all employers with fifteen or more employees. The term "employer" includes all private employers as well as state and federal governmental employers, employment agencies, labor unions, or employee-owned businesses.

The ADA prohibits discrimination by agents of the employer, such as doctors, employment recruiters, managers, or training personnel. Employers are required to post notices of the provisions of the ADA in the workplace.

If your employer has more than four employees, but fewer than fifteen, you are covered under the California law prohibiting discrimination based on your **physical** disability(s). You are not protected under the ADA unless your employer has at least fifteen employees (beginning July 26, 1994). If you face discrimination based on your **mental** disability(s), your employer must have at least fifteen employees before your are entitled to protection under either California law or the ADA. If your employer has fewer than five employees, you are not protected under California or federal law from discrimination resulting either from your mental or physical disabilities. However, I would always advise that you consult with an employment attorney before you make the decision that you have no rights, or no protection under the laws.

PEOPLE PROTECTED

The ADA extends protection to three groups of disabled individuals:

1) Those individuals who have a physical or mental impairment that substantially limits one or more of the major life activities.

2) Those individuals who have a record of such an impairment, or
3) Those individuals being regarded as having such an impairment.

What is significant about these three classifications is that protection is extended to individuals who suffer from discrimination as a result of conditions that no longer exist, and to those who suffer discrimination based solely on the perceptions and attitudes of other people towards them. In other words, if your employer perceives you as being disabled, then you may be, but remember, that the disability must affect a "major life activity.".

For example, if you are a reformed alcoholic and you no longer drink, you may still be disabled under this law. Your employer may not discriminate against you because of your history of drinking or his fear that you may relapse and begin drinking again. Alcoholism is a protected disability under the ADA.

If you are recovered from cancer or heart disease, mental illness, or any other disabling disease, you are covered under the ADA. You are covered if you have a physical condition such as a club foot, or a disfiguring scar, or you are HIV positive and your employer or prospective employer regards the condition as a disability.

The ADA includes attention deficit disorder as a protected disability. Attention deficit disorder deserves attention by employers and employees because it is so difficult to diagnose with certainty and the symptoms are so diverse. An employee with attention deficit disorder may demonstrate poor judgment, they may tend to act impulsively and are readily argumentative; they are very poor at completing job tasks and are easily distracted or forgetful; they don't work within job guidelines and seem to be in a daze. Under the ADA employers may be required to make reasonable accommodations to these employees, rather than fire them. Reasonable accommodations may include anything from simplifying and repeating instructions, to modifying their work areas to provide fewer distractions, to altering their entire job performance procedures.

Any reasonable accommodations required by the ADA must

be provided at the employer's expense.

The ADA protects job applicants, and job candidates, as well as current employees. "Job applicants" are job seekers who have not been extended a conditional offer of employment. "Job candidates." are job seekers who have been extended a conditional offer of employment but are not yet confirmed employees.

Being disabled does not guarantee that you will be protected under the ADA. You may or may not be entitled to protection depending on the job that you hold or seek. The determination whether illegal discrimination has occurred will depend on the relationship between the type of disability possessed by the applicant or employee and the essential skills and qualifications required for the job. See QUALIFIED INDIVIDUAL below.

MAJOR LIFE ACTIVITY

Protected disabilities are those that limit a "major life activity." Major life activities include such things as breathing, eating, hearing, learning, lifting, reaching, seeing, sitting, speaking, standing, talking, walking, and working. Any condition that impairs your abilities in any of the activities listed, is a disability. Some conditions that you might not normally think of as disabilities are listed below.

COMMON DISABILITIES COVERED

The we have seen, the ADA defines "disability" as a current condition, a past condition, or the appearance of a condition. Some of the conditions covered are:
- AIDS
- Alcoholism
- Attention deficit disorder
- Chronic fatigue syndrome
- Depression
- Diabetes
- Epilepsy
- Heart disease
- High blood pressure
- Learning disorders

- Mental retardation
- Migraine headaches
- Schizophrenia
- Sensitivity to cigarette smoke
- Stress disorders
- Past illegal drug use

"Disability" does not cover temporary conditions, such as broken bones, pregnancy, flu infection, or excessive weight due to overeating. "Disability" does not include personality traits such as bad temper, irritability, compulsive gambling, current illegal drug use, kleptomania, compulsive lying, any sexual behavior disorder, including, but not limited to homosexuality, bi-sexuality, pedophilia, exhibitionism, transvestitism, or voyeurism.

Economic or social disadvantages such as poverty, illiteracy, or inability to speak English are not "disabilities."

Current illegal drug use is not a protected disability. However, past illegal drug use may be protected. The use must have extended beyond casual use. It must have been serious enough to be regarded as a dependency which limited a major life function. If you were drug dependent enough to limit one of your life functions you would be covered under the ADA. However, if you lied about the drug use on a job application or in an interview the lie would make you "otherwise unqualified" for the position and you would not be entitled to protection.

DISCRIMINATION DEFINED

The ADA prohibits any employment related act that discriminates on the basis of a protected disability. The ADA broadens protection to the disabled by describing seven specific types of conduct that constitute discrimination:

1) Limiting, segregating, or classifying a job applicant or employee in a way that adversely affects his or her opportunities.
2) Participating in a contractual relationship that has the

effect of discriminating against a disabled employee or applicant.

3) Utilizing standards, criteria or methods that discriminate against the disabled or perpetuate such discrimination.

4) Excluding or denying equal job benefits to an individual as a result of his or her association with a disabled person.

5) Not making reasonable accommodations to a disabled applicant or employee or denying employment to a disabled applicant or employee in order to avoid making reasonable accommodations to the disabled applicant or employee.

6) Using qualification standards, employment tests or other selection criteria that screen out the disabled, unless the standard, or tests is shown to be job-related and is consistent with business necessity.

7) Failing to select and administer tests in a manner that ensures that the test accurately reflects the skills, or aptitudes it is meant to measure, rather than simply reflecting the deficiencies of the disabled applicant.

QUALIFIED INDIVIDUAL

The ADA imposes a crucial limitation on disabled individuals seeking protection. The ADA states that employers are prohibited from discriminating against "qualified individual(s) with a disability because of the disability of such individual..." This means that, besides being disabled, the person suffering discrimination must first demonstrate that he or she is "qualified" in order to be entitled to protection from discrimination.

What does "qualified" mean in this context? "Qualified" means a person who "with or without reasonable accommodation, can perform the essential functions of the employment position."

The EEOC provides some guidance in defining "qualified."

Qualified individual with a disability means an individual who satisfies the requisite skill, experience, education, and other job-related requirements of the employment position such individual holds or desires, and who, with or without reasonable accommodation, can perform the essential functions of such position.

A qualified individual is one who can perform the essential functions of a job. OK. Who determines the essential functions of a job? If the employer has no written description setting forth the essential functions, the courts or juries will make those determinations in each particular case. If the employer does have a written job description;

> consideration shall be given to the employer's judgment as to what functions of a job are essential, and if the employer has prepared a written description before advertising or interviewing applicants for the job, this description shall be considered evidence of the essential functions of the job.

Therefore, in order to be protected under the ADA you must be prepared to show that you are,
(a) qualified and,
(b) are able to perform the essential functions of the job with or without accommodation for your disability.

If the employer has drafted a written description setting forth the essential functions of the job, those functions are final unless a court or governmental agency determines that the essential functions are not really essential, or tend to unfairly discriminate against the disabled.

The EEOC provides a recommended two-step analysis of discrimination under the ADA.

> The first step is to determine if the individual satisfies the prerequisites of the position, such as possessing the appropriate educational background, employment experience, skills, licenses, etc. If you

do not satisfy the entry requirements, you do not qualify to receive accommodation for your disability under the act.

The second step is to,

determine whether or not the individual can perform the essential functions of the position held or desired, with or without reasonable accommodation.

One of the problems with EEOC's two step analysis is that the employer is not obligated to make reasonable accommodations for those disabled individuals who do not meet the initial qualification standards that the employer has established for the job. In order to avoid hardship under the two step definition, the EEOC has stated in its *Technical Assistance Manual* that,

if an individual meets all the prerequisites except those that he cannot satisfy because of his disability and the individual alleges disability discrimination, the employer must show that the prerequisites that screened him out are job-related and consistent with business necessity.

In other words, the employer has to show that the screening process is not itself discriminatory. It does not relieve the disabled person from having to satisfy the hurdle of the first test.

To summarize, in order to be protected from discrimination you must;

1) Have a protected disability.
2) You must be "qualified" for the job. This means that you have the proper skills, licenses, or other prerequisites required by the position.
3) You must be able to perform the essential functions of the job without accommodation for your disability. If there is a written statement setting forth the essential functions, that will control, unless the required functions are found

to be discriminatory.

4) If you cannot perform the essential functions without accommodation for your disability, the employer must determine whether reasonable accommodations would permit you to satisfactorily perform the essential job functions.

5) If the employer performs all reasonable accommodations, and you still cannot perform the essential functions you may be denied employment and it is not unlawful discrimination.

6) If you can perform the essential job functions with reasonable accommodation, you are protected and denial of the position based on your disability would be illegal.

7) You are also protected if the employer commits any of the prohibited acts described in DESCRIMINATION DEFINED.

You may still be "qualified" even if you are declared disabled and you qualify to collect disability benefits under SSI.

REASONABLE ACCOMMODATION

The act requires employers to make "reasonable accommodations" to disabled applicants and employees, unless the accommodation "would impose an undue hardship on the operation of the business." "Reasonable accommodation" includes:

1) making existing facilities used by employees readily accessible to and usable by individuals with disabilities.

2) job restructuring, part-time or modified work schedules, reassignment to a vacant position, acquisition or modification of equipment or devices, appropriate adjustment or modification of examinations, training materials or policies, the provision of qualified readers or interpreters, and other similar accommodations for individuals with disabilities.

As we pointed out earlier, the costs for any required accommodation must be borne by the employer. The employer cannot require an employee to pay for any accommodations his or her disability may require.

UNDUE HARDSHIP

Undue hardship is an action requiring significant difficulty or expense, when considered in light of the factors set forth below:

1) The nature and cost of the accommodation.
2) The overall financial resources of the facility; the number of people employed there, and the impact of the accommodation on the facility. A facility is a part or a branch of a business. A business may own and operate many facilities.
3) The overall financial resources of the business; the overall size of the business with respect to the total number of employees and the location, type and number of facilities, and
4) The type of operations of the business, including the structure and function of the work force, and the relationship between the facility and the business.

CALIFORNIA LAW

California has it's own version of the ADA. Like the ADA, California law makes it illegal to discriminate against persons with physical disabilities, and against persons with mental and learning disabilities.

If the employee or applicant falls within the protection of the act the employer or prospective employer is prohibited from discriminating against that person and the employer has the affirmative duty to make reasonable accommodations for the person's known physical or mental disability.

The employer is not required to make accommodations that would create a hardship for the business operation. Nor is the employer liable for discrimination if the disabled employee or applicant is unable to perform the essential duties of the job after the employer has made reasonable accommodations, or cannot perform the essential duties without endangering his or her own health or welfare, or the health and welfare of others.

California law differs from the federal law, in that, in California the employer has to actively attempt to come up with an accommodation for a disabled employee, without the employee having to first make the request. If the employer has no knowledge that the employee is disabled, then the employer has no duty to actively seek out an accommodation, but if the employer knows that the employee is disabled, then the duty attaches. The safe thing for the employee to do is always ask for an accommodation in writing. As in so many other situations, the employee may be well advised to consult with an employment attorney, even at this early stage where the employee is still employed and only seeking to obtain an accommodation, and not even contemplating a lawsuit.

DEFINITIONS UNDER CALIFORNIA LAW

MENTAL DISABILITY

"Mental disability" means any mental or psychological disorder such as mental retardation, organic brain syndrome, emotional or mental illness, or a specific learning disability. The act specifically excludes compulsive gambling, kleptomania and current illegal drug use.

PHYSICAL DISABILITY

This means "any physiological disease, disorder, condition, cosmetic disfigurement, or anatomical loss" that,

a) affects one or more of the following body systems: neurological, immunological, musculoskeletal, special sense organs, respiratory, including speech organs, cardiovascular, reproductive, digestive, genitourinary, hemic and lymphatic, skin, and endocrine; **and**

b) limits an individual's ability to participate in major life activities.

The act includes language specifically designed to include victims of HIV/AIDS. Such victims are regarded as having a physical disability for having a disease that has no current disabling effect but which later may develop into a disabling condition.

EMPLOYER

For purposes of discrimination based on a mental disability, the act applies to employers employing fifteen or more people. For purposes of other types of illegal discrimination, such as physical discrimination, the act applies to employers employing five or more people.

ESSENTIAL DUTIES

California follows the EEOC position in this definition. The employee or applicant must be able to perform the essential duties of the position in question before he can allege discrimination based on the disability. What constitutes "essential duties" will be a jury question in each case, but factors used in determining them are:

1) whether the reason for the existence of the position is to perform the duty.
2) whether there is a limited number of employees who can perform the duty.
3) whether the duty is highly specialized such that the person performing it was hired for his or her expertise, or ability to perform the duty.
4) the employer's judgment as to which duties are essential.
5) the written job description prepared to advertise the job.
6) the amount of time spent performing the duty.
7) the consequences of not requiring the performance of the duty.
8) the terms of any applicable collective bargaining agreement.
9) the work experience of past employees in the job.
10) the current work experience of employees in similar jobs.

REASONABLE ACCOMMODATION

"Reasonable accommodation" is said to include the same things mentioned above in the federal definition such as, modification of the existing business facilities to make them accessible to the disabled, job restructuring, part-time or modified work schedules, reassignment to vacant positions, or placement in an entirely new job, etc. See the federal definition above for a complete listing.

UNDUE HARDSHIP

Again, the California definition is an exact copy of the federal. For a complete definition see the federal definition, above.

DISCRIMINATION—BURDEN OF PROOF

In certain types of discrimination cases, such as racial, sexual or disability discrimination where the plaintiff is a member of an historically disfavored group, the courts utilize certain presumptions in favor of the plaintiffs in order to make the proof of discrimination easier.

For example, if a racial discrimination case is brought by a member of an historically disfavored group, such as African-Americans, the plaintiff need only show that he or she applied and qualified for a job, that he or she was rejected, and that the employer then sought out other applicants not within the disfavored group. The plaintiff has shown an apparent (prima facie) case of racial discrimination, and the burden shifts to the employer to prove that he was not motivated by racial discrimination. If the plaintiff is passed over in favor of a member of a racially favored group, discrimination is presumed to have occurred, unless the employer can prove otherwise.

The plaintiff is not required to present direct evidence of racial hatred, such as racial slurs, or statistical evidence of unequal treatment. The plaintiff is permitted to present any evidence that would tend to establish in the mind of the jury that it was more likely than not that the treatment experienced by the plaintiff was the result of racial discrimination.

The same presumption occurs in favor of women who have suffered from pay discrimination by receiving less pay than a man under similar circumstances. If a woman can establish that her job duties involve equal skill, effort and responsibility as a man's, that she faces the same working conditions, and that she earns less than the man, she has established an apparent case for wage discrimination and will win unless the employer can come forward and convince the court that there are justifiable reasons for the discrepancy.

AGE DISCRIMINATION

It is illegal to discriminate against an employee based on the employee's age if that employee is forty years old or older.

A recent California Supreme Court case has held that age discrimination violates a fundamental public policy. This means that all employers, no matter how few employees they have, are prohibited against discriminating against a person over the age of 40.

However, oddly enough this same Supreme Court ruled that it is not illegal for employers to discriminate against older employees on the basis that the older employees are more expensive than younger employees! In other words, if your employer wants to get rid of you because your salary is too high, he or she can now do so on that basis. I presume that the Supreme Court decision does not affect the current rule that an employer cannot terminate an older employee in order to deny them their rights under a qualified pension plan. See also, the section PROMISE OF GOOD FAITH AND FAIR DEALING on page 71.

It is illegal to advertise or otherwise state a preference for employees under the age of 40, or otherwise attempt to limit applications by people over the age of 40. If pre-employment physical or medical examinations are required (see JOB INTERVIEWS) the employer cannot require an applicant over the age of 40 to satisfy more stringent standards than are required of any other applicants.

In an age discrimination case the plaintiff need not show that the employee that replaced him or her was equal or inferior in qualifications. You may still have a case of age discrimination even though the replacement employee was better qualified! The replacement employee does not need to be especially young; he may be over forty years old himself, so long as he is substantially younger than the plaintiff.

If you are terminated as part of a reduction in work force, you will be required to present evidence that your termination was motivated by age discrimination. You may present circumstantial, statistical, or direct evidence that would tend to establish that age discrimination was present. The difficult case occurs when many employees are terminated at once. If just you, or a select group of older employees, are terminated in the work force reduction, you will have a much easier time showing age discrimination. If you are terminated as part of a reduction in work force you will need more evidence of discriminatory intent than a passing comment.

In one reduction in work force case a comment by a supervisor that, "We don't necessarily like gray hair," in combination with another written comment against older employees by a senior management executive, was not enough to establish a prima facie case of age discrimination.

It is illegal to reduce or terminate an older employees benefits in excess of the any difference attributable to increased cost. In other words, if an older employee costs the employer 5% more for health coverage, the employer can only reduce the older employee's benefit coverage by an amount necessary to lower the cost of coverage by 5% and no more. An employer cannot simply eliminate an older employee's entire benefits because they are "too expensive," nor may the employer eliminate the employee because the employee is associated with higher health costs. The reduction in coverage must be no more than required to offset the increase in associated cost.

Your employer must have at least five employees in order to pursue administrative remedies under FEHA. In addition the FEHA administrative remedies do not apply to nonprofit corporations, or religious associations. However, if your employer has fewer than five employees you are entitled to pursue an age discrimination case in the civil courts, based on broad public policy against age discrimination.

If you are over the age of 40 and you are asked to sign a release promising not to sue the employer as part of a retirement package, you must be given 21 days to consider the proposed release before you sign it, and an additional 7 days after you sign the release to back out of the agreement if you so desire. If you are part of a group of employees being asked to resign early, you must all be given at least 45 days to consider the proposal. If you sign the proposal, it does not become effective until the eighth day after signing.

An enforceable waiver or release must be written in common language understandable by the ordinary person.

An employee that signs an enforceable release must be promised something more than what that employee was already entitled to receive before signing the release. An employee must benefit from signing a release.

A release does not waive any rights or claims that may arise after the date of signing the release.

A release must state that it releases your rights under the Older Worker's Benefits Protection Act.

Prior to signing a release, the employee must be advised in writing to consult with an attorney.

Protection against age discrimination does not extend to employees of state military departments, such as the California National Guard.

WEIGHT DISCRIMINATION

It is illegal to discriminate in employment based on a physical handicap. The crucial question is, what is a protected physical handicap? Until recently, obesity was regarded as a physical disability entitling the obese person to protection if the employer regarded the fact of obesity as a disability and refused employment opportunities as a result. However, the Supreme Court has now held that obesity not caused by a genetic or other physiological disorder is not a protected disability, and as a result, fat people who cannot establish a physiological basis for their weight are not entitled to protection under FEHA. Obesity caused by the voluntary behavior of the obese employee is not protected.

How does this decision affect the principle that illegal weight discrimination can result from the employer's perception? The ADA makes perception the test as to whether excessive weight is a disability. If your weight is perceived as a disability by your employer, then the ADA holds that you are disabled. See ADA on page 16 for a further discussion.

Under the California decision the Court has placed the nearly impossible burden on the employee to establish that the employer perceived the obesity as resulting from physiological causes. Given the fact that employers are banned from making pre-employment inquiries about the existence, nature, and causes of an employee's disability, it makes one wonder how the employee or failed applicant is expected to come by this information. Is the employer supposed to be stupid enough to say "I can't hire you because I think your obesity is caused by physiological factors."? Not likely. The end result is, if your obesity cannot be proved to be caused by a physiological medical condition, the California court decision forces the victims into federal court.

RACIAL DISCRIMINATION

An African-American plaintiff may be subjected to racial discrimination, even if the discrimination results from the actions of another African-American person. In other words, African Americans can suffer racial discrimination from another African American.

You do not need to be an African American to be a victim of racial discrimination. Racial discrimination does not depend upon a scientific definition of race, and any non-Caucasian may be a victim of racial discrimination.

It is not racially discriminatory to "band" employees test scores, whereby small differences in test scores are ignored and minority employees are given preferences over other employees within the same "band" or range of scores.

It is illegal for an employer to discriminate against an employee because of the employee's interracial relationship.

RELIGIOUS DISCRIMINATION

It is illegal to discriminate in employment based on religious beliefs. To have a recognized religious belief, three components must be present:

1) The belief must be based on a theory of "man's nature or his place in the universe."
2) The belief must not merely be a personal preference

but has an institutional quality about it, and
3) The belief must be sincere.

An interesting example of personal behavior that did not
qualify for religious protection under the requirements set forth
above, was the person who insisted that eating Cozy Kitten cat food
was central to his religious beliefs and should therefore be protected
religious activity. The Court disagreed. Eating cat food is not protected religious activity. This illustrates the point that belief, expressed in bizarre or socially unacceptable behavior, will not be protected.

Protected religious beliefs include "non-belief." Therefore,
it is illegal to discriminate against atheists.

Employers are required to accommodate the employee's religious beliefs if accommodation does not impose an undue hardship on the employer, the employee's request is reasonable, the request does not infringe on contractual rights or duties, and other
employees are not discriminated against as a result of the accommodation.

Examples of accommodations that might have to be made
on behalf of an employee's religious beliefs include scheduling interviews, educational, or promotional exams so that they do not conflict with religious observances. If an employee's religion prohibits
the payment of union dues, the employer cannot force the employee
to maintain membership in a union.

Religious discrimination occurs if the employer provides
benefits, such as time off for employees of a particular religious
persuasion, without providing the same benefits for employees of
different religious persuasions, or employees with no religious beliefs.

Religious discrimination occurs if the employer punishes
religious beliefs by conditioning employment or employment benefits on the curtailment or abandonment of the religious beliefs.

Religious institutions, such as religious schools, newspa-
pers, or associations are permitted to discriminate in employment in
reference to religious belief. Religious discrimination is permitted
when religious belief is a bona fide occupational qualification.

Grooming or clothing rules that act to discriminate against religious groups may be illegal if the policies do not promote a business necessity and the employer refuses to attempt to make reasonable accommodations to the employee's religious obligations. For example, if female employees are required to wear short dresses and the employee's religion prohibits the wearing of short dresses, the employer may be required to accommodate the employee or be prepared to establish a "business necessity" defense for not doing so.

In religious discrimination cases, if the employee can show that he or she had a bona fide religious belief, that the employer was notified of this belief, the belief conflicted with a job obligation or duty, and the employer discriminated against the employee as a result of the belief, then the employer must show attempts to accommodate the employee's religious practices.

PREGNANCY DISCRIMINATION

Pregnancy discrimination is regarded as a form of sexual discrimination. All private employers with at least five employees are prohibited from discriminating against pregnant employees. The employees need not work full-time to be included in the five employee minimum.

It is illegal to discriminate against a female employee because of pregnancy, childbirth, or related medical condition. Discrimination includes refusal to hire, promote, refusal to select for training programs leading to promotion, reduced compensation or increased hardship in the terms, conditions or privileges of employment.

The employer must provide up to four months of pregnancy leave, if requested. The employee seeking the pregnancy leave must provide the employer with reasonable notice of the anticipated commencement of the leave and the anticipated duration of the leave needed. The employer must provide the same employment benefits for pregnant employees that the employer provides for other employees who are similarly restricted in their abilities to work. See also EMPLOYEE LEAVE on page 292.

The employer must permit the female employee to transfer

upon her request to a less strenuous or hazardous position for the duration of the pregnancy if the employer ordinarily has a policy, practice, or labor agreement to make transfers of temporarily disabled employees. Even if the employer has no such policy, it will be required if the woman's physician advises it and the transfer can be reasonably accommodated.

An employer cannot force a pregnant employee to go on leave or switch to a less strenuous position unless the employer can prove that the employee was disabled or that there is another valid occupational defense to the required leave.

Any transfer that requires the employer to create a position, or discharge an employee, or transfer another employee with more seniority, or promote an unqualified employee, is not required of the employer.

Pregnancy (and related conditions) discrimination is regarded as a form of sexual harassment. This means that the doctrine of strict liability may apply, as well as imposing liability on virtually all employers, no matter how small the company may be.

MARITAL STATUS DISCRIMINATION

It is illegal for an employer to discriminate based upon the marital status of the employee. This includes and employee's status as married, unmarried, divorced, widowed, or single, or otherwise. The employer cannot normally ask the employee about his or her marital status. An employer can ask an employee whether that employee is married to another employee at the same place of employment, but only to ensure that no problems develop with regards to morale, safety, supervision, or to ensure that the marriage relationship does not otherwise disrupt the work environment.

An employer that provides fringe benefits for the spouse or dependents of married employees does not discriminate against those employees without a spouse or dependents.

An employer cannot require a married woman to use her husband's surname.

SEXUAL DISCRIMINATION

It is illegal to discriminate against a person based on their

"Don't even ask."

sex. Employers are required to recruit applicants of both sexes equally and it is improper to classify jobs as either male or female in type.

If a job requires physical agility or strength the employer must permit all applicants the opportunity to demonstrate their ability to perform the functions of the job without regard to their sex. An employer cannot rely on height or weight standards that discriminate against women.

SEXUAL ORIENTATION DISCRIMINATION

It is illegal in California to discriminate against employees or job applicants based on their sexual orientation or their perceived sexual orientation. Complaints regarding sexual orientation discrimination are handled by the Labor Commissioner's Office, (the California Division of Labor Standards Enforcement) rather than the Department of Fair Employment and Housing (DFEH). Practically speaking, if you have a complaint for discrimination due to your homosexuality or lesbianism or appearance thereof, you are entitled to file a complaint, either with the Labor Commissioner's Office or in the courts, at your choosing. You are not entitled to the procedures and remedies available under the DFEH.

You do not have to be homosexual to be protected under the law prohibiting sexual orientation discrimination.

If you have been subjected to sexual orientation discrimination you must file a complaint within thirty days of the discriminatory act if you wish to proceed before the Office of the Labor Commissioner. Once you file a complaint with the Labor Commissioner's Office, the Commissioner's Office will assign a Discrimination Complaint Investigator (DCI) to investigate your case. The investigator will be responsible for contacting the parties and potential witnesses involved and, if appropriate, seek a settlement on your behalf. If no settlement is possible, then the investigator will make a written recommendation and present it to the commissioner for review. The DLSE will either accept the recommendations of the DCI (called a Facts and Conclusions report) and issue a decision based on the investigator's report, or schedule a hearing to take place on the matter. The hearing procedures are the same as set forth above regarding wage claim hearings. However, unlike other wage and hour matters, there is no right to "de novo" proceedings on appeal.

Note that, like sexual discrimination, the California courts take the "reasonable victim" standard in assessing the propriety of employer or employer-agent conduct. In other words, the court evaluates the severity of the employer's conduct from the perspective of a "reasonable homosexual." If a "reasonable homosexual" would consider the conduct sufficiently severe or pervasive so as to alter the conditions of employment and create an abusive working environment, then the plaintiff has established an apparent case of sexual orientation harassment. See the discussions on SEXUAL HARASSMENT on page 47.

Employers must also be cai ʾil about discriminating against an employee based on the employee's sexual practices. This is particularly true because of the employee's constitutional right to privacy in California. An employer who terminates an employee because that employee engaged in off-duty prostitution, or adultery, or who associated with persons of unusual sexual preferences, would be taking a serious chance of violating the employee's right to privacy. See also OFF-DUTY ACTIVITIES.

RACIAL OR NATIONAL ORIGIN DISCRIMINATION

Employment discrimination based on race or national origin is illegal. Below are examples of activities and policies that have been held to be discriminatory in these areas:

1) English-Only Rules: Rules which require employees to speak only English at all times are generally illegal as being discriminatory against national origin. Rules which require the speaking of English under particular employment situations may be legal if it results from business necessity.

Recently, cases have come up in which English-only rules were imposed to prevent employees from using their bilingual abilities to harass or slander other employees who did not understand their (non-English) native language. In one case the

English-only rules were upheld because under the circumstances of the case there were no non-English speaking employees and the restriction did not create a hostile work environment for the bilingual employees who were so restricted. The restriction was upheld even though it went against the long standing rule against such restrictions by the EEOC.

2) **Accent discrimination:** It is illegal to discriminate against an individual based on his or her accent or manner of speaking. In order to justify any such restriction the employer would have to demonstrate that the accent interfered with job performance.

3) **Height or Weight Requirements:** Such requirements may be illegal if the rules are so drafted to disproportionately disqualify individuals of a particular national origin or race. The restrictions must not discriminate against women. In order to be proper such restrictions must also further legitimate non-pretextual business interests.

4) **English fluency requirements, aptitude tests, and citizenship requirements or preferences:** All of the above may be illegal if they are either; designed or implemented in order to discriminate against individuals based on their race or national origin, or are applied unevenly amongst all applicants, or tend to disproportionately disqualify applicants of a particular race or national origin. In addition, such qualifying factors must be justified by legitimate business necessity.

JOB INTERVIEWS
The proliferation of anti-discrimination and harassment laws have made many aspects of employer behavior filled with risk.

Passage of the Americans with Disabilities Act (ADA) has made it illegal for an employer to discriminate against the disabled in interviewing for employment, or in the conditions of employment when hired.

The ADA has also made the interview situation a minefield for the employer. Not only must the employer phrase questions with extreme care, an employer is required to make reasonable physical accommodations for a disabled applicant. This may include such things as providing sign readers for the mute or deaf, or providing exams in braille for the blind. Due to the serious potential risks from any questions relating to disabilities, we shall discuss ADA related issues separately below.

In general, there are a number of areas of inquiry that should be carefully avoided by the hiring personnel in the employment interview.

It is illegal to ask about any disability possessed by the applicant!
It is improper to make any non-job-related inquiry, either verbally or through written questions on an employment application form, that relates to sex, sexual orientation, religious creed, color, national origin, ancestry, physical disability, mental disability, medical condition, or marital status.

The employer can only request information if the request is directly related and pertinent to the position being applied for, or directly related to a determination of whether the applicant would be a danger to his or her own health or safety, or the health or safety of others. For example, the following types of questions are illegal:

• Do you think that homosexuality is a
  disorder?
• Do you think that religious employees

are any more or less reliable than non-religious employees?
- What is your marital status?
- Do you have children? If so, what are your arrangements for child care?
- Do you plan to have children?
- Are you a US citizen? If not, what is your country of origin?
- How old are you?
- Have you ever been arrested?
- Do you eat a number of snacks at regular intervals throughout the workday?

It is illegal to request a photograph from an applicant as part of the application process.

JOB INTERVIEWS AND THE ADA

With the passage of the ADA the employer is prohibited from asking the applicant about such topics as his or her medical history, prior worker's compensation or health insurance claims, past treatment for alcohol or drug use, history of mental illness, or history of job absenteeism that resulted from illness or physical disabilities. Any such questions contained within a psychological profile questionnaire, or any other type of screening questionnaire are also illegal. If you have had a job interview where you faced questions regarding any of the above topics, it is likely that the questioning was improper.

The employer is only permitted to ask certain questions relating to a protected disability after the applicant has been offered a position and has become a "job candidate." Questions relating to disabilities prior to being given a job offer, are illegal. I will discuss this further below.

The ADA prohibits questions relating to disabilities. For Example, if you are interviewing applicants for a telephone lineman position which requires the applicant to be able to climb utility poles, and an applicant who appears to have an artificial leg applies for the position, the employer is prohibited from asking such questions as,

"Are you disabled?" or

" Have you lost your leg?" or

" How did you lose your leg?" or

" Do you think your loss of a leg will impair your ability to climb telephone poles?"

All of these types of questions involve an inquiry into a disability or the extent or nature of a disability. These types of questions are prohibited.

The employer is permitted to ask,

"This job requires you to climb utility poles. Can you climb utility poles with or without reasonable accommodation?"

What is the difference, you ask? The difference is, the second question focuses on the applicant's abilities in reference to performing the job functions. The other questions focused on the disability. Without a prior conditional offer of employment, the employer cannot ask anything about general or specific disabilities, period! The employer is not permitted to ask about the existence, nature, or severity of any disability, even if the applicant's disability would make it unlawful to hire the applicant for the position! For example, it is illegal to hire anyone with epilepsy for a position as an interstate truck driver. However, it is also illegal to ask the applicant,

"Do you have epilepsy?"

In fact, the employer may not ask,

"Do you have any disability that would prevent you from performing the job?"

All the employer is permitted to do is ask,

"Can you perform the functions of this job with or without accommodation?"

The employer can also ask,

" Do you possess a valid drivers license or Department of Transportation Certification required to drive a truck?"

If the applicant says no, the employer may ask.

"Do you plan to obtain the necessary licenses?"

The employer is also permitted to ask,

"Why don't you have the required license?"

The way the questions are phrased is very important. The employer can ask about the applicant's abilities to perform the job functions, but the employer is not permitted to ask about the applicant's disabilities or inabilities to perform the job functions.

The employer is required to offer the applicant reasonable accommodation to all job duties required by the position.

The employer is permitted to ask the applicant if he or she can perform specific job functions required by the job. However, be careful! The employer is not permitted to ask the applicant how the applicant expects to perform those job functions. That is regarded as inquiring about a disability, and is improper.

May the employer ask the applicant to demonstrate how the applicant would perform the required activities? Yes, however, the applicant is entitled to request a reasonable accommodation before the applicant is required to make the demonstration. If the employer is unable to reasonably accommodate the applicant, the applicant is entitled to describe to the employer how the applicant would perform the job duty with the reasonable accommodation. The applicant is not required to attempt to perform the activity without the reasonable accommodation.

The employer is not permitted to ask the applicant if the applicant will require reasonable accommodation to perform the functions of the job. For example, the employer may not ask the applicant with the artificial leg,

"Will you need any sort of reasonable accommodation or special equipment to perform the job duties?"

Furthermore, if the applicant volunteers information regarding a disability, and states that he or she will need a reasonable accommodation to perform the duties of the job, the employer is prohibited from asking what type of accommodation may be required by the applicant.

Follow up questions about an applicant's disabilities are strictly forbidden. For example, suppose the applicant states that he or she has attention deficit disorder or ADD. The employer is forbidden from asking anything about the disorder, or inquiring about what may be required to accommodate the applicant in minimizing the effects of the disorder until after the employer makes an offer of employment to the applicant. The employer is only permitted to ask what may be required to make a reasonable accommodation if the applicant states that a reasonable accommodation will be necessary for a pre-job offer demonstration of job skills or performance.

The employer is not permitted to ask any question relating to the applicant's ability to carry out any of life's normal daily activities. For example, the employer is not permitted to ask an applicant any of the following types of questions,

"Can you stand?"

"Can you walk?"

"Do you have normal use of all your limbs?"

" Do you have any impairment of your hearing?"

" What is your corrected vision?"

The ADA holds that these and similar questions about the average persons ability to perform normal life activities lead to improper inquiries about disabilities and are therefore, forbidden. Furthermore, questions which may be innocent when asked by themselves may be improper when combined with other questions. The following questions are legal if asked by themselves, but the group of questions become illegal when asked together. Basically, the line of questioning becomes illegal. It is difficult to know when the employer crosses the line.

"Do you have open skin sores?"

"Have you lost weight recently?"

"Do you have fever?"

"Do you have dark urine?"

"Do you tire easily?"

Employers are permitted to ask specific questions about above-average abilities, or special abilities not held by the general population, or specific job-related functions. This is a very dangerous and confusing area for employers as you will see by the following example.

Suppose the employer is seeking an employee whose job duties will include stacking two pound cans on shelves. The employer is forbidden from asking an applicant whether that applicant is capable of lifting and stacking two pound cans! The ability to lift and store two pound cans is regarded as the equivalent of the life activity of lifting. Any inquiry into your general ability to lift cans is regarded as a prohibited inquiry into a potential disability regarding the ability to lift.

If the physical ability required of the position goes beyond the capabilities of the average person, any inquiry is not thought to uncover information regarding disabilities and may be asked. For example, if the job requires the applicant to lift two pound cans for 12 hours a day at a high rate of speed, this is beyond the abilities of the average person and the employer may ask the applicant about his or her ability to stack cans according to those requirements.

The employer may also be permitted to ask questions relating to physical abilities if the questions are carefully worded to relate only to specific job duties. For example, where it is illegal to ask the question,

"Are you capable of lifting two pound cans?"

It is legal to ask,

"Are you capable of lifting two pound cans and placing them on five foot shelves in the order of their date of receipt?"

The second question specifically relates to the actual job duties and may be asked. The theory is, the last question focuses on the specific abilities required by the job, rather than focusing on abilities in general.

Questions which may not be asked in the pre-offer of employment stage, may be asked after the applicant has been given an offer of employment if the questions relate to determining the applicant's abilities to perform the functions of the job. The employer must also ask the question or questions to all applicants equally.

As we will see under INVESTIGATING APPLICANTS AND EMPLOYEES on page 83. the employer is prohibited from asking an applicant about his or her medical history before the applicant is offered a job. For example, the following types of questions are illegal:

- Do you have any physical or mental handicaps that will require the employer to make accommodations for you?
- Have you ever had back trouble?
- Have you ever been terminated or quit a job due to health problems?
- Have you ever been to a psychiatrist?
- Do you have any diseases?
- Have you ever attended a drug or alcohol rehabilitation program?
- How many days were you sick last year?
- How often do you need treatment for your disability?
- Have you ever taken AZT?
- If you drink alcohol, how many drinks do you generally have?*
- Do you have asthma?
- Do you take any lawful drugs?**

* The employer cannot ask if the applicant is alcoholic.
** This question may legally be asked only after the applicant has tested positive for current illegal drug use. However, see discussions regarding the limits on the employer's ability to require medical exams or drug tests.

The ban on these types of questions extends to any type of applicant questioning, including questions in job application forms.

The employer is not permitted to ask anyone else anything about the applicant that the employer is not permitted to ask directly. In other words, the employer cannot ask the family, friends, or past employer any questions that the employer could not ask himself or herself. For example, the employer cannot ask the past employer such questions as,

"Was the applicant sick often?"

"How is the applicant's health?"

"Do you know if the applicant has AIDS?"

If the applicant has not yet been given a conditional offer of employment the employer is only permitted to ask the applicant if he or she is capable of performing the essential functions of the job that he or she is seeking.

The employer is permitted to write down the essential functions of the job and ask the applicant if he or she can meet those requirements. For example, a position with a cable company may require that the employee be able to lift sixty pounds, climb utility poles and ladders, legally drive a car or van, and work regularly on weekends. If the employer sets forth the essential functions of the job, the employer may then inquire of the applicant to determine if the applicant can meet those functional requirements. For example, the following questions are permissible for the cable job:

• Do you possess a valid California driver's license?
• Do you possess all licenses required for this job?
• Would you be able to work regularly on weekends?
• Are you physically able to perform the
   requirements of the position?

Once the applicant is given a conditional job offer and the applicant is now regarded as a "job candidate," the employer is permitted to require the job candidate to undergo a physical or medical examination. The employer must still be careful to give the exam to **all** candidates equally. The information from the exam must be kept in a separate, confidential file, and the results of the exam must be used only for their legally permissible purposes of evaluating the candidate's suitability for the job.

Physical agility tests, or a physical fitness tests are not medical exams. These types of tests measure abilities, not disabilities, and are therefore properly required as pre-offer exams. If the tests scientifically measure the applicant's biological or physiological response to physical activities, then the exam is medical. For example, if the employer takes a measurement of the applicant's blood pressure, pulse or heartbeat after a physical test, such as running, the test would be medical and prohibited at the pre-offer stage of selection.

If the questioning or the medical exam screen out the applicant the employer must be able to demonstrate that the requirements which excluded the applicant are job-related and consistent with business necessity. The employer must also be able to demonstrate that the job duties cannot be performed by the applicant even with reasonable accommodation.

Under our example of the cable job, the employer is permitted to require the job candidates to demonstrate their abilities to drive a van, climb poles and ladders, and lift and carry heavy objects. Post-offer medical inquiries and exams are permissible when they are job related and necessary for legitimate business reasons, or they are related to a voluntary employee health program and the employee consents to the exam. Once again, medical exams are permissible if they are job related, and result from business necessity. It is unclear what is required of the employer to demonstrate "business necessity."

If an employer asks an applicant about prior job experience as a qualifying factor for employment, the employer must also take into consideration any volunteer or non-paid work performed by the applicant.

It is generally unlawful to test for AIDS without the prior written consent of the person to be tested.

SEXUAL HARASSMENT

Sexual harassment is regarded as a form of sexual discrimination. Before 1994 sexual harassment was only applicable within the context of the employment relationship. Now, however, sexual harassment may be found in the fiduciary relationship between a provider of professional services and the client. The new statute applies the concepts of sexual harassment to the attorney-client relationship, doctor-patient, priest-penitent, teacher-student, or any number of situations where you have a relationship of trust between the professional and the client. Our discussions of sexual harassment will use traditional employer-employee terminology, but remember that the concepts are now equally applicable to the professional-client situation, or even within the student-teacher relationship.

Traditionally there are two distinct types of sexual harassment.

The first type occurs when an employer or manager conditions continued employment or an employment benefit on the employee's engaging in some sort of sexual behavior, commonly described as the granting of sexual favors. This type of sexual harassment is known as *"quid pro quo,"* which means "something for something."

The second type of sexual harassment is commonly described as a sexually hostile work environment. This occurs when the work environment is so severely or pervasive abusive, hostile or offensive that the conditions upon which you were employed are altered by the offending behavior.

Quid pro quo harassment is committed by an employer, manager or supervisor against a subordinate employee, whereas "hostile work environment" harassment may be committed by anyone, including co-workers, subordinates, independent contractors, or even customers.

Sexual harassment is defined by the Federal Equal Employment Opportunity Commission (EEOC) as:

> Unwelcome sexual advances, requests for sexual favors, and other verbal or physical conduct of a sexual nature constitute sexual harassment when submission to such conduct is made either explicitly or implicitly a term or condition of an individual's employment, employment decisions affecting an individual, or has the purpose or effect of unreasonably interfering with an individual's work performance or creating an intimidating, hostile or offensive working environment.

The California Fair Employment Commission (FEHC) defines sexual harassment as:

> 1. Verbal harassment, *e.g.*, epithets, derogatory comments or slurs upon the basis of race, religion, color,

national origin, ancestry, physical disability, medical condition, mental disability, marital status, sex or age (if over 40);

2. Physical harassment, *e.g.*, assault, impeding or blocking movement, or any physical interferences with normal work or movement when directed at an individual (on the basis of sex, race, national origin, etc. as above);

3. Visual forms of harassment, *e.g.*, derogatory posters, cartoons, or drawings (on the basis of sex, race, national origin, etc. as above); or

4. Sexual favors, *e.g.*, unwanted sexual advances which condition an employment benefit upon an exchange of sexual favors.

The FEHC definition of sexual harassment is much broader than the sample EEOC definition. Verbal sexual harassment includes not only sexual comments, but racial slurs, slurs based on physical disabilities, etc. sexual harassment includes physical abuse, or the threats of physical abuse. For example, it may be sexual harassment to grab an employee's arm and shake them and yell at them.

The concept of sexual harassment has been expanded to prohibit any behavior which imposes unequal workplace burdens on a person because of the person's sex. Sexual harassment also includes harassment based on pregnancy, childbirth, or related medical condition.

REASONABLE VICTIM STANDARD

The prospects of winning a sexual harassment suit were significantly increased in California with the adoption of the "reasonable victim" standard in such cases. Under prior law a victim had to establish that the behavior or environment complained of constituted harassment as viewed by a "reasonable person." The court rejected the limitations imposed by the "reasonable person" test, choosing instead to focus on what was actually offensive to the victim. The Court recognized that behavior a man might find inoffensive or even complimentary, could be frightening to a woman. Under the "reasonable victim" standard the court attempts to analyze the behavior from the victim's perspective and use that perspective to determine the propriety or impropriety of the behavior in question.

The "reasonable victim" standard is also applied in sexual orientation cases where the victim is a homosexual or a lesbian and the applicable standard becomes what a "reasonable homosexual or lesbian" would find offensive, etc.

If the victim alleges conduct that would, for example, lead a reasonable woman to feel that the working environment has been altered by the behavior, then the victim has made an apparent case for harassment.

A recent case involving quid pro quo (or "something for something") harassment made clear the risks to management in these types of cases. In a case involving a supervisory postal employee and a junior female employee who was pressured into having sexual relations with the senior employee, the court held that liability could be found where the harasser either intended to harass, or the victim reasonably perceived the conduct to be harassment. The court expanded the potential for liability even further by holding that the demand for sexual favors did not need to be explicit, but could be inferred from the behavior of the supervisor. Liability can be found by looking at the connection between the promise of job benefits and the request for sexual favors.

UNWELCOME CONSENT

You may consent to the sexual requests or demands of the harassing party and still be a victim of sexual harassment. The issue is not whether or not you consented to the behavior but whether you "welcomed" the behavior. This is a very important concept to understand. Generally, the courts hold that if the victim did not instigate or solicit the behavior, then the victim's willingness to go along with the behavior does not mean that the victim "welcomed" it. In other words, if the victim did not make the first move, the behavior is probably not "welcome." Generally, if the sexual talk, activities, or whatever, are started by someone else, you may still be a victim of sexual harassment even if you join in or agree to the proposition(s). The concept of "welcomeness" is an attempt by the court to find out if the harassing behavior was truly offensive and undesirable to the victim. The courts recognize that many times the victim is afraid not to agree, or is powerless to refuse, or fears the loss of his or her job, etc.

HOSTILE ENVIRONMENT CLAIM

As we have seen, the hostile environment claim is much broader than the *quid pro quo* or "something for something" complaint. Unlike *quid pro quo*, the oppressive party need not be your supervisor or employer, and the victim need not be the object of the improper activity. If you are a member of a protected class, such as a woman, and you witness acts of sexual harassment against another woman, you may be a victim of environmental harassment yourself. You would have a claim for environmental sexual harassment even if the victim of the offensive behavior welcomed the behavior and did not feel that she had been harassed, and the offensive behavior was never directed against you.

The courts have held that "environmental harassment" exists when the employee:

1) was subjected to sexual advances, requests for sexual favors, or other verbal or physical conduct of a sexual nature,
2) this conduct was unwelcome, and
3) the conduct was sufficiently severe or pervasive to alter the conditions of the victim's employment and create an abusive environment.

The hostile environment claim addresses the problem of conduct that is either so extreme, though it may occur only once, or, in the alternative, occurs so frequently, that the effect of the conduct is to make the working environment oppressive for the victim.

UNINTENTIONAL BEHAVIOR

In a hostile environment claim the behavior of the oppressing party need not be intentional. Unintentional behavior can also lead to liability. Examples of behavior that may constitute environmental harassment include sexual jokes or innuendoes, displayed pornography, excessive personal interest displayed by fellow employees, unwelcome physical contact, cruel or aggravating pranks of a non-sexual nature, or failure of the employer to take immediate corrective action in response to harassing behavior. In EMPLOYER RESPONSIBILITY we will see that inadequate corrective action by the employer will be a basis for employer liability for sexually harassing behavior.

Sexual Harassment ncludes many types of non-sexual or unintentional behavior

NON-SEXUAL BEHAVIOR

In an environmental harassment claim the offensive behavior need not be sexual in nature. Note that this indicates a significant broadening of the traditional *quid pro quo* harassment concept.

Sexual harassment can now be found in behavior that is not directly sexual, such as verbal abuse, "angry" stares, talking about the victim with other employees, sabotaging the victim's auto, or behavior that simply makes the victim's work more difficult.

In an important California case, a woman police officer sued the city of Simi Valley for sexual harassment and constructive discharge for injuries she suffered as a result of being harassed by fellow male officers. She had been subjected to false statements about her work performance, she had been assigned double work assignments, excluded from group activities, and other officers mimicked her and disrupted her wedding. The court held that intimidation and hostility which is done for the purpose of interfering with the victim's work performance, is environmental sexual harassment.

The courts have held that where there are many incidents of harassing behavior against many victims, the cumulative effect of the behavior against all the victims will constitute unreasonable working conditions.

SEXUAL FAVORITISM

Favoritism based on the granting of sexual favors may be sexual harassment of the victim as well as sexual harassment of the other non-favored employees in the work force. Favoritism may result in either *quid pro quo* or environmental harassment.

The notion of trading sexual favors for advantages in advancement is the core of the *quid pro quo* claim. When employees are rewarded for cooperative sexual behavior, the environment that is created is "hostile" to the honest aspirations of the other employees in the workplace that see their opportunities for advancement made more difficult or even foreclosed as a result of the sexually charged atmosphere. The sexually hostile environment can exist for both men and women employees who find the behavior offensive.

NEPOTISM

Nepotism involves favoring relatives in employment and promotion over other, non-related employees. Nepotism is not illegal. Nor is it illegal to have anti-nepotism policies if the policies are narrowly drafted and are designed to achieve a legitimate business purpose. For example, a company may have a policy against having spouses working within the same department, or at the same site, or supervising one another. Such a policy will be upheld if it is designed to prevent favoritism and the resulting conflicts of interest. The employer's rationale for the anti-nepotism policies is very important.

ADDITIONAL CLAIMS

If you are a victim of sexual harassment you frequently have numerous other claims against the perpetrator or the employer as a result of the harassment such as, intentional or negligent infliction of emotional distress, assault and battery, reckless endangerment, negligent failure to warn or negligent hiring.

Sexual harassment which is designed to humiliate or demean an employee may be the basis for an infliction of emotional distress claim against the perpetrator and the employer.

If you quit or are terminated as a result of the harassment you may have claims for constructive discharge or wrongful termination, as well as defamation of character.

EMPLOYER RESPONSIBILITY

In a sexual harassment situation, the employer is held to a very strict code of responsibility. In California the employer is **automatically** held liable for the acts of a supervisor who sexually harasses a subordinate employee whether or not the employer knew of the sexual harassment. This is known as "strict liability."

It makes no difference that the employer did nothing wrong. It makes no difference that the employer terminated the harasser after the conduct was discovered. It makes no difference that the employer did everything he could to avoid the harassment in the first place. It makes no difference if the employer knew nothing. If a supervisor sexually harasses a subordinate employee the employer is held responsible!

Will the employer also be liable for punitive or punishment damages if the supervisory employee commits sexual harassment? Possibly. If the guilty employee is a "manager" and the employer ratified the improper conduct, then the employer will be held liable for punishment damages. A supervisory employee is regarded as a higher level "managing" employee when the employee has the authority to make decisions that determine corporate policy. An employer will be liable for "ratifying" improper conduct if the employer knows about the conduct and ignores it, or responds inadequately to stop the conduct.

If sexual harassment is committed by a non-supervisor, such as a co-employee, or a traveling salesman, or a customer or whomever, the employer will be held liable if he knew or should have known about the harassment and failed to take immediate and appropriate action to correct the situation.

Not only is the employer liable for acts of sexual harassment committed by managers, or supervisorial employees, the employer is required to take whatever action is necessary to end the harassment of other, non-controlling harassers, or face liability for their acts also. If the employer fails to do so, for whatever reason, the employer will be held liable.

There may be circumstances where the victim is excused from having to notify the employer of harassment by a co-employee. The victim may be excused if the harassment was so pervasive that the employer would be presumed to know, or if there is no reasonable means by which the victim could notify the employer, or if notice would be futile, for instance, if the harasser is the employer.

Employers are commonly found liable in situations where the immediate supervisors of the harassed employee ignored the employee's complaints. If the employee is forced to go up the chain of command to obtain relief from the harassment, the employer is at greater risk of being found liable. Similarly, if the employer delays in responding to the employee's complaints, the employer is more likely to be held liable.

The EEOC recommends that the employer's response to sexual harassment be "immediate and appropriate." The employer's response is "appropriate" when it, "fully remedy[s] the conduct without adversely affecting the terms or conditions of the charging party's employment in some manner (for example, by requiring the charging party to work ...in a less desired location."

In other words, both the EEOC and the courts hold that it is the employer's responsibility to end the harassment. The employer must end the harassment without burdening the victim. If the employer fails to do so, the employer will be held liable. This rule is definitely very tough on the employers.

The courts generally hold that the employer has acted appropriately in response to a sexual harassment complaint if the employer's response eliminated the problem complained about. This does not mean that the employer is required to fire the harassing employee. Nor does it mean that the employer has to discipline the harassing employee. The employer is only required to take effective measures to stop the harassment. This may be accomplished by educating all the employees, rather than disciplining them, if that works. But the employer's response has to be effective. If the employer does not discipline the offending employee, or disciplines that employee inadequately, and that employee continues to harass, the employer will probably be held liable.

The employer is required to respond immediately to a complaint by an employee. This means that the employer must at least start an inquiry or investigation of the matter immediately. It does not mean that the employer is required to respond with some form of discipline immediately. The employer is required to immediately find out what is going on.

As employees, you should also know that your employer is required to distribute an information sheet to you which details the employer's anti-harassment policies. The handout is required to contain legal definitions of sexual harassment, examples of sexual harassment, the company's internal complaint procedures, the remedies available to employees through DFEH and FEHC, how to contact the state agencies, and a statement that the complaining employee is fully job protected for filing a complaint, testifying, etc.

If the employer does not have a clearly defined anti-sexual harassment policy, in writing, the courts usually find the employer liable for any sexual harassment that has occurred in the workplace. The courts say that the employer approved or allowed the sexually harassing behavior by the employer's failure to have a clear policy against it. It is not good enough for the employer to say that he or she did not have a policy and formal grievance procedure because the issue never came up before. The employer is not permitted to be "deliberately indifferent" to the problem of sexual harassment. In fact, a recent California case held that sexual harassment is the type of claim, by its nature, that supports a plea for punitive, or punishment damages against the employer. This opinion arose in a case where the employer did not have a written anti-sexual harassment policy.

WHAT TO DO IF YOU QUIT BECAUSE OF THE HARASSMENT

If you are harassed so badly that you just can't take it any more and you feel forced to quit, consider the following:

1) Write your boss a resignation letter. In that letter tell your boss that you are being forced to quit because you informed your boss all about the incidents of sexual harassment that you suffered. List the facts concerning each incident. Point out that even after your boss was informed, he or she did nothing to stop the harassment, or their efforts were inadequate. Tell your boss that you have to quit because a correction of the problem appears hopeless.

2) Explain what the harassment has done to you emotionally, and psychologically.

3) Ask your boss one more time to immediately correct the problem, so as to avoid your necessity to quit.

If your boss is the harasser, then simply set forth all the facts and tell him (or her) that his behavior has forced you to quit.

If you quit, it should be close in time to the last harassing act. If the last act of harassment occurs in March, but you don't decide to quit until October, then you will have a real problem establishing that the harassment was the cause of your quitting. If the harassment occurs in March, and it is intolerable, then you will probably find yourself quitting in March. The longer you endure "intolerable" working conditions, the less likely are the chances that the court will find your working conditions actually "intolerable."

Identify any possible witnesses on your behalf. Obtain their addresses and phone numbers. Better yet, see if they would be willing to sign a declaration on your behalf. Before you have any potential witness sign a declaration, consult with an employment attorney for the necessary foundational elements, or information needed to be contained in any declaration. Don't just draft your own declaration. I guarantee it will be defective.

Before you quit any job, read the section on CONSTRUCTIVE DISCHARGE.

WHAT TO DO IF YOU DO NOT WANT TO QUIT

As in the situation where you feel you have to quit, set forth your concerns in writing to your boss. Consider asking for mediation to solve the problem.

Remember that if you attempt to stay, that will tend to show that the conditions you faced were not so bad. This is not to suggest that you quit. Simply be aware that much is expected of you by the court, whether you stay or quit.

Watch out for retaliation, and if it occurs, document everything that takes place. Remember, it is illegal for the employer to retaliate against the victim, and retaliation may include being forced to transfer, or take another position within the company, etc.

RIGHTS OF THE ACCUSED

What if you are an employee and you are the sexual harasser or you are accused of sexual harassment? What are your rights if the employer takes action against you? Some employees who have been accused of sexual harassment or terminated for sexual harassment have brought lawsuits on the basis of constructive discharge or wrongful termination. The accused have also brought lawsuits for libel and slander.

The general rule is, if the harassment included some sort of physical contact, termination is permissible. Termination may also be permissible if the conduct was outrageous, such as exposing oneself to another, even though physical contact did not occur. If the harassment was verbal, then termination may be regarded as excessively severe punishment. It is impossible to state a hard-and-fast rule. Each situation must be analyzed to determine the seriousness of the alleged misconduct and the appropriateness of the response.

If you have been accused of sexual harassment, it is improper for the employer, or agents of the employer, to publicize that fact within the company, or otherwise. If your employer "spreads the word around," he may be liable to you for defamation. But remember, truth is an absolute defense to defamation. If you find yourself in this type of situation consult a qualified attorney.

WRONGFUL TERMINATION

DOCTRINE OF AT-WILL EMPLOYMENT

You do not have an automatic legal right to be retained at any particular job without a contract guaranteeing you employment for a particular period of time. Your employer may terminate you at any time, or "at-will." California follows the "at-will" doctrine. The basic rule of at-will employment is set forth in California Labor Code section 2922:

An employment, having no specified term, may be terminated at the will of either party on notice to the other. Employment for a specified term means an employment for a period greater than one month.

The basic law that applies in California states that an employer can terminate any employee at any time for any legitimate reason or for no reason at all, or based on his whim, or fancy, or pleasure, or mood, or irrational act. However, the rule is littered with statutory exceptions that carve the rule like a Thanksgiving turkey. Even though the employer has the right to terminate you for cause or even lacking cause or rationality, he cannot terminate you if the reason for the termination infringes on a protected right or goes against public policy.

An employer can fire you for no reason at all but he or she cannot fire you for the wrong reason. If you should ever face termination (and again, who hasn't?) You owe it to yourself to study these exceptions to the "rule."

The wrongful termination doctrines that I will be discussing below apply to most private employees, including part-time employees, managers, executives, and in some cases, even probationary employees. It is doubtful whether independent contractors are protected by these wrongful termination doctrines that limit the employer's right to terminate you. An independent contractor could possibly be protected if the court finds that it would be against a public policy interest to uphold the termination It would be a very rare situation where all the factors are present to obtain such a result. The court would look at such factors as the relative bargaining position between the parties, the motivations of both parties, the public interests involved, the existence of any fiduciary responsibility and the bad faith of the employer.

Bank employees are employees at will and are not entitled to protection from wrongful termination. This applies to all employees of any bank covered by, or chartered under;

1) The Federal Home Loan Bank Act, or
2) The Federal Reserve Act

If you are an employee for a bank chartered under (1), or (2) and your termination was done, approved or ratified by the bank's board of directors, then you have no contract rights to your job. You can be terminated at will. So, if you were fired, check to see if maybe the board of directors was not informed of the actions and did not approve, or ratify the acts of those that fired you.

If you are an "officer" of a bank chartered under the National Bank Act, you can be terminated at will. If you are a regular employee, (not an "officer") of a bank chartered by the National Bank Act, then you may have a contract right to your job.

Generally employees and officers of federally-chartered savings and loan associations do not have contract rights to their jobs.

Bankers have influence in Congress. However, there is some hope for bank employees, as expressed in a recent California discrimination case. Although bank employees have no contractual rights to employment, a recent California case held that the bank (employer) cannot terminate an employee if the termination is the result of wrongful discrimination. This means that if you are a bank employee you may entitled to sue for wrongful termination if you can show that the termination was motivated by discrimination based on age, sex, race, national origin, religious creed, color, ancestry, marital status, pregnancy, childbirth, medical condition, or physical or mental disability.

In general, do not presume that your employer can terminate you for no reason, or if you were provided with a reason, don't presume that it was proper and sufficient cause, even if you are employed under a written contract that states that you may be terminated at any time, i.e. a contract with an express "at will" provision. Numerous requirements must be met even in a harshly drafted agreement. If you have an employment agreement that has an "at-will" provision the following four conditions must be met for the provision to be enforceable against you.

1) It must be an actual agreement and not a solicitation for employment.

2) The written agreement must contain the entire agreement between you and the employer. This means that there are no additional terms of employment that are agreed to verbally, or are set forth in some other docu ment, or are simply excluded.

3) The agreement must be one that both parties honestly bargained for.

4) The agreement must not have been modified by subsequent acts of the parties. In other words, neither you nor your employer have changed the terms of the agreement as they are written.

Take some time and think about these four requirements. If you think there might be a small possibility that one or more of the conditions are not met, consult an attorney before you give in or give up.

What if the "at will" provision was in an application form and not an employment agreement? The California courts are split over whether an "at will" provision in an application form constitutes a "contract" that determines your "at will" status in the job. Some courts hold that if the employment application is executed (signed by you) and states that it is to be the final agreement between you and the employer, the application becomes the employment contract and you are an "at will" employee, even if the employer promised you otherwise. The "at will" provision in the application may apply even if you later sign a written agreement for employment and that agreement is silent on the issue of "at will."

Some courts hold that the application form is not a

contract and it's provisions do not control. Unfortunately, it will ultimately depend on the political leanings of your particular superior court judge.

EXCEPTIONS TO AT-WILL TERMINATION

Due to the complexities involved in any potential wrongful termination or harassment case it is recommended that you do not attempt to handle the matter on your own. Consequently, I will not discuss each of the exceptions in any detail. It is important only that you are aware of the activities for which you cannot be terminated and the bases for termination that are improper for the employer to assert as a basis for your termination. If you think that your employment situation may involve one or more of the following, then you may want to seek further advice. Consider preserving evidence at this time.

The following is a list of exceptions to the at-will doctrine of employee termination. The items in the list that are followed by a "FLSA" indicate that you local Office of the Labor Commissioner is authorized to help you with complaints based on those particular violations. You may either contact the local office of the DLSE or write to the Discrimination Complaint Investigative Unit set forth on page 280 of the appendix.

WARNING: If you wish to go before the Labor Commissioner with a complaint you must file your complaint within 30 days of the occurrence of the improper act for those violations listed below that are followed by a "DLSE."
It is illegal to terminate, or otherwise punish an employee as a result of the employee either doing or refusing to do any of the following activities, or for the employee having any of the qualities so described:

1) Over the age of 40 because of the employee's age.
2) Political activity.—DLSE
3) Refusal to participate in Abortions.
4) Reporting patient abuse.

5) Refusing to submit to polygraph or lie detector tests.—DLSE

6) Wage garnishment.—DLSE

7) Election officer service.

8) Military service.

9) For discussing or disclosing wages, or refusing to agree not to disclose wages.—DLSE

10) Attending an alcohol or drug abuse rehabilitation program.—DLSE. See ADA.

11) Refusing to authorize disclosure of medical information.

12) Refusal to buy from the employer.

13) Activity within employee organizations or designation of an employee representative.

14) Refusal to commit an illegal act.

15) Sexual orientation, actual or perceived.—DLSE

16) Exercising rights under the Federal Clean Air Act.

17) Enforcement of benefit or pension rights under ERISA.

18) Initiating or attending proceedings before the Labor Commission.—DLSE

19) Union membership, organizational activities, or other "protected, concerted" activities.

20) Refusing to perform dangerous work, or work in an unsafe work place, or for exercising rights under OSHA.—DLSE

21) Pregnancy, childbirth or related medical conditions.

22) Jury duty if the employer is given reasonable notice.—DLSE

23) Race.

24) Sex.

25) Color.

26) Religion.

27) National origin.

28) Ancestry.

29) Physical handicap or disability. See ADA.

30) Medical condition. See ADA.

31) Marital status.

32) Re-employed veteran within one year of re-employment without good cause.

33) Exercising rights under the Water Pollution Control Act with respect to employer's compliance.

34) Filing of a workers' compensation injury claim. See ADA.

35) Disclosing information regarding violations of federal or State law to a governmental agency.—DLSE

36) Exercise of rights under the Agricultural Labor Relations Act (ALRA).

37) A termination in violation of a substantial public policy.

38) A termination in breach of an implied promise of good faith and fair dealing.

39) A termination in breach of an implied promise not to terminate except for good cause.

40) Infection with HIV virus or AIDS or the appearance thereof. See ADA.

41) Attempting to prevent sexual harassment.—DLSE

42) Being infected with a contagious disease but able to perform all job functions and not posing a health or safety threat to others. See ADA.

43) Mental disability. See ADA.

44) Attempting to prevent discrimination.

45) Disclosing fact of illiteracy.

46) Taking time off to attend school where employee's child or ward has been suspended, upon notice to employer.—DLSE

47) For visiting a child's school up to (4) hours per child—DLSE This exception has been expanded to permit parents, legal guardians, or grandparents the right to take 40 hours off from work a year, but no more than 8 hours each month in order to participate in school activities. The employee is obligated to provide reasonable notice in advance.

48) Taking time off to perform emergency duty as a volunteer fireman.—DLSE

49) Attending a judicial proceeding as a witness, or "witness duty."—DLSE

50) For complaints regarding receiving different wages based on gender.—DLSE

51) For refusing to work hours in excess of those permitted by the Industrial Welfare Commission (IWC).—DLSE

52) For an employer failing to provide an employee with a copy of a shopping investigator's report before discharging or disciplining an employee.—DLSE

53) For complaining or testifying regarding non-compliance with the Hazardous Substances Act.—DLSE

54) For complaining about violations of the Health and Safety Code Sections dealing with the operations of a Child Care Center.—DLSE

55) Participation in an interracial relationship.

56) Filing a petition in bankruptcy.

57) Alcoholism, See ADA.

Among the categories listed above, the concept of termination in violation of public policy and the concept of the implied promise of good faith and fair dealing are not readily understandable and require a few words of explanation. In addition, we will expand on several of the other exceptions to the "rule" of "at-will" employment, as well as the concepts of being employed as a "for cause" employee, or as an employee hired for a specific period of time, such as being hired on a two year contract.

EMPLOYMENT FOR "CAUSE" —EMPLOYMENT FOR A SPECIFIED TERM OR LENGTH OF TIME

Although all employment is presumed to be at-will, unless set forth otherwise, there are many instances where you may be employed other than at-will. Probably the most common occurrence of "for cause" employment arises within the context the permanent public employee, those that are employed under the rules of civil service. Employees are often hired "for cause" by the express contract offered by the employer. Employers that follow strict and consistent "progressive discipline" personnel policies often times establish "for cause' bases for their employees. Employers often have to establish "for cause" bases for employment in order to attract and keep talented workers, or to comply with union bargaining demands. For further discussion of these issues see EMPLOYEE HANDBOOKS.

Unlike an "at-will" employee, an employee hired "for cause," cannot be terminated simply upon the passing fancy or sudden whim of the employer without any "real" reason. An employer must demonstrate "good cause," or "just cause" in order to terminate or demote or otherwise punish an employee hired "for cause."

What is "good cause" for terminating someone? What comes to your mind? For most of us, when we think of "good cause" we think of an employee who has committed bad acts, or done shoddy work, or has a bad attitude, or consistently shows poor performance, or inability to get along with co-workers, and most likely, a combination of all the above.

What if I told you that you could be terminated for "good cause" if you did absolutely nothing wrong, but your employer honestly thought that you did something wrong, wrongfully accused you, and thereafter terminated you as a result? Would you regard that as "good cause" for you to lose your job? Hardly. Sadly enough, one California court has so held, and although the case is being reviewed by the California Supreme Court, no decision on this matter has been provided for us yet. With that limitation in mind, let me explain what the better rule is regarding "good cause."

In order for the employer to be justified in terminating or demoting a "for cause" employee that employer must satisfy three separate tests.

1) The employer must be acting in "good faith." This means that the employer is acting under a fair and honest cause, regulated by good faith. The employer must be acting "fairly" and "honestly."

2) The stated reason for the termination must reflect a serious business concern of the employer. As was stated by the court in one case, the reasons provided by the employer for the termination must not be "trivial, capricious, or unrelated to business needs or goals. This means that the reason(s) provided by the employer must legitimate, and not just a pretext to cover up some other real motive, like anger or ill-will towards the employee.

3) The facts underlying the stated reason for the termination must be substantially accurate. This means that if the employer accuses you of some bad act, and terminates you, he or she had better be right. You're accused of stealing? It had better based on some good facts supporting the allegation. If not, see the section on DEFAMATION.

Wait! I need to mention one "exception" to this rule requiring "good cause" as defined above. If the employer is facing financial difficulties, and is forced to reduce the size of his or her business by terminating many employees, referred to as a RIF or a "reduction in force," then that financial pressure may constitute "good cause" to terminate you. In order for the employer to be able to rely on this rationale, the financial pressure must be real, the reduction in force had better involve terminating more people than just you and the employer still must be acting fairly, honestly, without discrimination and not in retaliation for some protected act on your part.

The RIF defense for terminating a "for cause" employee does not work for the employer in attempting to terminate an employee hired for a specific time. The only reasons that the employer may make use of for terminating such an employee are set forth below.

Another situation where an employer needs "good cause" to terminate an employee is when the employee is hired for a specific period of time. What is a good example? How about any professional athlete? For example, suppose Dennis Rodman, the basketball player, is hired for one year and is paid a salary for his services on the basketball court. This is a contract for a specified period of time. One year. After the year is up they negotiate a new agreement, but, his employer cannot terminate that agreement before the year is up unless Mr. Rodman commits some breach of that agreement himself, thus providing the employer with "good cause" to terminate the employment relationship.

If you are an employee hired to work for a specified period of time, set forth in advance, then you can only be rightfully terminated if you commit the following acts;

1) You willfully breach your duty to your employer in the course of your employment; or

2) You habitually (consistently, all the time) neglect your duty to your employer; or

3) You are continually incapable of performing your obligations to your employer under the terms of your agreement.

As described above, the "financial pressure" or RIF argument for providing the employer with a legitimate reason for terminating you in violation of the agreement is not available. A "for term" employee cannot be lawfully RIFFED by the employer. If it happens, the employee can sue.

TERMINATION IN VIOLATION OF PUBLIC POLICY

It is improper for an employer to terminate an employee if the reason for the termination violates a "public policy." For a termination to violate a public policy the reason given for the termination must affect a duty which exists for the benefit of the public at large, rather than for a particular employer or employee. In general, the courts say that a public policy "concerns what is right and just and what affects the citizens of the state collectively."

The public policy affected must be firmly established at the time of discharge. In other words, the issue must not be one involving any measure of social dispute or argument. For example, in one case the employee was terminated for refusing to take a drug test. The court held that it would not have been against public policy for the employer and employee to have mutually agreed to a drug test. Furthermore, the court held that the public opinion on drug testing was so unsettled that no clear public policy, for or against the use of drug tests, could be stated.

In contrast to the drug test case, whistle-blowing on co-employees who were currently engaged in ongoing illegal activities, such as bribery, kickbacks, tax evasion, drug trafficking, or money laundering, stated a settled public policy against the furtherance of criminal activities, and a dismissal resulting from the whistle-blowing would be against public policy.

Other cases that have found the termination to be in violation of public policy include an employee who was terminated after refusing to deliver spoiled milk, and instead reported the incident to the local health department; an employee who notified the government that the employer was fraudulently charging the government for time not actually worked; an employee who refused to provide false reports to a state investigator, an employee who protested the employer's strip-search policy, and an employee who refused to assign other employees to job duties that would have exposed them to health risks in violation of safety regulations.

It is a matter of public policy when an employee attempts to ensure that his employer complies with building and construction codes.

Is it a violation of public policy to terminate an employee for threatening to file a lawsuit against his employer? No. The courts have said there is no constitutional or legal provision guaranteeing free access to the courts without fear of retaliation by your employer.

In other recent public policy cases the courts have held that it is against public policy to discharge an employee for attempting to make his company comply with anti-discrimination laws, even though the employee himself was never subject to unlawful discrimination. Contrast this with a case where the employee refused to drive a truck that he thought was not properly registered. He was terminated for his refusal to work and the court held that the termination was not against public policy. Several things distinguish that case from the others.

First of all, in this case the employee was wrong in his analysis of the law. The truck had a valid three month waiver of the registration requirements and it would not have been unlawful to drive the truck. The employee had made a mistake.

Secondly, the employee was not whistle blowing or otherwise attempting to prevent criminal activity, he was simply refusing to work.

Lastly, the registration of vehicles is not in furtherance of a general public policy, unlike the elimination of discrimination, or sexual harassment, or ongoing criminal activity. In the registration case, the court said that driving the vehicle would not have been unlawful, therefore the public policy against criminal activity didn't apply. If course, if the employee had been right, it would have been unlawful, which makes the court's reasoning particularly harsh. The lesson to be learned from the last case is, if you think that you are being asked to do something illegal, and it doesn't relate to something clearly anti-social—be sure you are right because you will bear the risk if you turn out to be wrong.

The courts have listed four areas of employee activity that are protected under public policy grounds.

1) Refusing to violate a statute.
2) Performing a statutory obligation.
3) Exercising a statutory right or privilege.
4) Reporting an alleged violation of a statute of public importance.

Recent court cases have stressed the need for the employee to be able to demonstrate a statute that prohibits the alleged improper employer activity. By statute, I mean a law passed by the state or federal legislature, not just a rule or regulation passed by a regulatory body or government agency. Do you think your employer did something, or asked you to do something in violation of public policy? **Show me the statute that prohibits the behavior!**

If you think that the circumstances of your discharge involved matters of public policy, seek out professional advise within one year of your termination, the sooner the better. This is a complex area of the law, and it will cost you nothing more than a telephone call to obtain my opinion, for example.

EMPLOYMENT CONTRACTS

An employment contract is an agreement which establishes the terms and conditions of an employment relationship. In order to be enforceable such agreements must satisfy the same requirements as any other contract. For example, generally the agreement must provide for the parties to the contract, the nature of the services to be performed, the compensation to be paid, and the term or duration of the employment relationship.

Must an employment contract be in writing to be enforceable? Probably not. A contract normally must be in writing if the obligations under the contract cannot be performed within one year. However, nearly all contracts can be performed within one year because the employee can quit or the employer can terminate the employee for cause.

Even if you have a written contract, outside evidence may often times be introduced to explain the terms of the contract. If you have a written employment agreement that you feel prevents you from having recourse for some action that your employer has taken, have the contract analyzed by an employment attorney.

TERMINATION IN VIOLATION OF THE IMPLIED PROMISE OF GOOD FAITH AND FAIR DEALING

When you enter into a contract in California, any contract, the court implies a promise, or covenant, by both parties to act in good faith towards the other party. Sound reasonable? I think so. The court imposes within every contractual agreement the enforceable presumption that both parties have agreed to act in good faith, and fairly, and not attempt to deprive the other party of the benefit of the mutual agreement.

Now, let us suppose that you enter into an at-will employment relationship with your employer. You can quit your job at any time. Your employer can terminate you at any time, with or without good cause. But, your employer still has to act in good faith towards you, because you have entered into an employment **contract**! Remember, the court implies an obligation placed upon both parties to act in good faith, and in fairness towards one another. The courts say that the employer has to act towards you the same as he or she would act in furtherance of their own interests.

The violation of good faith and fair dealing is relevant when you have some promise made to you that relates to a promise, other than whether or not you could be fired for cause, and that promise is relevant to why you took the job. For example, you are hired as an at-will employee, but you are also promised that you will be provided with certain stock benefits if you join the company, or meet a sales quota, etc. Maybe you are an immigrant employee and you are promised help in obtaining a "green card" if you come to work for the employer. In each of these situations, if the employer later refuses to give you your stock, or refuses to help with obtaining your "green card,' and thereafter terminates you for asking for your stock or your "green card," such behavior by your employer may be in violation of the promise of good faith and fair dealing, even though employer may have otherwise had the right to terminate you.

The promise of good faith and fair dealing imposes two obligations on each party to every employment agreement:

(1) Each party has to act towards the other in good faith. i.e., honestly. and sincerely, and,
(2) Each party has to act fairly.

This means that your employer may say to you in all honesty, "I don't think that I should have to pay you the stock benefits that I originally promised. I think that the sales quota was set too low. You met the quota too easily." This statement and act by your employer may be in "good faith," meaning that he is telling you honestly that he doesn't think that he should have to pay you, but it may not be **fair** for him to do that. If his actions are regarded as honest but unfair, then he may be in violation of the implied obligation of good faith and fair dealing.

WRONGFUL FAILURE TO HIRE

A cause of action for wrongful failure to hire may arise in those situations where a prospective employer has promised a position, either verbally or in writing, to a job applicant who has relied on that promise by placing himself in a worse position (such as moving or quitting his present job) and the employer fails to provide the job as promised. You may be entitled to sue even though the job that was promised was at-will and you could have been legally terminated at any time for any reason at all after you started working. Even if the promised job is at-will, you are still entitled to be given the opportunity to show that you could have performed the job satisfactorily.

In one case the applicant met all the advertised job require-

"Thanks for coming, but I decided we don't need you."

ments and quit his job based on verbal assurances that the new job was his. The prospective new employer ran a credit check on the applicant, discovered that the applicant had poor credit, and refused to hire him based on his credit history. The court barred the employer form relying on a "hidden" contractual term that had not been disclosed, bargained for, or agreed to, and held that the employer had to follow through with the promised position. In addition, the court noticed that the employee had relied on the employer's promise to his detriment. See also EMPLOYER MISREPRESENTATIONS on page 101.

RESUME FRAUD AND "BAD ACTS"—THE AFTER ACQUIRED EVIDENCE DOCTRINE

If you falsify your resume or answer falsely on an employment application in order to get a job you may be barred from receiving damages against your employer if you are later wrongfully terminated. The federal courts have held that such behavior may prevent the terminated employee from being entitled to recover from the employer, even when the employee has been improperly terminated. This theory has also been applied in situations where the employer has uncovered bad conduct by the employee totally unrelated to the reasons for the employee's discharge.

For example, the employer may terminate the employee for reasons that are illegal and discriminatory, and then discover afterwards that the employee was stealing, or doing drugs, or some other improper activity. The discovery of the "bad acts" may insulate the employer and prevent the employee from any recovery for being fired illegally. Any act that would have been cause for firing or would have prevented you from being hired in the first place could be disastrous for you. The doctrine is called "after acquired evidence" because the employer relies on evidence discovered or acquired after the fact, and uses that evidence to shield themselves from liability for acts that were otherwise completely improper or illegal.

Do not lie on your resume, and be very careful of other behavior that would give your employer grounds to escape liability should you ever be wrongfully terminated or discriminated against.

RETURNING VETERANS

If an employee is called to active duty in the armed forces, or volunteers for active duty, his employer is obligated to grant him a leave of absence. The employer is obligated to provide a leave of absence for a period of up to four years. If the employer sells his business, his buyer assumes the obligation of providing the position for the veteran when he returns.

The employee has up to ninety days to apply for reinstatement after his discharge from active duty. If the employee is hospitalized from injuries received in active duty, the employee has up to one year after his release from the hospital to apply for reinstatement. Once the employee has applied for reinstatement, the employer must immediately place him back to work. The returning veteran is also entitled to the same position, or one "of like seniority, status and pay." If the position has experienced increased pay or benefits, the reinstated employee is entitled to receive them.

If the returning veteran has been disabled and cannot perform his old duties, the employer must provide alternative employment equal to the old position in seniority, status and pay.

Enforcement of your rights is handled through the United States Attorney's office.

DISCHARGE OF EMPLOYEE

An employee is discharged by any combination of behavior or language that indicates to the employee that his or her services are no longer required or accepted.

An employee that is hired for a particular position is discharged when he is discharged from that particular position.

A substantial reduction of the employee's wages and position contrary to the agreed-upon rate and status may constitute a discharge. Normally, "substantial" is regarded as a 20% or more reduction in pay.

If your employer suddenly reduces your pay, or demotes you or otherwise "breaches" or violates what you thought your employment agreement was, can you sue and win? If you are an at-will employee, your employer can terminate you at any time, so... He reduces your wages... are you terminated? Yes. Can you sue and win? No. Probably not, unless you can establish that you had an agreement that your employer could not terminate you except upon a finding of good cause. Your employer can reduce your wages at any time. The courts regard that act as, in effect, a termination, followed by a new offer of employment at the lower wage, that you "accept" by continuing working for the employer. Seems a little farfetched? I agree, but that's how the courts rationalize it.

An at-will employee is not entitled to a reason for his or her discharge at the time of discharge. However, it may be wise to inquire of the employer or the agent of the employer; the employer may slip and tell you a reason for discharge that is illegal, treads upon a statutory or constitutional right, or goes against public policy. If the employer responds in any such manner, preserve your evidence of this as best you can by following up your "termination" conversation with a letter to the employer or employer's agent that discharged you that restates the reasons for your termination. For example, the letter might include something like the following;

> Dear Mr. Bumsly;
> I wanted to talk to you a little bit about our conversation that took place yesterday, July 28, 1993, where you told me that I was no longer welcome on the premises of Acme production, Inc. If I understood you correctly, I was terminated because you felt that my attendance at a drug rehabilitation program only showed what a poor employee risk I was. It was such a shock. I really don't know what to say. I realize that you have nothing personal against me but I do not think that it was a wise managerial decision, given my devotion to Acme all these years.
> You must know that I have never been on drugs while at work, or let drugs influence the quality of my work for you, and I have never missed work

because of drugs. I would like to ask you to reconsider this hasty decision and give me a chance to prove myself.

By setting forth the reasons given to you for your discharge, and if the reasons set forth are not thereafter disputed by the employer, you provide support for your contentions that the discharge was due to the improper reasons as described in your letter (which you will present to the labor commissioner at the hearing or at trial). Without this evidence of the conversation you can be sure that by the time this matter proceeded to a complaint stage the reasons for your discharge will have been completely "laundered" to eliminate any suggestion of improper motives. By making a record of things as they took place, when they took place, you have a better chance of preserving evidence not influenced by your employer having had "time to think things over."

It is important in any employment dispute situation to try to gather and preserve evidence or proof of your claim. In the above example, if there were witnesses to the event, obtain a signed testimonial from the witnesses while their feelings of concern for you are fresh. Do not delay until later in the proceedings, they will have cooled on the idea and doubts will have surfaced justifying a refusal of your request. Do not permit your employer to make up a defense for firing you out of evidence that you failed to document in a timely fashion in its original and unmodified state.

What if it is unclear whether or not you have been discharged? Occasionally a crafty employer will place you on "suspension" pending some sort of investigation or inquiry to determine whether or not you are to be terminated. In reality, the employer may be stalling you for his own purposes, and at a moment that is convenient for him, informs you of your "immediate" termination and provides you with your final check. If this ever happens to you, file a claim with the DLSE for the penalties owed for the delay in payment of your last check.

If you were not suspended "with pay," the "suspension" was really a termination and you should have been paid immediately at the start of the "suspension."

CONSTRUCTIVE DISCHARGE

The California courts hold that constructive discharge occurs when

> "an employee is forced to resign due to actions and conditions so intolerable or aggravated at the time of his resignation that a reasonable person in the employee's position would have resigned and whose employer had actual knowledge of the intolerable actions and conditions and of their impact upon the employee and could have remedied the situation, but did not."

In another case the court stated that, "the intolerable conditions must be sufficiently extraordinary and egregious to overcome the normal motivation of a competent, diligent and reasonable employee to remain on the job to earn a livelihood and to serve his or her employer."

In constructive discharge cases the employee is not fired, he quits. Most employers don't realize that they can be legally liable for wrongfully terminating an employee when that employee quits, but it is true.

It is impossible to specify the exact conditions that would constitute intolerable working conditions. However constructive discharge is often found in cases where the employee is denied promotion, is passed over by less qualified personnel, or is unfairly demoted or subjected to personal ridicule or punitive work assignments. Look for a **pattern** of employer behavior that makes working conditions so difficult or unpleasant that a reasonable person would feel compelled to resign.

Under constructive discharge,

> "The employer must either deliberately create the intolerable working conditions that trigger the resignation or, at a minimum, must know about them and fail to remedy the situation in order to force the employee to resign."

The employee need not prove that the employer intended to force the employee to quit.

How soon must the employee resign after the onset of the intolerable behavior? Is there an exact time limit within which the employee is compelled to act or be barred from seeking legal remedies thereafter? No. There is no set time frame within which the employee must act; the reasonableness of the employee's resignation, including any delay, is a jury question, not determinable by a statute of limitations. However, recent cases indicate that the longer an employee waits to quit after the onset of the intolerable conditions, the more likely it will be that the court finds that the employee was not forced to quit due to the intolerable working conditions.

The courts hold that an employee must act within a "reasonable" period of time after the onset of the horrible conditions in order to be able to sue for constructive discharge. This means that an employee cannot stay on the job indefinitely, waiting to find a new job before quitting the old one, and still sue for constructive discharge. The court will require the employee to quit much sooner than the normal statute of limitations period, which means that the employe will normally be required to quit well before the passage of one year under the "intolerable working conditions." It doesn't matter that quitting may pose a severe financial burden on the employee. The court will require the employee to demonstrate that the conditions were really, in fact, intolerable by quitting promptly. If the employee does not quit promptly, the employee's suit for constructive discharge will probably be dismissed.

What if the intolerable conditions end before the employee quits? Is the employee still entitled to sue for constructive discharge? No. In order to pursue a claim for constructive discharge you must quit while the terrible conditions are still present.

The improper actions that compel the employee to quit need not be performed by the owner. If the actions are taken by someone else, such as a manager, or an employee, or customers, or the general public, the owner may be liable if he or she knew about the situation, had a duty to remedy the situation and could have, but did not.

Up until July of 1994, employers would be liable for constructive discharge if the employer had "constructive knowledge" of the actions that prompted the resignation. In other words, if the employer did not actually know about the actions against the employee, perhaps committed by a lower level supervisor, but the employer should have known, then the employer would be held liable. This is no longer the rule. Now the employer must actually have known about the actions of the supervisor or whomever before the employer will be held liable for their actions.

In order to hold the employer liable, the employer must have either deliberately created the intolerable working conditions that caused the employee to quit, or the employer actually knew about the intolerable working conditions and failed to do anything about it.

If you find yourself in a situation that you regard as unbearable or impossible I suggest two things;

1) Bear it! Stick it out! Do not quit! Let the employer terminate you if at all possible. If he will not, but intends to torture you in a variety of subtle ways, then, of course, you have no option but to quit. Know that many judges cast a negative eye on employees that quit, no matter how awful the employer was.

2) Make sure you inform your employer of the horrible nature of the working conditions, or the impossibility of the tasks placed before you. Tell your employer in writing. Extend an offer in writing to do what you can to correct the situation. Be the voice of reasonableness and conciliation. Tell your employer that you consider his or her acts an attempt to terminate you in violation of your agreement. Tell her that she is making you quit. When your employer ignores your letters, or e-mails, you will be in a much stronger position if you find you must quit.

In the case of agricultural employees the proliferation of labor contractors may reflect a mechanism responding to the potential liabilities imposed by vicarious liability. Labor contractors, who are normally regarded as independent contractors in relation to the growers, shield the growers from liability. If the labor contractors, who are responsible for paying the field workers, abuse the field workers, liability does not extend to the growers. The workers are regarded as being the employees of the labor contractor, not the grower. On the other hand, the labor contractors, known as "day haulers" are themselves liable as the effective employers of the workers. If a worker is mistreated, his or her recourse is to proceed against the labor contractor.

California uses an objective test to determine whether the pattern of employer behavior would cause a reasonable person to resign. In other words, the employee does not have to establish that the employer subjectively intended to force the employee to quit. The employee is spared the difficult task of proving the employer's subjective mental state. The employer's actual intentions or motivations are irrelevant. The employee only has to establish the objective results of the employer's behavior, without worrying about what the employer really intended by his behavior.

You will find that the theory of constructive discharge may be important in cases of discrimination, such as sexual orientation harassment. See SEXUAL HARASSMENT, on page 47.

See also TERMINATION IN VIOLATION OF THE IMPLIED PROMISE OF GOOD FAITH AND FAIR DEALING for your right to sue for damages if you have been improperly disciplined or demoted, even though you were not terminated or forced (chose not to) to quit.

GOOD CAUSE

"Good cause" for termination is "a fair and honest cause or reason regulated by the good faith of the employer." A violation of the implied promise to act fairly towards you and in good faith occurs when your employer terminates you alleging "good cause" but does so as a pretext for some other real reason. The courts have held that it is a violation of good faith if "the existence of good cause for discharge is asserted by the employer without probable cause and in bad faith, that is, without a good faith belief that good cause for discharge in fact exists."

A violation of the implied promise of good faith and fair dealing exists if the discharge is trivial, capricious, pre-textual, or unrelated to business needs or goals.

It has been held to be good cause to terminate an employee that habitually called in sick. Disobedience of reasonable and lawful orders, as well as habitual neglect of duty, or incapacity to perform your job duties are grounds for discharge. Criminal behavior or behavior reflecting "gross immorality," even though not related to employment, would be grounds for discharge if the activities were detrimental to the employer's interests. Habitual drinking or drug abuse are grounds for discharge, but past abuse is not. Alcoholism is also a protected disability, though drinking on the job is not. See AMERICANS WITH DISABILITIES ACT on page 16.

Good cause can exist for reasons unrelated to the conduct or performance of the discharged employee. If the employer reorganizes the business, or curtails a branch of the business and terminates employees as a result, it is for good cause. In this situation "good cause" is based on legitimate business reasons. This means that if you are an employee hired under an implied agreement not to be terminated except upon good cause, if your employer's business starts doing badly and he needs to terminate one or more employees, as part of a "reduction-in-force," he will be entitled to terminated you on that basis, even though your work was good, and you did nothing wrong. If, on the other hand, you are hired for a specific period of time, such as one year or two years, then a reduction-in-force is not a good enough reason to terminate you. Your employer must establish that you committed a willful breach of duty, or habitual neglect or continued incapacity. See the section

Does an agreement not to terminate you for "good cause" apply to demotions or disciplinary actions? Yes. A recent case involving two PG & E employees held that where the employer demotes or disciplines the employee in violation of the employer's own personnel rules, the employee can sue for damages. The employee may sue even though the employee is still employed.

Under the previous rule the employee had to have been fired or had to have quit under the theory of constructive discharge before they could sue for damages.

For a detailed discussion of quitting or being terminated for good cause see the following discussion on unemployment compensation. Some examples of good cause for terminating an employee are; the employee's failure to perform properly assigned job tasks, a reduction in force (RIF) due to a decline in the employer's business, falsifying employer documents, fighting with other employees, or customers, assisting a competitor or engaging in acts that violate your employee responsibility of loyalty to your employer, or failing to meet reasonable sales quotas.

Whether or not you find yourself terminated for good cause is relevant,

a) if you have an agreement that prohibits discharge except upon "good cause," or

b) for purposes of qualifying for unemployment compensation.

See the discussion under WRONGFUL TERMINATION for more information dealing with good cause.

INVESTIGATING APPLICANTS AND EMPLOYEES

INVASION OF PRIVACY

Under the rules of common law you are entitled to sue someone (you are said to have a "cause of action") if he or she makes public a protected private fact about you. Publicizing a private fact does not mean that the person publishes the fact in the paper, or goes on television, or yells it from the balcony at City Hall. "Disclosing to the public" means only that the person told or conveyed the private information to someone else. Under relevant California constitutional law you are not even required to show that the person invading your privacy told someone else about the private facts concerning you.

California expands the common law concept by making it an invasion of privacy if the employer improperly used information that had been properly obtained. For example, if your employer obtained a copy of your credit report, citing "business reasons" for requesting the report, but later used the report for purposes of collecting money you owed to the employer, then your employer has committed an invasion of your right to privacy. In another example, if your employer discloses information from your personnel file to a third party, the employer has invaded your privacy through the misuse of the confidential information. Invasion of privacy includes misuse of protected, private information.

Can your employer search your personal items that you keep at work? The answer depends upon whether, under the circumstances, you had a reasonable expectation of privacy regarding the items searched.

If you are a public employee you are protected under the fourth amendment to the United States Constitution prohibiting unreasonable searches and seizures. If you are a private employee you are not protected under the fourth amendment because your employer is not an agent of the state. However, employer searches may be an invasion of your reasonable expectations of privacy as protected under the California Constitution.

The California Supreme Court recently held that the California constitutional right of privacy applies to private employers, as well as governmental employers.

Your employer, private or governmental, is only permitted to invade your right to privacy in the workplace by showing a competing interest which overrides your right to privacy under the particular circumstances. Employer conduct which invades employee privacy is evaluated by whether or not the conduct is necessary to accomplish an important employer or social interest. If the employer can show an important reason for the invasion of employee privacy, and the employer can show that he or she used privacy safeguards, protective measures, and used the least intrusive method available to accomplish the investigation, then the invasion of privacy may be legal.

The court will also evaluate the employee's reasonable

expectations of privacy under the circumstances, as described below.

If your employer acts excessively, his or her actions will probably be declared illegal.

Your employer is not required to have a warrant in order to conduct searches which investigate suspected violations of workplace rules.

The right to privacy is a fundamental right in California.

If you had your purse in the back room at work, you probably have a reasonable expectation of privacy that your purse will not be searched by anyone, for any reason. What if you have a personal locker? If the locker is unlocked, there is probably no reasonable expectation of privacy that the locker would not be opened. That still doesn't give anyone the right to search through your purse or other items located within the locker. What if you lock your locker with your own lock? Now you have a reasonable expectation of privacy that extends to viewing the items within the locker itself. Any entrance into the locker itself would be an invasion of privacy.

Your right to privacy is not absolute and depends on several factors. If you have been given prior notice by the employer that employee lockers would be subject to unannounced searches, then you have no reasonable expectation of privacy. The reasonable expectation of privacy requirement is an objective test, it is not merely what your personal expectations may happen to be. Furthermore, the right to privacy is not absolute and may be overridden by legitimate business needs.

You may reduce or waive your privacy expectations by specifically agreeing to searches in a search agreement, or company policy brochure. If you have the choice of using a company lock or your own lock, use your own— that will increase your reasonable expectations of privacy.

The right to be free from unreasonable searches in the workplace is protected under the Fourth Amendment to the United States

Constitution. Fourth Amendment protection against unreasonable searches applies only for employees that work for the state or federal governments. Private employers are not subject to Fourth Amendment restrictions. The limitation on searches that we have discussed that applies to private employers flows from the employee's right to privacy under Article I of the California Constitution.

Employees have the right of sexual privacy regarding the nature of their sexual relationship (if any) with their superiors at work. See OFF-DUTY ACTIVITIES on page 283.

Employees have a right of privacy to their personnel files. As an illustration of how the employee's right of privacy limits employer activity, if you are terminated your employer is prohibited from disclosing the reasons for your termination to other employees or any one else. That information is private information related to your personnel file. You have a right to sue your employer if he or she posts on a bulletin board, or announces in a company memo, or states in an employee conference, etc., the reasons for your discharge as a warning to other employees, or for any other reason.

What happens when the right to privacy comes into conflict with the need to acquire evidence of employer misconduct? In other words, what are the rights of co-employees in litigation? There is no simple answer, and much depends on the judge overseeing the litigation. If the plaintiff demonstrates a compelling reason why the plaintiff cannot properly prosecute his case without the protected information of the co-employee, the judge will likely order the information released, unless the affected employee specifically objects. The judge may look to see if there are less intrusive means of obtaining the information, such as denying the release of the employee's personnel file in favor of asking questions of the employee.

DRUG OR ALCOHOL TESTING

Testing employees for drug or alcohol use pits the employee's fundamental constitutional right of privacy against the employer's right to ensure a safe and drug-free work environment. In balancing these conflicting interests, the courts have distinguished between employees and applicants, and weighed the degree of intrusion caused by the particular testing procedure. Procedures that cause only slight intrusions into protected expectations of privacy, such as the taking of fingerprints, are more readily upheld than more intrusive methods.

Some state courts have held that an employee's right to privacy in relation to drug testing is not waiveable. In other words, the courts have held that employees cannot agree to be tested in violation of their rights as part of an employment agreement. Such an agreement is regarded as being in violation of public policy. The courts are still split on this issue. The decision in your case may depend on which court hears your case.

In dealing with employees, the employer must first demonstrate a compelling business interest before the propriety ("O.K.ness") of an invasive drug test may be contemplated. If the employer demonstrates a compelling business interest, an invasive test such as urinalysis, pupil dilation or blood testing, may be upheld as valid if,

> a) the employee to be tested engages in employment duties that involve direct and immediate risk to the general public (a safety-related employee), or
> b) there is probable cause to believe that the employee's performance has been impaired by drug or alcohol abuse.

Invasive drug tests of "safety employees," such as armed security guards, train engineers and other employees of the Federal Railroad Administration (FRA), FAA air traffic controllers, employees of the Federal Highway Administration (FHA), employees of the Federal Transportation Administration (FTA), or employees whose duties, if impaired, would directly result in an immediate and unavoidable threat to the public are those that may be tested. Under option (a) the testing involves groups of employees. The suitability of the testing flows from the nature of the tested employee's job responsibilities under situation (a). The employee's individual behavior is not relevant, nor has it prompted the test. In contrast, the testing in (b) results from the employee's suspicious behavior and does not occur as a result of a general policy applicable to all employees within the classification. The focus under (b) is strictly on the individual.

Remember that under either situation— public safety, or probable cause to suspect the individual, the employer must first demonstrate a compelling business interest justifying the invasive test before we go any further with the analysis. The employer must show a compelling interest, otherwise the test is improper at the outset.

Employer attempts to conduct random or group drug tests for reasons other than safety, such as maintaining a drug-free workplace, or protecting the public image of the company, are not "compelling" reasons, and are therefore illegal.

Local ordinances may impose even greater restrictions on the employer's ability to test for drugs. The city of San Francisco only permits drug tests if the employer has a reasonable suspicion that the suspect employee is physically impaired from drugs or alcohol and where the impairment causes a clear and present physical danger to the employee or to others. The employer has to permit independent testing and the tested employee has to be permitted to challenge, or explain, the positive test results. In addition, the employer must pay to have the drug test conducted. The City of Berkeley goes even farther by prohibiting drug testing of applicants or employees under any circumstances.

Another potential problem with drug tests is that some drugs will show residual presence in the body over a period of days or weeks after the drug was taken. If the employee is tested and indicates positive, the employee may have a valid argument that the test showed "past" drug use, not "present," and reflects an inquiry by the employer into a "protected" area. The employer may run afoul of the ADA or employee privacy rights.

The employer need satisfy a less stringent "reasonableness" test when testing job applicants. Drug screening of job applicants will be upheld if the testing is conducted in accordance with procedural safeguards, the results are kept confidential, and the applicant is given written notice of the drug test requirement. Applicants are regarded as having a lesser expectation of privacy in the job screening process. This rule providing a lesser right to privacy for applicants was overruled in the recent Soroka case but the case was settled prior to review by the California Supreme Court and consequently cannot be relied upon as current law. The case is at least an indicator that the courts in California may be willing to require the higher standard for applicants. At this time the law is unsettled.

Neither employers, nor health care providers contracted by employers, are required, upon request, to disclose the results of physical exams to job applicants who took the exams. Applicants are not "employees" and are therefore not entitled to inspect personnel files. Furthermore, job applicants who have been referred to a health care provider are not "patients," and are therefore not entitled to inspect their medical records.

The right to privacy extends beyond prohibiting governmental intrusions. All private employers are subject to the laws protecting individual privacy rights.

LIE DETECTOR TESTS

Both public employees and private employees working in California are protected from being required to take polygraph (lie detector) tests. Private employees are protected under both state and federal law; public employees are protected under state law.

California prohibits employers from requiring applicants or employees to take polygraph tests, or from retaliating against employees who refuse to take such tests. The California law is similar to the federal law, described below, but if you work in California there are no exceptions which require to you take a test or risk your job for refusing to do so. The federal law described below highlights additional limitations on the employers. I have deliberately omitted the exceptions under the federal law because they do not apply to people who work in California.

One aspect of the California law that you must be careful of is the employer is permitted to **ask** you to take a lie detector test, though not permitted to **require** you to take a test. Don't ever let yourself think that you have to take such a test. If your employer asks you to take a polygraph test, the employer must first inform you in writing that you are not required to take the test, either as a condition for obtaining a job, or as a condition of retaining your job. Your employer must tell you in writing at the time the test is to be administered. Failure to do so is a crime.

Under the federal law, the Employee Protection Act of 1988 prevents most private employers from using polygraph exams to screen job applicants or to test current employees. Polygraph exams include all forms of lie detector tests, voice stress, or psychological stress exams. If the employer conducts such an exam, the act prohibits the employer from using or disclosing the test results.

Federal law prohibits employers from discharging employees for refusing or failing to take polygraph tests, or on the basis of an unlawfully administered test. The act prohibits retaliation against employees who assert rights under the act. If an employer violates any of the provisions of the act the employer may be liable for civil penalties up to $10,000. In addition, the employee may sue the employer in federal or state court, and if the employee wins, may be awarded attorneys fees, in addition to all other remedies.

HONESTY TESTS

Employers have attempted to get around the ban on lie detector tests by using written "honesty tests" that are designed to test the applicant's measure of honesty or inclination to lie, cheat, or steal. The tests probe, through written questions, the applicants feelings and perceptions regarding honesty. So far, the legality of "honesty tests" has not been determined in the courts. Therefore, if you are asked to take such a test you will either have to do so, or take the employer to court.

Honesty tests are likely in violation of the California ban on polygraph-type tests, and are an invasion of privacy, but it hasn't been determined yet.

PSYCHOLOGICAL TESTS

Psychological tests are legal if the questions are not otherwise prohibited by the ADA, or Title VII, or the other statutes that limit applicant questioning. See JOB INTERVIEWS on page 38 for a discussion of permissible areas of questioning.

Whether psychological tests for applicants must first pass a "compelling business interest" test to be valid is still unsettled law in California. The point is, if your (potential) employer requires it, you may have to comply or else fight it out in court.

ARREST RECORDS

It is improper for an employer or prospective employer to ask an applicant or employee to disclose arrest information about the employee that did not result in a conviction. In other words, it is generally illegal for an employer to make blanket hiring decisions based on the disclosure of applicant's arrest records. It is also illegal for the employer to gain access to such information through other sources.

It is also illegal to discriminate against an employee or applicant based on an arrest, or history of arrests, that did not lead to a conviction.

If the arrested individual participates in a pretrial or a post-trial diversion program, that is not considered a conviction, and any requested disclosure or discrimination resulting from the applicants participation in the diversion program, would be illegal.

However, it may be proper for an employer to consider information of criminal behavior of an applicant or employee that is provided by a third party, such as a witness or informant. If, for example, an employer is told that an employee was recently involved in a bar fight which led to an arrest and there is evidence that the employee may be a safety risk to other employees, the employer may terminate the employee or take other protective measures.

An employer is permitted to ask an employee or applicant about an arrest for which the employee or applicant is out on bail, or out on his own recognizance (O.R.) pending trial, but the employer is not permitted to discipline the employee or otherwise act against the employee or applicant based on the information. The employer can ask but he cannot act on the information!

There are several exceptions to the rule restricting employer questioning. Health care employers may question applicants about arrests for sex offenses if the applicants are to interact with patients. Health care employers may ask about drug arrests for applicants that will have access to drugs. Utility employers may ask about arrest records if the applicants are to have access to the homes of private individuals. There are also numerous exceptions for federal and state law enforcement agencies.

Employers are permitted to ask about past arrests that resulted in a conviction. Employers cannot ask about marijuana possession convictions that occurred more than two years prior. Employers are permitted to refuse to hire an applicant based on his or her history of criminal convictions if there is a sound business reason for doing so. A blanket refusal to hire based on conviction records is probably discriminatory. An employer may ask,

"Have you ever been convicted of a felony?"

However, the employer must also tell you at the same time that a felony conviction does not disqualify you for the job.

If an employer improperly inquires about your criminal history you may be entitled to sue the employer, and receive your costs, attorneys fees and $200. If the inquiry is an intentional violation of the rule against asking about criminal history that did not result in a conviction, you may be entitled to three times your damages or $500, plus costs, and attorneys fees. Such an inquiry is also a crime.

For a further discussion on questioning applicants see JOB INTERVIEWS on page 38.

FINGERPRINTS OR PHOTOGRAPHS

If an employer requires either fingerprints or a photograph from the employee or applicant, such information must be kept confidential. It is a crime to furnish an employee's or applicant's fingerprints or photograph to another person, ex-employer, or potential future employer.

Employers are entitled to keep fingerprints and photographs for their own use.

It may be improper for a prospective employer to request

fingerprints or photographs from job applicants. Such requests may be shown to be discriminatory on the basis of race, age, or national origin.

SHOPPERS OR SPOTTERS

"Shoppers" and "spotters" are undercover employees who monitor the honesty of other employees by observing them in the workplace. "Shoppers" or "spotters" pretend to be customers, wander throughout the business and observe other employees. If you are an employee that has been caught by a shopper or a spotter, you must first determine if the undercover employee works only for your company or was hired as an independent contractor.

If the shopper or spotter was hired as an independent contractor to perform investigative work, the employer must provide the employee suspected of doing something improper, with a copy of the investigative report prior to disciplining or discharging the employee. Similarly, if the employer plans to question the employee about his or her honesty, and termination is a possible outcome of the questioning, then the employee must be given a copy of the latest investigative report before the end of the interview.

If the shopper or spotter works for the employer on an exclusive and regular basis, and the shopper works only in connection with the employer's business, then the employer does not have to provide copies of the reports to the suspected employee, as described above. In addition, the shopper must be regarded as an employee of the employer authorizing the investigation and the shopper must conduct the entire investigation for the employer.

EMPLOYEE QUESTIONING

If an employee is interviewed for suspicion of wrongdoing, the employee should be aware of several things. It is illegal for an employer, or an agent of the employer, to detain or question an employee against his or her will, by threatening to use force against that employee. If the employer does so he is guilty of false imprisonment. Holding an employee against his or her will, is illegal even if the threat of force is only implied.

For example, you are invited into your supervisor's office,

the door is closed behind you and a security guard places himself in front of the door, blocking your exit. No one has threatened you with physical force, but the threat of force can certainly be implied from the circumstances. You have been falsely imprisoned. This assumes, of course, that the detainment was against your will. The suspected employee may suffer from illegal restraint even if the restraint is not physically confining. For example, as in the example above, you are called to your supervisor's office, the door is left open and there is no guard—but your supervisor tells you that if you do not cooperate with his investigation, the police will be called in and criminal charges will be filed against you. Is the threat of bringing in the police, a threat of force? Yes. You have been falsely imprisoned.

In the example above, what are your rights if the employer calls the police and insists that you be arrested? If the employer knew that you were innocent and gives the police false information in order to get you arrested, the employer is guilty of false arrest.

If the employer acts in good faith, not knowing that you are innocent, he is not liable to you for false arrest. The employer may also be liable to the employee for defamation, intentional or negligent infliction of emotional distress, or other personal injury claims.

CREDIT CHECKS

Access to consumer credit reports such as Trans Union, TRW or Equifax are governed by federal and California law. The Federal Fair Credit Reporting Act (FCRA) lists the permissible reasons for disclosing your credit report to another party, including your employer. The list is exclusive, and access to your credit report for any reason not listed, no matter how reasonable or important, is illegal under federal law. The permissible purposes for obtaining your credit report are:

1) In response to a court or grand jury subpoena (order).
2) In response to written instructions from the consumer to whom the report relates.
3) Disclosure to persons who the reporting agency has reason to believe will only use the report,

a) in a credit transaction with a consumer,
b) for employment purposes,
c) for underwriting insurance involving the consumer,
d) in connection with a determination of the consumer's eligibility for a license or grant by a governmental entity required by law to consider an applicant's financial responsibility or status, or
e) where there is otherwise a "legitimate business need" for the information in connection with a business transaction involving the consumer (such as a credit purchase).

The federal statute defines "(b) for employment purposes" as,

... a report used for the purpose of evaluating a consumer for employment, promotion, reassignment or retention as an employee.

Your employer may examine your credit history and use that information for evaluating you for employment, promotion, etc. However, the employer may not obtain credit information on any person other than the applicant or employee in question and most importantly, **the employer must obtain the prior written consent of the consumer whose report is being obtained,** as set forth under the California Consumer Credit Reporting Agencies Act (CCRA). Under the CCRA, before the employer can obtain the individual's credit report the employer must,

1) Provide the employee with written notice that the employer is requesting a consumer credit report.
a) The notice must inform the employee that a report will be used for employment purposes, and
b) Identify the source of the report. This includes a statement of the name, address, and toll-free tele

phone number of the consumer reporting agency.
2) The employee may request to receive a copy of the
report at the same time that the employer receives it.
If the employee so desires, the employer is obligated
to request a copy of the report for the employee at no
cost to the employee.

**May your employer use credit reports for purposes of litigation
in a labor dispute or other litigation?** No. The employer may use
a credit report only for the listed and authorized reasons: hiring,
promotion, reassignment, or retention of an employee. Obtaining a
credit report for purposes of litigation is not a "legitimate business
need," and is therefore not permissibly obtained under that rationale. Under a new law, the employer must have a written certification form on file with the reporting agency before a report is requested on an applicant or employee. The certification form must
contain a statement by the employer that the information in the credit
report will not be used in violation of any state or federal laws.

May your employer grant anyone else access to your report?
No.

**Are job applicants entitled to written notice that a credit check
will be used in determining job qualification?** Yes. The California law requiring disclosure, set forth above, applies to applicants,
as well as employees. If the applicant is denied employment as a
result of the credit report, the employer must inform the applicant
of that fact, in writing, and furnish the applicant with the name and
address of the credit reporting agency that supplied the report. The
employer must notify the applicant, in writing, that the applicant is
entitled to a free copy of the report.

An employee or job applicant is entitled to receive a record
of all the parties that have received a copy of the employee's report
for employment purposes within the last two years. The employer
must also tell the applicant, in writing, that the applicant is entitled
to dispute the information in the report
A tip to remember— Get a copy of the report and look at the dates

of any negative information about you. Most items that are more than seven years old can be removed upon your request. Unsatisfied judgments will stay on your report for ten years and bankruptcies for fourteen years.

Another tip to remember—If you become involved in litigation with your employer, contact the major credit reporting agencies and obtain a copy of your credit report. The report will state who has made recent inquiries regarding your credit. In your request for a copy of the report, ask the credit agency to make a complete disclosure of the nature and scope of the investigation that was requested by the employer. If your employer or his lawyer has run a credit check on you since the beginning of the dispute, you should allege a violation of FCR or CCRA, as applicable. I should point out that you cannot bring this type of complaint before the DLSE. They can't help you. This tip is relevant if you or your lawyer plan to sue your employer in court.

NOTE that bankruptcy is listed under the exceptions to the at-will doctrine of employment, which means that it is illegal to terminate an employee or discriminate against an employee or applicant because the employee or applicant has filed for bankruptcy.

You cannot be denied employment because you have filed for bankruptcy, or had a bankruptcy in the past.

CONSUMER INVESTIGATIVE REPORTS

Consumer investigative reports are like credit reports but contain much more detailed information about the person being investigated. Consumer investigative reports generally include interviews with people that know you, such as past employers, friends, neighbors, and relatives. Your rights regarding consumer investigative reports are nearly the same as with credit reports. For example, the employer faces the same restrictions on reasons for acquiring such reports, as well as restrictions on notification of the employee, etc.

One difference between credit reports and investigative reports is that if the employer seeks an investigative report for employment reasons other than promotion or assignment, the employer must notify the employee in writing within three days after requesting the report. Credit report notices must also be given. However, the statute does not list the three day requirement. The notification must also explain the nature and extent of the investigation, the name of the source of the report, and the right of the employee to review the report.

You are not entitled to notice of the report if the employer's purpose in getting the report is to determine whether or not you will be terminated, or whether or not you are engaged in criminal activities likely to result in losses to the employer.

TESTING FOR AIDS

Employers may require medical exams of employees that disclose the existence or absence of AIDS or HIV status. However, employers are prohibited from basing any employment related decisions on the results of these tests. Furthermore, it is a crime for the employer to disclose the results of the tests to any third person.

In order to test for AIDS, the employer has to obtain the prior written consent of the person to be tested. See also MEDICAL RECORDS on page 279.

PHYSICAL OR MEDICAL EXAMS

The Americans with Disabilities Act (ADA) prohibits an employer from requiring a physical exam of an applicant without first making a conditional offer of employment. Employers are also prohibited from asking medically related questions of the applicant without first making a conditional offer of employment. In other words, the employer can say,

"The job is yours if you pass the physical."

but the employer cannot say,

"All applicants must take this physical and upon passing the physical, we will consider whether any of you may be appropriate for this position."

It may be illegal for an employer to utilize a medical exam or test that tends to discriminate against an applicant based on his or her race, sex, national origin, etc. For example, tests for sickle cell anemia will tend to discriminate against persons of African or Middle Eastern descent. If genetic tests are conducted that unfairly burden one racial group over another, the tests are probably discriminatory.

Under the ADA, tests for drugs or alcohol cannot be expanded to include a comprehensive physical exam unless a conditional offer of employment is first extended to the applicant.

ELECTRONIC MONITORING OF EMPLOYEES

Under California law your employer cannot monitor or intercept your telephone conversations without the consent of both parties to the conversation. Therefore, the consent of the employee is not enough to permit the interception. The person on the other end of the line also has to agree. Unlike the federal law, California does not permit the employer to listen in on extension lines. Nor may employers listen in on confidential conversations with the aid of an amplification devise. If you are having a conversation under circumstances that would lead a reasonable person to believe that your conversation was private, your expectations are protected and any intrusion into that conversation is illegal. Your conversation need not be over an electronic medium.

Conversations held over electronic mail (E-mail) or bulletin boards are not protected. In one California case, the court held that the employer may monitor electronic mail or electronic bulletin board information.

Although it is not electronic, it is illegal to make use of two way mirrors in any restroom, shower, locker room, fitting room, or hotel room.

ELECTRONIC MONITORING BY EMPLOYEES

Employees sometimes record conversations between themselves and their employers. This activity is illegal if both parties to the conversation do not knowingly agree to the taping. Although I obviously cannot recommend this activity I have seen cases where the evidence preserved by such a tactic worked wonders for the employee. If you choose to record conversations to establish evidence of what you may have been promised be very aware that the tactic may backfire on you.

A recent example of the danger of illegally taping conversations occurred in a case where an employee was suing his employer for sexual harassment. In order to collect evidence against the employer the employee secretly taped over 160 conversations without permission of the other parties. The court responded by dismissing the sexual harassment suit and fining the employee $132,000! The employee was ordered to pay the $132,000 to the employer and eleven other employees. Fair warning!

ANTI-RETALIATION LAWS

There are numerous laws forbidding the discharge, discrimination, or punishment of an employee in retaliation for the employee's reporting, or participation in, proceedings to determine whether there have been violations of federal law, including;

1) Fair Labor Standards Act (FLSA).
2) Migrant and Seasonal Agricultural Worker Protection Act.
3) Surface Mining Control and Reclamation Act.
4) International Safe Container Act.
5) Contract Work Hours and Safety Standards Act.
6) Service Transportation Assistance Act of 1982.
7) Federal Racketeer Influenced and Corrupt Organizations Act (RICO).
8) Americans with Disabilities Act (ADA) of 1990.
9) Family and Medical Leave Act (FMLA).
10) Employee Retirement Income Security Act of 1974 (ERISA).
11) Civil Rights Act of 1974, Title VII.
12) National Labor Relations Act.

The ADA is typical of anti-retaliation laws in that it prohibits an employer from retaliating against an individual who opposes a practice made unlawful by the act, or who participates in a proceeding brought under the act, or exercises rights under the act. The above list is certainly not exhaustive. If you think that you have been retaliated against for activities related to any federal or state law, you should seek the advice of counsel. See EXCEPTIONS TO AT-WILL TERMINATION on page 62.

CAL OSHA ANTI-RETALIATION PROVISIONS

It is illegal in California to discharge or otherwise retaliate against an employee who files a health complaint against his or her employer.

ARBITRATION AGREEMENTS

If you sign an arbitration agreement you promise and agree to take any complaints against your employer to binding arbitration, rather than to a civil court of law. This means that you give up your right to a jury trial, you give up the right to question witnesses by deposition, and you give up your right to appeal. You are constitutionally entitled to a trial by jury in any matter at common law exceeding $20 in dispute. Arbitration waives that right.

Arbitration can be astonishingly expensive for the litigants. You may be required to pay unbelievable fees to proceed in arbitration. By signing an arbitration agreement, you are waiving your right to sue your employer. This is a fair warning to those who may be asked to sign such an agreement.

See also UNIONS on page 327 regarding your right to take wage claims to the Labor Commissioner even though you have agreed to accept arbitration instead.

EMPLOYER MISREPRESENTATIONS

California enacted a law to protect agricultural workers from being told exaggerated promises, made to persuade them to relocate to work in the fields, only to find that the job opportunities were not as they were promised. Employees or job applicants are entitled to double damages if an employer knowingly makes any false statement, either spoken, written, or advertised, which concerns the kind, character or existence of work being offered, and the employee or applicant is persuaded or influenced to move as a result of the false promise.

It is illegal for the employer to misrepresent the length of time the work will last, or the pay that is to be offered, or the housing or sanitary conditions to be encountered, or the existence or nonexistence of any strike or other labor dispute. The employee or applicant is protected if the employee is persuaded to make even a temporary move. In other words, the employee need not have to move permanently.

This law gives greater protection than merely not being hired as promised. See WRONGFUL FAILURE TO HIRE on page 72.

Under this law the employee or applicant can get double damages for being hired at a lower wage rate, or for a shorter period of time than promised, or for being offered a job that was not as good as was promised, etc.

The law applies to employers, or anyone making the promises on behalf of the employers, such as officers, managers, and agents.

The difficult component to gaining protection under this law is proving the "knowing misrepresentation" by the employer or his or her representative. Very rarely are you provided with written documentation of any verbal promise, and often the promises are implied or understood, rather than defined. Be aware of any promises made to you. Try to document or confirm through witnesses what promises were made. Do you have anything that would tend to show that the employer knew that the promises made to you were not true?

If you cannot prove that the employer or manager made a "knowing misstatement," you may still have a good case under a theory of "negligent misrepresentation." A recent case has held that if the employer makes you these promises and was negligent in making the promises, even though the promises were not "knowingly false," you can sue. The theory is that the employer did not act with due care (he or she was negligent) in making these promises to you.

EMPLOYER HEALTH & SAFETY OBLIGATIONS

Your employer has an obligation to provide you with a safe and healthful place of employment. Furthermore, your employer has an obligation to "provide and use safety devices and safeguards reasonably adequate to render the employment and place of employment safe, or do every other thing reasonably necessary to protect the life, safety, and health of employees." For example, employers are required to provide toilet facilities and fresh drinking water for employees. Employers must maintain a medical or surgical chest if power machinery is used.

Every employer in California is required to develop and maintain a written Injury and Illness Prevention Program (IIP). An IIP is a written program showing how the employer will attempt to prevent and respond to injuries at the workplace. This (IIP) requirement applies to all employers, including employers of only seasonal or intermittent employees.

Employers in low-hazard, or non-high-hazard industries, or employers of seasonal or intermittent workers do not need to develop an individualized written program. Cal-OSHA has developed model IIP programs that these employers can use.

Your employers safety obligations are set forth in the Occupational Safety and Health Act (OSHA). If you think that your employer is in violation of OSHA's rules, contact your local Division of Industrial Safety, within the Department of Industrial Relations.

EMPLOYMENT CONTRACTS "FOR LIFE"

If you enter into an employment agreement where the employer promises you "employment for life" or something similar, the agreement is interpreted to be a contract for employment for an indefinite period and is terminable at will by either party! There is no security flowing from the agreement. Some cases have held that a contract for permanent employment is construed as a contract of employment for a reasonable period of time. Such a contract is enforceable according to it's terms and may not be terminated by the employer without good cause.

Contracts for life are not enforceable where the contracts

are not precise regarding wages, working conditions, and the nature of the work to be performed.

EMPLOYMENT CONTRACTS FOR A SPECIFIC PERIOD OF TIME

Being hired for a specified period of time provides you with the strongest job protections. You are hired for a specified period of time if the date that your job ends is spelled out when your job begins. For example, you are hired for one year, or two years, or if the termination of your employment is readily capable of determination from a known fact or condition.

The question arises, what if it is not clear from your agreement, the exact date that your job will end? Are you hired for a set term? For example, you are hired to harvest all the lumber from a tract of land. When you have completed the harvesting of lumber from the land, your job will end. Is this a set term? If the land is so large that the lumber is removable within a known or knowable period of time, then the contract would appear to be for a set term. Your employment is not indefinite, since the lumber will someday be gone, and that day is subject to reasonable calculation.

If you are hired for a specified period of time, and your employment will end after that date, you cannot be terminated except upon the happening of at least one the three following events:

1) You commit a willful breach of duty to your employer. In other words, you intentionally do some bad act towards your employer.
2) You habitually neglect your duty to your employer. This suggests a requirement of continuous and repeated neglect.
3) You demonstrate continued incapacity to perform your job duties. Again, this suggests more than one incident of incapacity. The code requires continued incapacity.

See also EMPLOYMENT FOR CAUSE on page 65.

EMPLOYER PERSONNEL POLICIES/EMPLOYEE HANDBOOKS

In nearly any employment related problem that you may face as an employee the importance and impact of employer rules,

"I wish I hadn't signed that contract for life..."

regulations, policies and procedures cannot be understated. Your employer has the right to set up rules, procedures, etc. for the operation of his or her business enterprise. You will be required to abide by those rules, etc. so long as they are reasonably related to achieving a legitimate business purpose, they are non-discriminatory in purpose and application, they are not designed or applied to harass or punish you, and they do not infringe upon any of your employee rights. There are many exceptions and qualifications that attach to this last statement, but the statement provides a valid perspective from which to analyze employment problems.

Very rarely will you have a single coherent source available to you of all your employer's rules and policies. The rules you are required to abide by may be written, verbal, or simply conduct by managers, supervisors or other employees that is never formalized either verbally or in writing.

Your employer may have a written employee handbook or personnel manual which briefly explains your job rights (or more likely, lack of), grievance procedures, benefits, employee obligations and company adherence to state and federal policies respecting employment.

The employee handbook or manual may be changed at any time by your employer. Your employer is normally not required to inform you of any changes. Nor is your employer automatically bound by the handbook if changes are made in benefits or policies. For this reason, and others, obtain a copy of any handbooks, manuals or policies, and retain them in a safe place for future reference. You may find yourself arguing that you were promised certain benefits at your time of hiring which were reflected in a handbook that no longer exists. The new handbook may contain no promises of such benefits. Your introduction of the handbook may convince the trier of fact that your employer should be prevented (estopped) from denying you the benefits, promises of which you (may have) relied on when you agreed to work.

Your employer's personnel policies or rules may be legally binding under theories of contract, or estoppel, or other bases in equity. Your employer's policies need not be set forth in one document. You are permitted to piece together your employer's policies from many sources. For example, your employee handbook may state that you are an at-will employee with no job security but you may still be entitled to security if you can show that your employer promised you job security verbally, or by his or her conduct, or by statements by a manager, or by statements made to other employees that the employer knew you would hear, or by any other intentional act or statement. If your employer does or says anything to contradict the at-will language of the written manual **and you can prove it**, you have a good chance of winning. Your employer will be estopped or prevented from withdrawing the later promise that modified the written policy. Always bear in mind that having a right without out proof of what was said or done, may be like having no right at all.

If you can establish that your employer has set forth a particular policy or procedure, your employer is bound to follow that policy or procedure. Your employer is not permitted to act erratically, or follow his or her own procedures only when he or she chooses to. For example, if your employer has established a procedure where an employee is entitled to two written warnings prior to termination for cause, it would be improper to terminate you without benefit of the warnings, even though the written warnings are not otherwise required by law. Your employer is not permitted to avoid following his or her own procedures on the basis that the procedures are not otherwise required.

If the employees are aware of the employer policies and rely upon the policies to be fairly applied, the employer is bound. In fact, the employee is not always required to prove that he or she relied on the employer's stated policy. Courts have held that if the employer promises that a particular procedure will be followed, or that certain benefits will be offered, or that the employees can rely on job security, that the employer will be bound by the promise even where there is no evidence that the employee actually relied on the promise.

The bad news with handbooks, or other writings that you have signed, and with that signature, tossed away your rights, is that the courts will often let you do this. If you argue that you were not given a choice in deciding whether or not to sign the documents, the courts sometimes take the tough approach that you always had the right to quit your job, rather than sign the documents demanded by your employer. Some choice! By not quitting, and by continuing to work, you have impliedly consented to the change in terms of your employment thereafter, and you cannot complain. This "consent" can enable your employer to reduce your wages, demote you, take away non-vested benefits, change your job duties, or almost anything else. Is there anything that you can do when your employer places a document in front of you and says, "Sign!"?

When all else fails, and you are backed up against the wall, you may try signing your "name" as follows:

Mr. I Protest

Scribble this "signature," and maybe your employer won't notice that you never signed at all, but rather, protested his new policies. I have never tested this in litigation, but, hey, you may have no other alternative.

FREE SPEECH

Do employees have the right to freedom of speech in the workplace? Employees think that the United States Constitution somehow provides a guarantee of "freedom of speech" in the workplace. It does not. The Constitution protects an individual's freedom of speech from intrusion by the government, not by a private employer, and not by the government, when the government is acting in the capacity or role as an employer. You are not entitled to say what you like at your place of employment and be protected from retribution from your employer.

A recent case involving the freedom of speech rights of federal employees held that the employees are protected in speaking out on topics of "public concern." However, the employees are not protected and can be fired if the employer "reasonably believed" that what the employee(s) said did not concern a matter of "public concern." Therefore, what the employee may have said is irrelevant. What the employer reasonably thought the employee said is the critical issue. The rule to remember is, be careful what you say and be careful who you say it to, and be careful who can overhear you.

DEFAMATION

Defamation is an injury to the reputation or character of someone resulting from the false statements or actions of another. Defamation is a false attack on your good name. Your good name is regarded as a proprietary interest, not a personal interest. Defamation is an improper and unlawful attack against your proprietary right to your good name, your reputation.

Defamation is a general term for the false attack on your character or reputation through either libel or slander. Libel is a term describing visual defamation, usually in the form of lies in print, or misleading or deceptive photographs.

Libel exposes or subjects you to hatred, contempt, ridicule, or disgrace, or causes you to be shunned or avoided, or injures you in your occupation.

Slander is a term describing defamation that you hear, not see, usually in the form of someone talking trash about you or spreading or repeating lies and unfounded rumor.

Slander is an oral statement that tends to injure you in respect to your office, profession, trade or business. The statement or statements generally suggest that you lack integrity, honesty, incompetence, or that you possess other reprehensible personal characteristics.

Defamation is an important concept to know for anyone working in California. Why? Because you may be an at-will employee subject to being terminated at any time for no reason, but if your employer, or his or her representative defames you, you will be entitled to sue for that attack on your reputation or character, even though you have no contractual right to your job and you would not be able to sue for wrongful termination based on a contractual theory. Furthermore, if the false attack on your character or reputation causes you to be terminated as a result you can sue for wrongful termination in violation of public policy, which will entitle you to seek damages far greater than the usual wrongful termination case based on contract. This means that if you were terminated as a result of the defamatory statement, you then will have the right to sue for wrongful termination in violation of public policy even though you were an at-will employee and you could have otherwise been terminated for no reason at any time.

A legal claim based on defamation entitles the victim to recover against the defamer for his or her emotional damages. In addition, the victim will be entitled to sue for punitive, or punishment, damages.

There are other critical differences which make defamation important to be aware of. You can prove defamation on your word alone, even though it is always better to have some confirming evidence. (a letter, a memo, an e-mail, statements from fellow employees confirming the defamatory remarks about you, etc.) You can testify in court as to statements made by others about you. This means that the "hearsay" rule does not apply to the testimony in court which repeats defamatory statements made out of court.

You do not have to prove damages in defamation cases. Damages are presumed. This means that you do not have to testify that you were emotionally destroyed or had to see a psychiatrist or other mental health specialist or doctor.

The defamatory comments do not have to be stated (this is described as being "published") to someone outside the company. Purely internal memorandums or comments that falsely attack you can be defamatory. If another employee heard or read the comment then the defamatory statement has been "published" sufficiently to support a charge of defamation.

Each repetition of a defamatory remark is a new injury. This means that you can obtain damages for each time the defamatory statement is repeated.

You may even be entitled to receive damages every time you repeat the defamatory comment to someone else! Yes, if it was reasonably foreseeable that you would feel compelled to repeat or explain the defamatory comment, your employer may be liable each time you repeated his comment!

For example, suppose your employer charges you with stealing or lack of loyalty to the company and you are terminated as a result of those false accusations. Suddenly you find yourself unemployed and looking for a new job. You feel compelled at interviews to explain why you can't offer a good referral from your prior employer.

"He said I stole from him, or he alleged that I wasn't loyal to the company."

Under these circumstances your repeated explanation of the defamatory comments may itself be defamation that you are entitled to be compensated for! See the additional discussion of this topic below.

The biggest problem in alleging defamation in the workplace is the concept of privilege. In some instances the defamer may be privileged or entitled to make the defamatory statements. It is not defamation if the person making the statement is privileged in doing so.

The defamer may have an absolute privilege for statements made in judicial proceedings, and a limited privilege for defamatory statements made in the employment relationship.

For example, suppose you have an overtime claim that you are pursuing in the office of the labor commissioner. In that hearing your employer says that you not paid certain overtime because you stole money and the employer felt thought that he could withhold overtime as compensation for that theft. At another time or place the statement by your employer would be slanderous if it were false, but in the context of the labor hearing the statement is absolutely privileged. No defamation results from the defamatory statements.

The privilege protects statements made before the beginning of a civil or criminal proceeding, if the statements are part of the "preparation" for that proceeding.

Anytime you have a proceeding that is judicial in nature, the statements made there are absolutely privileged. Most proceedings involving wage or job related claims are judicial in nature, and statements made in those hearings are privileged. This means that your employer may say things that are untrue, even if he knows that they are untrue, and says them intending to injure you or make you look bad, or ruin your reputation. He can do so without fear of being liable to you in any subsequent lawsuit against him. That is simply the way the system is set up. Defamatory statements made in an employment dispute before a government agency are absolutely privileged, and you are simply out of luck. Even though defamatory statements made in judicial proceedings are privileged, don't despair. There are many situations other than judicial, where the privilege is only partial, and that privilege can be lost under a number of circumstances.

In order for the defamer to be protected by the absolute privilege, at least one of the following four factors must be satisfied. Analyze these four factors to see whether statements made against you might not be protected. Absolute privilege is provided if;

1) The statement was made in a judicial proceeding.
2) The statement had some connection or logical relation to the judicial action.
3) The statement was made to achieve the objects of the litigation.
4) The statement involved litigants or other participants authorized by law.

Any doubts as to whether judicial privilege applies is decided in favor of the privilege. Although the privilege was meant to apply to defamation, the privilege applies to almost all personal injury claims, such as intentional or negligent infliction of emotional distress or interference with prospective advantage.

Probably the most important situation involving qualified privileges are those where your work is being evaluated in performance reviews or other evaluations of your conduct in the workplace.

Can your employer defame you in a performance review without being liable to you for defamation? Maybe. Maybe not.

An employer loses his or her qualified privilege to make defamatory comments in critiquing you or your work when the defamatory statement is made,

1) Without a good faith belief in the truth of the statement; or
2) Without reasonable grounds for believing the truth of the statement; or
3) With a motive or willingness to vex, harass, annoy, or injure you; or
4) Is exaggerated or not fully or fairly stated; or
5) The result of a reckless investigation; or
6) Motivated by hatred or ill will towards you.

Examples of statements by employers in the employment context that have been determined by the courts to be defamatory are those that involve; allegations of embezzlement, lying, irresponsibility, lack of integrity, dishonesty, laziness, incompetence, not being eligible for rehire, insubordination, being a traitor to the company, or having committed a criminal act.

As you can see, there are numerous situations where the employer risks losing his or her qualified privilege and if the privilege is lost, any publication of the false comment becomes defamatory and you will be entitled to damages for the injury to your reputation.

Other factors that may be considered in making a finding of defamation are whether the person making the statement knows or believes the statement to be true; whether the statement is the result of anger, jealousy, resentment, grudges, quarrels, ill-will or other conflict between you and the person making the statement.

In order to be defamatory the statement must be, of course, false. The employer has the burden of proving that the statement is not false. In other words, the employer has to prove that the statement was true. The statement must also seem to state a fact, or that it is based on fact, rather than an opinion, or based only on opinion. **A statement made as a statement of opinion, rather than as an allegation of fact, is not defamatory.**

Are statements made about you by a supervisor that are placed in your personnel file possibly defamatory? If the statements are statements of opinion, rather than false statements of fact, they are not potentially defamatory. The question to ask is, does the statement of opinion suggest that it is base on fact or is provable as a fact? Statements that may support a claim of libel are; false accusations of criminal conduct, lack of integrity, dishonesty, incompetence, or reprehensible personal moral behavior. For example, if you found in your personnel file, a false statement accusing you of suspected theft, such a statement would be defamatory. Such a statement would imply to the average reader that it is confirmable as a fact, and is not just an unfounded personal opinion.

Be aware that a defamatory statement in your personnel file defames for as long as the statement exists in your file. What does this mean? This means that defamatory statements made 5, 10, or even 15 years ago, and placed in your personnel file may be subject to a lawsuit if they are still there in your file "attacking" your reputation or your good name up to the present time. The statute of limitations does not protect the employer on "old" statements that are still around to be seen or heard.

If you are an employee or supervisor-employee and you are falsely accused of engaging in sexual harassment or some other offensive activity and the fact of the accusation is "published," your employer may be liable to you for defamation. If the employer notified other employees or other parties of the allegations against you , such conduct by the employer may be defamatory against you.

If you are defamed, the injury to your reputation affects a proprietary or "ownership" interest and is not a personal injury. This means that damages from defamation are not pre-empted by workers compensation. You are entitled to sue for damages in civil court.

If the damages from defamation were thought to arise as a normal risk from the employment relationship and were regarded as a form of personal injury, rather than an injury to your ownership interest in your reputation, you would be forced to file a worker's compensation claim. You would not be able to sue in civil court.

As we mentioned earlier, an interesting situation that sometimes occurs is when the publication of the slanderous information is made by the employee being slandered, rather than by the employer. This is described as "self publication." For example, suppose your boss brings you into his or her office and informs you that you are no longer needed because he suspects that you are a drinker and he states that he does not regard you as competent in your work.. Suppose further that your employer makes these comments only to your direct manager, and repeats these comments to no one outside the company. Suppose after your boss informs you of these "facts," you feel compelled to tell your fellow employees what has happened to you. After all, everyone wants to know. Under these circumstances the employee himself publishes the defamatory statements. Have you been defamed by your employer?

Is your employer liable for defamation when you have repeated and published the statements? Your employer will be liable where he or she knew or should have known that someone facing circumstances similar to yours would have been compelled to "self-publish" the defamatory statements, and did nothing to prevent it. The question the court asks is, was the self-publication foreseeable under the circumstances? If so, the employer may be liable. The difficulty with "self-publication" defamation for the employee is that the employee has the burden of proving that he or she was psychologically compelled to repeat or publish the defamatory statements.

What if you leave your old job for a new one and find out that your ex-employer has been saying bad things about you? Bad-mouthing an employee, or a former employee is known as "blacklisting" and is potentially illegal as a form of defamation just described.

BLACKLISTING

It is illegal for an employer to make a misrepresentation which prevents or attempts to prevent a former employee from getting a new job. This rule applies to your employer, his agents or officers. A misrepresentation can include any act, suggestion or inference that leads the listener to believe something untruthful or misleading about the employee in question. It need not be a direct statement. Even gestures, or tone of voice, or a raising of an eyebrow could qualify as an illegal misrepresentation.

The real problem in blacklisting is proof, or rather, lack of proof. Very rarely will you have evidence that your old employer sabotaged you. More than likely, you will never discover anything other than you were suddenly terminated, or you didn't get the job that had seemed so promising moments before. This is one situation where an ounce of prevention is worth a couple of pounds of cure.

The best thing you can do for yourself to prevent being black-listed is to obtain a written letter of recommendation or a job referral before you are terminated. If you have even the slightest feeling that something isn't going well, or that changes may be coming that might involve the elimination of your job, get a supervisor or the employer to sign a statement that you can use to present to a prospective new employer. You do not want the new employer calling your old one and permitting him or her the opportunity to damage you now that you are gone. Of course, often this is simply not feasible, and in such situations, you too may be compelled to "self publish" the defamatory story made against you in an attempt to disarm it.

If it is possible, present the good reference to the new employer yourself. The preferable situation is to write the letter of recommendation yourself and have the (ex-)employer sign it. This permits you the opportunity to make sure the right things are said about you. Be positive. You can omit mentioning your weak points but be truthful about what you do say. Find your good qualities and emphasize them. You will be surprised what your ex-employer will be willing to sign if he or she is presented with the choice at the moment that you are being terminated. The employer that doesn't like you still wishes to avoid a confrontation, or worse, a threat of legal action, and will make concessions to you in order to make you disappear.

Restrain any desire to "tell off" your employer. Obtain a letter of recommendation and leave. Never burn bridges if you can avoid it. He or she doesn't need to know how you feel.

If your old employer is a complete jerk and refuses to sign any letter for you, then present that information to the prospective employer at your earliest opportunity. Be straightforward. Tell the new employer that there was a conflict and that a positive referral is unlikely. By informing the new employer, you have lessened the impact of a bad referral by making it anticipated. You have also possibly "self published" and your statement would be admissable in court to establish that you have been defamed by your own disclosure of the original false statement that was made against you.

If an employer volunteers to another person or another employer, the reason or reasons, for an employee's discharge or reason for quitting—that employer is guilty of a crime. The employer will also be liable to you for triple damages in a civil lawsuit. The rule applies to the past employer, or agent, employee, superintendent, or manager of the past employer.

The past employer is only permitted to disclose the truthful reasons for the discharge or voluntary termination of the employee if the past employer is specifically asked without prompting.

GROOMING AND CLOTHING

Employers are entitled to enforce reasonable grooming and clothing rules as a condition of employment. Grooming or clothing rules may be declared improper under two theories prohibiting discrimination.

The first theory declares the employer's grooming or clothing policy illegal if it is applied differently to similarly situated employees based on their religion, national origin, race, or sex. For example, if the employer has a policy prohibiting long hair on men, which is enforced, but the employer fails to enforce a long hair limitation against women, the grooming policy would be improperly discriminatory. This is called "disparate treatment." Disparate, or unequal treatment occurs when the rules are unfairly enforced against one group but not another. This theory also applies to clothing standards.

For example, if the employer has a "no pants" policy applicable to women, if the employer has a uniform policy requiring women to wear short dresses
the policy would be arguably improper as discriminating against women if there were no corresponding limitations placed on the male employees. A corresponding, or comparable limitation on other employees need not be identical to be fair. For example, male employees don't have to be subjected to a "no dress" ""no long pants" policy; a corresponding or comparable "tie required" policy would

be adequate to negate a charge of discriminatory rules. We also see that it is not discriminatory if one group of people have a negative restriction placed on them, for example, a "no pants, or no long hair" policy, and the other, non-affected employees have a dissimilar, positive restriction place on them, such as "white shirt and tie required."

The second theory is the "adverse impact" theory. Under this theory, a grooming or clothing policy is improper if it is drafted so as to have an "adverse impact" on a particular group of employees as a result of their race or national origin. For example, a policy banning "afro" hairstyles may constitute a prohibited limitation on African-American employees if there is no corresponding appearance limitation placed on non-African-American employees. Many courts require that the employer's policy or rule affect an "immutable" or unchangeable racial characteristic of the employee before the rule is regarded as unfairly discriminatory under the theory of adverse impact. Unlawful "adverse impact" rules are unfair because they focus on, and punish, racial characteristics that people have no control over.

Clothing policies that require female employees to dress provocatively may be illegal if the dress code causes them to be subjected to sexual harassment.

If the employer can show that there is a safety concern or legitimate business reason for the grooming regulation, such as a "no beard" policy, then the restriction will most likely be upheld.

If you insist on wearing long hair you may be compelled to wear a hair net or similar device as a reasonable health measure. New legislation makes it illegal for an employer to have a "no pants" policy applicable to the female employees. If the employer requires employees to wear uniforms, and the uniforms for females do not include an option for pants, the employer will have to seek an exemption from the Fair Employment and Housing Commission. The employer will have to show good cause for obtaining the exemption.

See also RELIGIOUS DISCRIMINATION on page 31, and VIOLATING EMPLOYER RULES on page 241.

Chapter Two
SUING YOUR EMPLOYER FOR UNPAID WAGES AND OTHER BENEFITS

WAGE AND HOUR LAW

A BRIEF SUMMARY OF THE SYSTEM

Much of California Wage and Hour Law is drafted by the Industrial Welfare Commission (IWC) in the form of wage orders. The IWC was originally established to regulate the wages, hours and working conditions of women and children. It's authority was later expanded to regulate the hours, minimum wages and working conditions of all private employees in the State of California.

The rules that we shall discuss regarding wages, hours and working conditions apply only to employees of private employers. Public employees' wages, hours and working conditions are generally covered by agreements known as memorandums of understanding. The agreements are drafted by their employee organizations, agreed to by the governor and approved (if necessary) by the legislature. In addition, the benefits common to public employment make considerations of minimum wage irrelevant. Questions regarding overtime or working conditions of a like nature should first be directed to representatives of your employee organization. Discussions in this book regarding the broader issues of discrimination, sexual harassment and employee leave are certainly pertinent to public employees, as well as private employees.

The laws that are created by the IWC are enforced by the Division of Labor Standards Enforcement (DLSE), otherwise referred to as the Office of the Labor Commissioner, or Labor Commissioner's Office.

The responsibility of the DLSE is to interpret and enforce the intent of the IWC. The California labor laws are modeled after section 7 of the Fair Labor Standards Act of 1938 ((29 U.S.C. §207(a)(1)). The federal laws regulating working hours and overtime were intended to encourage more employment and reward employees for the burden of working long hours.

The Labor Commissioner or Commissioner deputies have the authority to enter any place of business located within the State of California. The Labor Commissioner has the authority to require any employer to furnish relevant information or documentation, such as books or records, when requested. The Labor Commissioner can also compel people to appear to testify. In order to insure compliance with Commissioner orders, the Office of the Labor Commissioner maintains field enforcement offices that specialize in enforcing the labor rules and regulations. A list is provided in the appendix section.

As with most employees working in California you are protected under both the California and federal laws regulating employment. Since the state and federal laws are not always identical, whether you will rely on California law or federal law to protect yourself will vary depending on your particular situation. It is not important for you to know the basis for your rights as I will explain them. The important thing is simply knowing what your rights are. If you know what you are entitled to, you become much less susceptible to exploitation or mistake.

I have found that the California state laws generally afford more protection or greater benefits for employees, however it is not always the case. Should the situation arise where the California law provides less protection to the employee (not the employer), then the federal law controls. State and local laws control in the wage and hour situations only where they provide greater benefits to employees than the relevant federal statute. This book is written for employees working in California, and therefore the rules set forth are those that apply in California. The rules may vary in other states.

The following wage and hour rules apply to most non-governmental employees. The subsequent sections dealing with discrimination, harassment, leave and privacy rights apply to most all employees, public or private.

DEFINITIONS AND RELATED LAW

EMPLOYERS

California Labor Law states that an employer is "...any person ...who directly or indirectly, or through an agent or any other person, employees or exercises control over the wages, hours, or working conditions of any person." The definition of employer depends on the legal context within which the term is being used. Generally, an employer is any person or business unit that hires or permits a person to perform any type of service, legal or illegal, whether for the benefit of the person doing the hiring or for any third person. Generally, if one party has the right to select and control another person to perform a service and direct his method of performing the service, there is an employer-employee relationship. The fact that one person is performing work for another is evidence of employment.

GOVERNMENT CONTRACTS

If you work for a private employer, you are protected under the wage and hour laws. This is true even if the work you perform is for the government under a governmental contract. Your employer is still private, even though the work performed is on behalf of the public sector.

PREVAILING WAGE ON PUBLIC PROJECTS

The purpose of prevailing wage laws is to protect employees working on public construction projects. The "prevailing wage" is a wage that is commonly paid to employees on like projects in like employment categories. The Director of the Department of Industrial Relations (DIR) determines the prevailing rate of wages in the local area for work of a similar character and the agency's determination is final. For all public projects that cost more than $1,000, employees must be paid no less than the prevailing wage as determined by DIR.

The prevailing wage includes not only the hourly wage but all commonly received benefits, such as medical and dental coverage, retirement benefits, vacation and sick leave, and insurance.

Generally, it is a public project if the private firm gets paid out of public funds for construction, repair or demolition projects.

If the entity employing your firm is a governmental body, such as a city, municipality, public utility, the work is part of a public work. If a public entity will lease the facilities at the completion of the work and the lease with the public entity was entered into prior to the commencement of the work, then the work by the private firm on a private building is still a public project.

If the prevailing wage rule is applicable, then the prevailing wage must be paid by all subcontractors on the job, as well as by the primary contractor.

EMPLOYEES

An employee is any person employed by an employer. You are employed if you provide services to an employer. Like the term "employer," "employee" has no fixed meaning. It all depends upon the context within which the word is being used.

Prison inmates are not regarded as employees under the FLSA. However, prison inmates who manufacture goods or perform services under a joint venture agreement between the Director of Corrections and any employer must be paid wages comparable to the employer's non-prison employees for similar work. If the employer does not have any non-prison employees, the wages are determined by examining wages in the local community for similar work. The Director of Corrections is permitted to deduct up to 80% of the prisoners gross wages for federal, state, and local taxes, charges for room and board, payments for restitution of victims, and family support orders of the prisoner, if any.

You are not regarded as an employee if you work as a volunteer for charitable or nonprofit organizations as part of a rehabilitation program. For example, if you work as a volunteer for the Salvation Army Thrift Stores as part of your rehabilitation off alcohol, you are not an employee. If the work you provide is part of a program to serve your own personal interest, you are not entitled to overtime.

Undocumented workers, commonly referred to as "illegal aliens" are "employees" within the meaning of the National Labor Relations Act (NLRA) and the FLSA. Furthermore, the Equal Employment Opportunity Commission (EEOC) has consistently interpreted Title VII of the Civil Rights Act to include illegal aliens within the definition of "employees." See EMPLOYEES VS. INDEPENDENT CONTRACTORS below for a further discussion of employees.

PART-TIME EMPLOYEES

There is no set definition for a part-time employee. We know that the state law says that full-time is generally no more than 40 hours in a seven day workweek, but you and your employer could agree on a full-time workweek of fewer hours if you wanted to, such as 33 or 38 hours, or whatever. It doesn't really matter what part-time is defined as, because part-time workers are entitled to all the rights set forth for full-time employees.

Occasionally, employees will find themselves in a position where the employer classifies them as part-time employees in order to deny them benefits available to full-time employees. The employer will be able to do this if the denial is not determined to be fraudulent, is not a breach of your employment agreement, or designed to discriminate against a protected classification, or does not, in fact, discriminate against a protected classification.

UNDER THE TABLE OR CASH EMPLOYEES

Employees who work illegally on a cash basis are still entitled to the rights set forth in this book. If you are an employee concerned about wage and hour matters, say you worked for someone "under the table" and they failed to pay you fairly, you can contact your local office of the Labor Commissioner and file a claim just like anyone else. The real question is, will the tax authorities come after you if you file a claim? If a person files a claim against an employer the DLSE will generally notify the field enforcement unit to investigate the employer. If it is determined that the employer has been operating illegally, then the enforcement unit will notify the agencies that may be concerned about workers compensation payments, or social security payments, or whatever. The DLSE does not notify the IRS that you received income "under the table," however the DLSE cannot promise you that your receipt of income will remain undisclosed to the IRS.

AM I PROTECTED?

It is impossible to attempt to list those occupations that may be excluded from protection in California from portions of the wage and hour law under the executive or managerial exemption. See OVERTIME AND THE SALARIED EMPLOYEE on page 186. However, it is important to point out that California provides much broader protection than the federal laws. For example, the federal laws exclude from protection, partially or completely, any person employed in; agriculture, agricultural production, raising or caring of livestock, landscaping, forestry or lumbering, fishing and seafood work, hospitals and nursing homes, irrigation system work, maple syrup production, transportation of fruits or vegetables, cotton ginning, aircraft, boat, or trailer sales, and amusement or recreational businesses.

The federal laws also do not completely protect full-time students, handicapped people, baby-sitters, airline employees, employees who sell or service cars or truck or farm equipment, domestic servants, gardeners, local truck drivers, employees of movie theaters, certain newspaper employees, certain railroad employees, seaman, and taxi drivers. The important thing to remember about being protected under the federal laws is—IT DOESN'T MATTER! DON'T WORRY ABOUT IT! California provides wage and hour law protection for nearly all the occupations that the federal laws omit, and the California laws control in California.

Employees are protected under the Wage and Hour Rules. Independent contractors are not.

EMPLOYEES OF TEMPORARY OR LEASING AGENCIES

Temporary agencies have become popular because they provide the client "employer" the opportunity (they think) to convert part of their work force from employees to independent contractors. The client leasing the employees seeks to avoid obligations and liabilities commonly associated with employees. After all, they are not hiring employees, but merely purchasing or leasing the services of independent professionals. By leasing employees from an agency can the client avoid the responsibilities of being an employer? No.

Employees who are temporarily placed or leased by their employers to work for another company are regarded by the Labor Commissioner as employees of both the placement or leasing firm and the client purchasing the help. The leasing firm and the client purchasing the services are regarded as "joint employers" and both are liable for any wage and hour violations or obligations falling under the authority of the Labor Commissioner.

For complaints brought before FEHA the client-employer is regarded as an employer if the client controls the terms, conditions or benefits of employment of the person being "leased."

Both the leasing company and the client are liable to maintain workers' compensation coverage for the leased employees. It is not adequate if only either one of the parties maintains workers' compensation coverage for the leased employees. Both must do so.

An employer cannot avoid the requirement to provide workers' compensation coverage by providing an ERISA type health plan for employees.

If an employer fails to maintain proper workers' compensation coverage for employees, the employer is subject to a "Stop Notice and Penalty Assessment" from the Labor Commissioner and fines of $1,000 per employee, up to a total of $100,000 in fines. If an employee is injured and the employer is uninsured, the fines go up to $10,000 per employee.

If an employee is injured while working for an uninsured employer, the employer is automatically presumed negligent and the employee can sue for damages.

EMPLOYEES VS INDEPENDENT CONTRACTORS

It seems as though even the simplest concept becomes confusing when it involves transferring money out of your employer's account into yours. You thought that because you went to work for your employer, he was your employer and you were his employee. As far as you always knew, he was happy with that arrangement, that is, until you demanded your rights as an employee. Now, he is quite certain that you are an "independent contractor" and always were.

What is an "independent contractor?" Practically speaking, that is someone to whom the employer does not owe overtime or related wage and hour benefits: Someone who is in business for himself. An independent contractor is not an employee. An independent contractor is not entitled to overtime or other wage order protections. You are in business for yourself.

The employer may owe you money as an independent contractor but the employer does not have the responsibilities he would have if you were an employee. The relevance of the legal concept is, are you going to be regarded as someone who was in the employ of another and consequently fell under the protection of the California labor laws, or were you on your own, running your own business and not entitled to protection? Under most circumstances the answer will be clear enough. You are an employee clear and simple. But what if things are not so clear? What if, for example, you are a welder, hired to do a job for a company and you bring your own tools to the job site? What if you provide your own insurance coverage, list yourself as self-employed on your tax returns, and provide your own business cards and letterheads? Are you an employee or an independent contractor? Oddly enough, under these facts the welder in the case was determined to be an employee!

You may be regarded as an independent contractor for purposes of IRS classification or under the common law definition and still be regarded as an employee under the rules of employment law. For purposes of the employment laws the court looks to what is described as the "economic reality" test.

The court asks itself, in terms of economic reality is this "employee" dependent upon the "employer" for his livelihood? If so, then he is probably an employee and not an independent contractor.

The court will look at many factors; do you have other "employers" that you do work for, are you hired for a specific job that will terminate at a predetermined point in time; do you determine how and when the job will be performed; are your skills specialized and unique; do you provide your own tools; is the work performed at the "employer's" place of business or elsewhere; how are you paid; by the job or by the hour; is the method of performing your work subject to supervision and control; what is the intent of the parties involved; and are you really in business for yourself? These and many more factors may be considered.

Sometimes particular governmental agencies will use what is referred to as the "smell" test. The "smell" test is similar to the "economic reality" test but is more subjective and highly dependant on the prior decisions of the particular government agency doing the analysis. Factors taken into consideration are; the language in any agreement between the parties, whether the "independent contractor" received any benefits normally provided to employees, whether the "client" or "employer" filled out a 1099 form, and whether the "independent contractor" filed estimated tax returns. The bottom line is, each agency will conduct its own analysis to determine, under the circumstances, what the actual relationship is between the parties.

Do not assume that you are not entitled to wage and hour protection. Take your case to a hearing officer of the Office of the

Labor Commissioner and, if you present your case properly, they may agree with you. If you run a business with just one client, that client may be your "employer." Remember that how you describe yourself, or how your "employer" describes your relationship, is irrelevant.

OUTSIDE SALESMEN

The protection of the wage orders do not apply to outside salesmen. Outside salesmen are employees who sell the employer's products or obtain orders for the employer's services away from the employer's place of business for more than 50% of their total work time. The distinguishing characteristic of the outside salesman is working away from the employer's place of business, beyond the ability of the employer to monitor the salesman's hours. It is the employer's lack of control over the salesman's hours and working conditions that provides the rationale for the employer to avoid responsibility for overtime and the other wage and hour provisions.

The rationale is not consistent because outside sales work does not include promotional work performed away from the employer's place of business. Time spent doing promotional work away from the office is no more easily monitored than sales efforts.

In any event, if you promote the employer's products, rather than sell them, you are protected. Promoting an employer's product without having sales as the primary focus of the job may involve such duties as putting up displays and posters, removing damaged or spoiled stock from the merchant's shelves or arranging shelf displays. These employees are regarded as outside salesmen only if they are actually employed for the purpose of making sales or contracts, and are, in fact, doing so. If the employee is engaged in promotional activities designed to stimulate sales that will be made by someone else, their work is entitled to protection. In borderline cases the test is whether the efforts of the employee are aimed at increasing the sales of the company in general (protected) or whether the efforts are designed to increase his or her own specific sales (not protected).

Under the federal rule, if you are an outside salesman and you spend at least 20% of your work time doing protected activities (you aren't selling away from the employer's business) you are regarded as a protected employee. One day a week is equal to 20% of your total work time if you work full-time.

If you are an outside salesman, arguing for overtime or other benefits before the DLSE (which is a state, not federal, department), you will want to point out that the federal rule requires that only 20% of your time be devoted to protected activities, not 50% as under the state rule. You will want to point out that the federal rule should be followed where, as here, it provides greater protection for the employee.

DRIVER SALESMEN

Sometimes employers will employ drivers to deliver products to customers. The driver's duties also include many functions related to selling the goods that they deliver. In determining whether the driver is an outside salesman, the issue is, what is the chief duty or primary function of the employee? The determination of the primary function must be made in terms of the basic character of the job overall. All the employee's duties must be considered to figure out the employee's primary function, and the time devoted to the various duties is relevant, but not controlling, in determining the relative importance of each duty. For example, a route driver who transports products sold through vending machines and keeps such machines stocked, in good operating condition, and in good locations, is not employed to make sales, even though his efforts are very important to the promotion of sales. He is employed to maintain and supply the employer's equipment. Therefore, he is protected.

As with many of your rights described in this book, I cannot tell you in advance whether or not you are entitled to protection if you work as a driver salesman. The best that I can do is tell you the factors you need to be aware of in order to successfully argue that you are entitled to protection and what to do to best present your case.

SEASONAL LABORERS

Under the California labor code, seasonal labor is defined as all labor performed by any person hired in this state to perform services outside the state for a period longer than one month, where the wages are paid at the termination of employment, rather than at fixed intervals. This definition of "seasonal labor" is not what you would normally imagine it to be. See SEASONAL LABOR under PAYROLL WITHHOLDING and SEASONAL LABOR under FREQUENCY OF PAYMENT—REGULAR PAYCHECKS on page 222 and 206.

WORKING FOR RELATIVES

You are not protected under the labor laws relating to minimum wage, or hours and working conditions, if you work for your parent, child, spouse or if you are the legally adopted child of your employer.

EMPLOYEE RIGHTS OUTSIDE THE UNITED STATES

Although I began by stating that this book sets forth the law as applicable in California, a footnote is in order regarding employees of California (or other U.S.) Companies who may find themselves working in a foreign country. In 1991 the Civil Rights Act was enacted which extended civil rights protection against job discrimination to U.S. Employees employed by U.S. Companies abroad. The 1991 act overruled previous court decisions which held that the protections of the 1964 Civil Rights Act did not apply to U.S. Employees working abroad. The act also extends the protection of the Americans with Disabilities Act (ADA) overseas. Therefore, if you are a U.S. Employee in a foreign country, working for a U.S. Firm, you are protected from discrimination under either the provisions of the ADA, or the provisions of the 1964 Civil Rights Act.

NON-CITIZENS

Non-citizens have the same employment rights as citizens. The only difference between citizens and non-citizens is that certain governmental positions may require citizenship as a condition of employment.

ALIENS

UNDOCUMENTED WORKERS

The common description of an undocumented worker is an "illegal alien." Are illegal aliens entitled to employment protection under the laws of California? Yes.

Illegal aliens occupy an awkward and unusual position in this society. Congress passed the Immigration Control Reform Act (IRCA) in 1986, which shifted the burden of identifying and eliminating illegal aliens from the work force from the Federal Government to private employers. IRCA made it illegal for an employer to hire an undocumented worker. It became the employer's obligation to see to it that no undocumented workers were permitted employment. Furthermore, it is illegal for an alien to seek employment without authorization to do so from the Immigration Naturalization Service (INS). Yet, despite these laws, if an undocumented worker obtains employment, then he or she is entitled to the protections afforded to all other employees, citizen or non-citizen, legal or illegal.

Illegal aliens are protected employees under the provisions of the FLSA, which sets forth the wage and hour provisions, and under Title VII of the Civil Rights Act of 1964, which provides that it "...is an unlawful employment practice for an employer to discharge any individual or otherwise to discriminate against any individual...because of such person's race, color, religion, sex or national origin..."

The Equal Employment Opportunity Commission (EEOC) has held that "any individual" includes aliens, legal and illegal.

If you are an illegal alien or a legal alien who does not have authorization to work, you may still pursue most of the remedies set forth in this book for work that you have performed while in this State, even if it was illegal for you to have worked in the first place.

You have the right to join unions or form labor organizations, elect worker representatives and enforce all FLSA and NLRA laws and safety and health laws! The theory behind this policy is that to do otherwise is to encourage employers to exploit a powerless and disadvantaged class of people who have nowhere to turn for help. Employers should not be permitted to benefit from improperly hiring undocumented workers, or be encouraged to do so by being permitted to exploit them by having the undocumented stripped of all rights.

Illegal aliens are entitled to employment protection.

Undocumented workers are entitled to the protections extended by the **federal** labor laws, not the California labor laws. What is the significance of this? The federal labor laws do not protect employees working in agriculture or numerous other occupations. See AM I PROTECTED? on page 124. The California Office of the Labor Commissioner extends protection to these occupations but only "officially" to documented workers. Undocumented workers are not "officially" protected in California. But, here's where it gets tricky—California has a "no ask" policy regarding the legal status of employees seeking help through the DLSE. This is extremely important because undocumented employees who work in any of the federally excluded occupations and are therefore not protected under the federal laws should not be entitled to protection in California either, but since the DLSE doesn't ask, the employees that come before the DLSE are assumed to be legal (even if you do not speak English) and are entitled to the full coverage offered under California law.

We have seen that undocumented workers have certain rights concerning conditions of employment, but do they have a right to employment itself? What are the rights of the undocumented worker in the event of a discharge by an employer? This is a touchy situation.

Undocumented workers are entitled to protection from discrimination based on race, national origin, ancestry or skin color under Title VII of the Civil Rights Act. However, undocumented workers are not entitled to work without I-9 compliance, which, by definition, they do not have. The practical result is that in defending himself against a Title VII discrimination complaint or a wrongful termination complaint, the employer will probably assert the employee's lack of I-9 documentation. See the next section for further explanation of the I-9 form. Will the employer win? Unfortunately, it is impossible to predict. Although, in the cases I have seen where the employer alleged the employee's illegal status in defense of labor claims brought by the undocumented workers the employers have lost! I do not believe that the "bad acts" doctrine has been applied in this employment context. See RESUME FRAUD AND "BAD ACTS" on page 74.

The courts have held that the legal status of the employee cannot be used as a shield by the employer to foster improper employer activities. Furthermore, employers are not permitted to make determinations that are only properly made by the INS. Although it would seem clear that the employer would be able to assert the employee's illegal status in the first instance as a defense to any such suit, much depends on the rationale relied on by the employer for the termination. If the employer terminated the employee for reasons other than lack of I-9 compliance, the judge or arbitrator may prohibit the employer from alleging lack of documentation as a basis for termination. If the judge or arbitrator determines that the employer did not have a proper basis for terminating the undocumented worker, or did so in retaliation against the worker, or for some pretext, the judge or arbitrator can order the reinstatement of the worker and the employer must comply with that order. An undocumented worker is entitled to reinstatement as ordered by a judge or arbitrator.

What if the employer retaliates against the undocumented employee by informing the INS of the employee's illegal status? The Supreme Court has held that alerting the immigration officials in retaliation against an undocumented worker for asserting his rights, is illegal under the NLRA. If the INS does come calling, they are authorized to inspect employer records and conduct investigations without first obtaining a warrant.

You may have noticed that I have said that undocumented workers fall within the protection of the FLSA, which is the federal law regulating wages and hours. But the federal law does not protect employees in agriculture or numerous other occupations. See AM I PROTECTED? on page 124.

Since undocumented workers derive their protected status from the federal laws, are they entitled to protection if the federal laws do not protect their particular occupation? For example, do illegal agricultural workers have protection in California since the federal laws do not protect agricultural workers, and the California laws only protect legal agricultural workers? This would seem to be a serious problem. Fortunately, California follows a "don't ask" policy with regards to employees that come before the DLSE for help. The Office of the Labor Commissioner treats all employees as employees under California law. The DLSE does not ask if you are documented and does not care. Consequently, undocumented workers are able to gain protection under the California laws that protect agricultural employees (and most other occupations) even though the federal laws would not provide the same protection.

AUTHORIZATION OF EMPLOYEES HIRED BEFORE NOVEMBER 7, 1986

If you were hired before November 7, 1986 you are not now required to present evidence that you are authorized to work in the United States. However, this exception is very limited. If your employer discovers somehow that you are not authorized to work, the employer is obligated to terminate your employment.

In addition, you will have to show current eligibility for employment if, at any time after November 7, 1986, you either quit your job, you are terminated, or you are deported from the United States. In other words, the only time you do not have to show continued eligibility to work is if you have the same employer (not the same job) that you had before November 7, 1986. If a new company has "bought out" your old employer, the new employer is regarded as the same employer and you do not have to show current employment eligibility.

DOCUMENTATION PROCEDURES FOR ALIENS

The employer has an obligation to verify the work eligibility of all of his employees by completing an INS I-9 form. The I-9 form provides personal information on the employee, including provisions for establishing employee identity. A sample I-9 form is provided on page 337. The employer is obligated to verify identity and employment eligibility of all employees, and at the same time the employer risks charges of discrimination or fines if he asks for more or different documents than required by the INS.

The employer is entitled to copy documents submitted by the applicant to confirm status and eligibility. If the employer makes copies of any documents provided by the applicant the documents must be attached to the I-9 form. If your employer requests to copy documents submitted by you but not from any other employe, your employer may be liable to you for discrimination.

There are three types of acceptable identification set forth by the INS: List A, which establishes both identity and employment eligibility; List B, which establishes identity; and List C, which establishes employment eligibility.

If the employee or applicant presents an acceptable List A document that satisfies both identity and eligibility, the employee cannot be compelled to provide additional documentation. In other words, the employer cannot additionally require the employee to show a List B or C document. In fact, the employer can face serious fines for even requesting additional documentation in the mistaken belief that it is "better to be safe than sorry." Under these circumstances, it is not "safe" for the employer to request more documentation than he or she is entitled to by law, and if he or she does so, they will be real "sorry" they did. If the employee or applicant presents an acceptable List B document, he or she must also present an acceptable List C document. The employer is not entitled to demand that the employee show a "green card" or INS-issued documents as proof of eligibility to work. "Green cards" are actually "pink" in color. The acceptable documents in each list are as follows:

Documents that Establish Both Identity and Employment Eligibility
LIST A: U.S. Passport

Certificate of U.S. Citizenship
Certificate of Naturalization
Unexpired foreign passport,
with I-551 stamp
Alien Registration Receipt Card
Unexpired Temporary Resident Card
Unexpired Employment Authorization Card
Unexpired Reentry Permit
Unexpired Refugee Travel Document
Unexpired Employment Authorization
Document w/photo

Documents that Establish Identity
LIST B: State driver's license or ID card w/photo or
descriptive information
Federal or state ID card w/photo or
descriptive information
School ID card w/photo
Voter's registration card
U.S. Military card or draft record
Military dependent's ID card
U.S. Coast Guard Merchant Mariner Card
Native American tribal document
Canadian Driver's license
For minors:
School record or report card
Clinic, doctor, or hospital record
Day-care or nursery school record

Documents that Establish Employment Eligibility
LIST C: Social security card
Cert. of birth abroad issued by Dept. of State
U.S. Birth certificate or certified copy
Native American tribal document
U. S. Citizen ID Card
ID card for use of U.S. Resident citizen
Unexpired INS employment authorization
document

The employee is entitled to present, and the employer must accept, whatever documents the employee chooses to offer as proof of eligibility, so long as the documents appear to be genuine, and establish employment eligibility.

As an illustration of our discussion, the employee is entitled to present a driver's license and a social security card for verification of eligibility. The employer must accept those documents and not request another document. The employee is entitled to show either a List A document or a combination of List B and C documents (one each) of his choosing to establish his employment eligibility.

TEMPORARY LEGAL ALIENS

Many legal aliens enter the United States and are authorized to work for limited periods of time under limited circumstances. Nonimmigrant aliens who commonly fall into this category are students under an F-1 visa, temporary workers under the TN-1, H1-A, H1-B, H2, H2-A visas or, exchange visitors under the J-1 visa.

When employees in this category are hired their employer enters into an agreement with the INS which states that the employee is being hired for a specific term or period of time. Is this "agreement" between the employer and the INS, taken under penalty of perjury by the employer, evidence that the employer intended to hire you for a definite period of time? If the answer is yes, not only are you not an at-will employee, under California Labor Code §2924 you can only be terminated for habitual neglect of duty, continued incapacity to perform your duties as an employee, or willful breach of the employment agreement. This is even more protection than afforded regular "for cause" employees. I cannot state that the H1-B or other application will establish you as an employee hired for a specific period, however I am currently litigating this issue in different judicial districts in California, so we shall see. For further references see, FOR

CAUSE EMPLOYEES and EMPLOYMENT CONTRACTS FOR
A SPECIFIED PERIOD OF TIME, at 65.

    Bear in mind, as in most employment situations, that it is
very important for you to collect and preserve evidence that
supports your theory of employment; Documents that evidence
the verbal promises made to you, e-mails, confirming letters back
to the boss, etc. and please, do this **before** everything goes bad on
you.

"I wonder if I have any illegal aliens working for me?"

WAGE AND HOUR LAW

EQUAL PAY

Federal law requires that all employees are entitled to equal pay for similar work. Differences in pay cannot be on account of one's sex. This law originated in the desire to get rid of pay discrepancies against female employees. This is not to suggest that men are not protected. Men are protected. In fact, many equal pay claims in California have been filed and won by men.

The law applies to virtually all employees, including executives, managers, and professionals that are otherwise excluded under the wage and hour laws.

The employer cannot equalize the pay between employees of different sexes by lowering the pay of one sex to equal that of the lower paid sex. The employer must raise the pay of the employees who have been discriminated against.

Equal pay includes all forms of compensation, including fringe benefits. This means that the employer may not discriminate based on sex in terms of salary, retirement benefits, pension plans, stock options, bonuses, or other forms of compensation.

An employee who has been discriminated against in pay on account of sex can recover damages even though they may have voluntarily agreed to work for less. If you think that you have been paid less because of your sex, if you hire an attorney to represent you, if you win, you will be entitled require your employer to pay attorneys fees.

The equal pay act is enforced by the EEOC, which is a federal agency. See also EQUAL PAY on page 139 for a further discussion of what a person needs to show to establish a pay discrimination case that he or she can probably win.

WORKDAY AND WORKWEEK

A workday, for the purposes of computing overtime on the daily threshold, is a consecutive 24 hour period beginning at the same time every day. You can begin the workday at any time of day, and different employees can have workdays begin at different times. A workweek, for the purposes of determining overtime based on the weekly threshold, is any 7 consecutive 24 hour periods, in other words, any 7 days in a row. "Daily and weekly thresholds" are two different situations where the employee was entitled to overtime prior to January 1, 1998. We retain these definitions for those readers who may have overtime claims for work performed before January 1, 1998. For more discussion of this see OVERTIME on page 167.

The workweek can start on any day of the week, but it must start on the same day every week. Like the workday, the workweek can only be changed if the change is intended to be permanent and is not done to avoid the wage and hour laws. It is not the policy of the Division of Labor Standards Enforcement (DLSE) to tell the employer or employee how to set up their workweek. However, in the absence of any agreement between the employer and employee to the contrary, the DLSE sets the workweek as beginning 12:01 a.m. Sunday, and ending at midnight the following Saturday.

An employer is not required to provide the same workweek for all employees.

A workday is 8 hours.
A workweek is 40 hours.

The hours used to compute a workday are 8 hours, and the hours used to compute a workweek are 40 hours. An employee's regular rate of pay must be based on no more than the legal maximum regular hours, normally a 40 hour workweek and an 8 hour workday. The regular rate of pay includes every form of regular payment, such as salary, hourly, piece rate, bonuses, and the money

value of meals and lodging. See OVERTIME AND THE REGU-
LAR RATE OF PAY on page 175. **Every person employed in any
occupation is entitled to one day off every seven days.** This applies to employees that work at night. Generally, no employer can
require an employee to work seven days a week, but there are several exceptions to this rule:

1) The rule does not apply to emergencies.
2) The rule does not apply to work regarding the care of
   animals, crops, or agricultural lands, or to work
   relating to the protection of life or property from loss `
   or destruction.
3) The rule does not apply if you worked less than 30
   hours in the week.
4) The rule does not apply if you worked 6 hours or less,
   at least one day during the week.

If the nature of your work requires you to work seven days a
week, as set forth above, you are entitled to receive your accumulated required days off at the end of the month and no later than that.

MAXIMUM WORKDAYS

Some occupations limit the number of hours that an employee may be required to work. For example, if you work in underground mines or underground workings, or smelters or refining
plants, you are limited to 8 hours for every 24 hour period, except
for emergencies. If you are employed in a pharmacy you are not
permitted and cannot be required to work more than 9 hours per
day. If you work for a railroad as either a brakeman, conductor,
engineer, fireman, motorman, telegraph operator, or train dispatcher,
you are not permitted to work more than 12 consecutive hours on a
work shift. If you are one of the employees named above that has
been on continuous duty for at least 12 hours you must be provided
with a least 10 consecutive hours off duty thereafter. If you have
been working at least 12 hours within a 24 hour period, even though
the 12 hours was not consecutive, you must be provided with at

least 8 consecutive hours off work.

For further discussions see REQUIRING OVERTIME on page 178.

72 HOUR WORKWEEK LIMITS

If you work in an industry that prepares agricultural products for sale you cannot be required to work more than 72 hours in the workweek. If you refuse to work more than 72 hours in a workweek, your employer is prohibited from firing you or otherwise discriminating against you in any manner.

The 72 hour limitation also applies if you work in canning, freezing and preserving industry; the professional, technical, clerical, mechanical and similar occupations; or in industries handling products after harvest.

If you work as a personal attendant you cannot be forced to work more than 54 hours a week, nor more than six days a week. If an emergency forces you to work longer hours you must be paid overtime.

HOUSEHOLD LIVE-IN EMPLOYEES

If you are a live-in employee in a household occupation, such as a butler, maid, chauffeur, cook, companion, groom, gardener, day worker, graduate nurse, practical nurse, house cleaner, house keeper, tutor, valet, or similar occupation, you have the following employment rights:

1) You are entitled to a least 12 consecutive hours off for every 24 hour workday.
2) Your workday shall not exceed 12 hours except:
   a) You can agree to accept shifts where you have 3 hours free time during the 12 hour shift. The free-time need not be consecutive.
   b) If you work during your 3 hours of free-time or during the regular 12 hour off-duty shift you are entitled to be paid overtime.

Live-in employees are protected by the three threshold overtime rules. In other words, if you work 12 hours a day and receive 12 hours off-time you are entitled to overtime for hours worked in excess of 8 hours per day, hours worked in excess of 40 regular hours per work week, or hours worked on the seventh consecutive day of work.

In addition, if you are a live-in employee you are entitled to 24 hours off every five days, except in emergencies. If an emergency forces you to work on the sixth day you are entitled to overtime for the first 9 hours, and double-time thereafter, extending to the seventh day, if necessary.

An emergency is defined as an unpredictable or unavoidable occurrence at unscheduled intervals requiring immediate action. An unpredictable occurrence is unplanned and unanticipated. An unavoidable occurrence permits you the advance knowledge of the likelihood of the event. You can see that an emergency can be either anticipated or unanticipated if the emergency cannot be avoided and it requires your immediate action to correct the problem.

"Baby-sitters" are not covered under this wage order. Nor are you covered if you work in a private household to supervise, feed, or dress a child or supervise a person who is unable to care for themselves as a result of old age, physical disability or mental disability.

MOTEL MANAGERS

A recent case has held that live-in hotel and motel managers who are required to remain on the premises 24 hours a day during the days that they work are only entitled to be paid for the time that they actually perform job duties. Such employees are not entitled to be paid for the entire 24 hours if they actually worked less than that.

See also OVERTIME on page 167.

MINIMUM WAGE

The minimum wage in California as of March 1, 1998 is $5.75 per hour. This means that if you work for someone in California, your employer is obligated to pay you at least $5.75 per hour for every hour you work for him or her. If you agree to work for less in order to get the job, you are still entitled to be paid at least $5.75 per hour, despite your agreement to work for less, or even for free, but see TRYOUT TIME on page 146.

The minimum wage applies regardless how your wage is computed, whether by hourly wage, or piece rate, or commission or otherwise. If you work on a piece rate basis and your average weekly production pays you less than the minimum wage, your employer is obligated to pay the difference to ensure that you receive the minimum wage. The same is true for commission wages. If your commissions are not sufficient to pay you the minimum wage for all your hours worked, your employer must pay the difference to bring your pay up to minimum wage. The minimum wage also applies to part-time workers, no matter how few hours you work.

Your rights to minimum wage are not waiveable. In other words, your rights cannot be taken from you or voluntarily given up by you. You are not permitted to sign your rights away even if you wanted to. Any promise by you to give up your rights or trade them away will simply not be enforced against you despite any promises by you to the contrary. If you cash a check which states that it is payment in full but which, in fact, does not pay you in full, or you sign a receipt for full payment when money is still owed you, such items are not conclusive evidence that you have been paid in full. You still have the right to seek complete payment.

You may normally delay up to two years before you take legal actions to collect any monies owed you, although delay is not recommended. In some cases you must file a complaint within 30 days of the action you are complaining about. For a further discussion of this issue see HOW SOON MUST YOU ACT on page 219.

If you work for someone and you are being paid less than

$5.75 an hour, you have the right at any time to go to the employer and demand to receive the difference between what you were being paid per hour and $5.75 per hour. If your employer refuses to pay you what you are owed, you may contact your local DLSE office (see the listing on page 331) and file a claim, or you may sue your employer yourself, either in small claims court, or in other civil court proceedings, as is most appropriate. If you win in the civil proceedings, you will be entitled to recover the balance due, plus interest that has accumulated, plus reasonable attorneys fees and all costs of bringing the legal action.

If you are seeking substantial money for unpaid overtime, and by that I mean generally over $5,000.00 you may be better off by hiring an attorney, rather than doing it on your own through the Office of the Labor Commissioner. First of all, there may be other causes of action that you are unaware of, and secondly, even if you do win before the Commissioner, this decision will be automatically appealable to civil court by the employer and you may be forced to begin again. In addition, you may not be adequately skilled to present your argument on your own, and bringing your claim on your own may not be in your own best interests. On the bright side, if this does occur, the Office of the Labor Commissioner will probably provide you with a lawyer free of charge.

If you hire a private attorney and you win, you will be entitled to collect attorneys fees for your lawyer from your employer. This provides a real motivation for a private attorney to take your case.

TIPS AND MINIMUM WAGE

California does not permit an employer to reduce your wage below the minimum wage if you receive tip or gratuity income in addition to the minimum provided by the employer.

Federal law would permit your employer to reduce your wage. This is one of many instances where California law is better for the employee than the federal law.

California does permit the employer to enforce a company policy (if there is one) of "tip pooling" where a portion of your tips are required to be shared with other non-tipped employees, such as busboys or dishwashers. Tip income is not included in your base wage for computation of overtime pay. Overtime is based on what your employer pays you, not on what you receive from other people. You cannot receive overtime based on your "tip" income.

MINIMUM WAGE AND PIECE RATE

Piece rate is a method of payment where you are paid based on your production. This method of payment is often used in the agricultural occupations. If you work under a piece rate system or other incentive plan system where you are paid according to how much product you produce, the employer is obligated to provide the employees with a statement of the piece rates paid or an explanation of the incentive plan being used and the employer must maintain an accurate production record for each employee. You are entitled to receive the minimum wage of $5.75 an hour, even if your own piece rate output provides you with less than the minimum wage. The employer is obligated to provide piece rates that yield at least the minimum wage. If your production yields less than that, then the employer is obligated to pay the difference to ensure that you earn the minimum wage.

LEARNERS

If you are learning a new occupation, your employer is permitted to pay you $4.90 per hour (85% of the minimum wage) for your first 160 hours (4 weeks) of work if you have no prior experience in the type of work you are doing. If you begin working for a new employer and you have prior experience in the type of work you are doing for him, you must be paid $5.75 an hour, even though it is the first time that you have done this type of work for this employer. If you have done the same or similar work for someone else before, you are not a learner. Be sure to tell your employer you have prior experience if there is any possibility that he may be planning to pay you only $4.90 an hour.

TRYOUT TIME

You may agree to work for a short period of time for free in order to see whether you find the work to your liking. Free tryout time cannot extend for more than two hours. If you work longer than two hours you must be paid.

PERMITTED FORMS OF PAYMENT

All wages must be in the form of cash or payable in cash on demand. "Payable in cash on demand" is a fancy way of saying you are paid by a check or something that "looks like" a check. If you are paid by check, the check must be cashable for 30 days after you receive it. If the form of payment is protested or dishonored, your employer may be charged with a misdemeanor crime. It is a crime to refuse to pay wages due and payable after demand has been made by the employee. It is also a crime for the employer to deny that you are owed money or assert that you are owed less than you really are, with the intent to force you to accept less, or with the intent to annoy, harass, oppress, hinder, delay or defraud you.

Your employer is not permitted to require you to sign anything that waives any of your legal rights regarding your wages as a pre-condition of your being paid. In other words, don't sign anything that says that you are giving up any of your legal rights.

GROUP PIECE RATE

Group piece rate pay is where the employer totals the production output of a group of employees, divides the total production by the number of employees and pays each one an equal portion of the total wages due. The regular rate of pay for overtime is computed by dividing your pay by the total number of hours you worked for the relevant pay period.

NET PROFITS

What if you have an agreement with your employer to be paid out of, or share the net profits of the business? The first step in determining what you are entitled to under this type of arrangement is to look to your agreement. Net profit is generally figured out according to the intentions of the parties who have entered into the agreement. If the agreement is uncertain, or poorly drafted, then the acts and conduct of the parties may be used to determine their intention. There is a general policy of interpreting a confusing contract against the person that drafted the contract. If you have a written agreement to pay you a percentage of profits, you may be able to convince the hearing officer that the employer, who normally has a much stronger bargaining position, either drafted the agreement, or controlled the terms of the agreement. Any confusing or vague conditions should properly be interpreted in your favor. If no agreement exists to define the net profit, then "net profit" is that money which remains after payment of expenses.

If your agreement promises you a percentage of profits and you are terminated, you are entitled to pro rata payment up to the time of termination. This means that you are entitled to your share for the amount of work that you put in so far, or up to the time of your termination. You are entitled to interest on profits after the profits become due and payable, until they are paid, unless it is agreed that the profits are to be left in the business until termination of the agreement or the occurrence of some other condition. In that case, interest is payable from the time of the termination of the agreement or the occurrence of the condition. As you must realize, these are all factors that must be analyzed on a case by case basis.

COMMISSIONS

You are considered as paid on a commission basis, or commission plan if you are;
(1) involved in selling a product or service; you are not making the product or rendering the service, and
(2) you are paid a percentage of the price of the product or service.

As with the discussion of net profit, you must always analyze any agreements in force to determine what the parties intended. Your commission agreement with your employer can be verbal or in writing.

Generally, salesmen are entitled to commission from any sale where the salesman was the procuring cause of the sale, even though other people may have participated or assisted in completing the sale. Although you have to have a completed sale to be entitled to commission, you do not have to have completed the sale yourself to be entitled to commission. You have to be regarded as a "procuring cause," which is defined as the originating cause that ultimately led to the sale, or the cause that set into motion the chain of events that ultimately resulted in a sale. For example, you may be the procuring cause to a sale even though your boss stepped in at the last moment and completed the sale. If it was your efforts that got the buyer to come in or got the buyer interested in the first place, you probably "procured" or "got" the sale and you should be paid commission, even if you were shoved aside later on.

Generally, once commissions are earned they cannot be forfeited. Once you have earned a commission your employer cannot add additional conditions on you before you are entitled to be paid your commission.

No deductions, other than standard payroll deductions, may be made from an employee's commissions.

If you are terminated, your commissions, if they are capable of being calculated, must be paid to you at that time.

If you quit, and you provide the 72 hours notice of quitting, your commissions are payable to you on your last day of work.

What if you are asked to sign an employment contract that provides that you will only be paid commissions on sales that have actually been collected prior to your final day of employment? This, or any similar harsh contractual provision may be avoided if you can establish one or more of the following conditions ; The contractual provision was presented to you without any real ability on your part to bargain over the inclusion of the provision, the provision was presented as a "mere formality," enforcement of the provision would result in a miscarriage of fairness, the provision was commercially unreasonable in exacting a penalty far in excess of any harm suffered by the other party.

See also COMMISSIONS AND OVERTIME on page 176.

BONUSES

The option of providing a bonus is up to the employer. However, where a bonus is promised to either a prospective employee or to a current employee, there are several theories applied to require the employer to make good on his promise. If you are a prospective employee and the employer promises you a bonus to entice you to work for him and later recants or takes back the promised bonus after you have accepted an offer of employment, the employer is held to the promise. The employer is forced to abide by the promise to provide additional compensation as part of the job offer.

If you are already employed and under a preexisting duty to work for the employer you are still entitled to the promised bonus. The courts explain that the promised bonus acts as an inducement for the employees to put forth extraordinary efforts beyond what was required of them by the preexisting employment relationship. By promising you a bonus you were encouraged to work harder than you otherwise had to and the employer should pay you for that. In other cases, the promised bonus is said to induce the employee to continue in employment by causing the employee to forego rights to seek other employment and therefore causes the promise to be enforceable.

The courts sometimes prevent the employer from withdrawing a promised bonus, explaining that once the employees have relied on the employer's promise, it is only equitable or fair that he be held to the promise. In legal terminology this is known as "promissory estoppel."

Promised bonuses are generally enforceable.

If you have an employment contract, any terms to the contract that would result in a loss of employee's bonus earnings are not favored by the courts, and are construed or interpreted against the employer. If any of the terms of the agreement, either verbally or in writing, are confusing, the benefit of the confusion is interpreted against the employer and for the employee.

An agreement to pay a bonus need not specify the amount to be paid or even the formula to be used in computing the payment in order to be enforceable. The law implies an agreement to pay the reasonable value of the services, as determined by all the circumstances of the case.

What if the employer promises a bonus dependent upon the occurrence or non-occurrence of some condition? For example, the employer promises to pay you a bonus at the end of the year "if business is good," or "I will pay you a $100.00 bonus at the end of the month if we meet our sales projections, and if we don't, I will pay a bonus of $50.00." Although the two examples may seem the same, they are very different. Under the first example the employer did not promise either the amount of a bonus or even the guarantee of any bonus at all. This is often referred to as a "discretionary bonus," because the employer retains the right to change his mind, both as to the existence of the bonus and to the amount of the bonus, until the happening of the condition upon which the bonus is based. If the occurrence or non-occurrence of the condition is within the control of the employer, then the employer has really committed himself to nothing. If the employer is the one who determines that "business is good, or business is bad," it appears as though the employer has not promised anything! If you find yourself in this unpleasant situation, you need to point out to your hearing officer that the labor laws require, under all circumstances, that the employer act in good faith and deal fairly with the employees. If you can establish that the employer made "false or empty promises" or otherwise acted unfairly, or in bad faith, or attempted to take advantage of your lack of knowledge or sophistication, then you have a good chance of making him pay up on his worthless promise.

In the second example, the employer committed himself to paying a bonus, although the amount of the bonus was subject to a condition. If the condition occurs, the employer has promised a big bonus, if the condition doesn't occur, then the bonus is smaller. Under the second example, you are promised a bonus of some amount, no matter what, and you must be paid. Under the first example you may be out of luck unless you can show that the promise was made in bad faith, or to trick you, or was just unfair under the circumstances.

WHEN BONUSES MUST BE PAID

If a bonus is promised for some future time, for example,

the end of the season or the end of each week, then it must be paid when promised. If the bonus is based on a percentage of production or some formula, then it must be paid with the other wages for the pay period. If you have earned overtime, the bonus overtime must be paid at the same time as the other wages for the period, or no later than the next regular payday according to the regular payroll period.

SEPARATION OR SEVERANCE PAY

There is no legal right to severance pay as a normal condition of employment. The right to severance pay depends on the particular agreement between the employee and the employer.

Severance pay differs from other forms of employee compensation in that it is given in recognition of past services and in recognition of their past value. It is a form of accumulated compensation for services already rendered. Once it is earned, in other words, after you have performed your labor upon which the severance pay is based, the severance pay becomes payable no matter what happens thereafter. If you are later fired for cause, you are still entitled to your severance pay. It has already been earned.

If the employer thinks that he is due a setoff (a setoff is a reduction in what you are owed for something else that you owe him), he can file a claim against you, but he cannot resort to self help except under the limited situations laid out in CASH SHORTAGE OR EQUIPMENT BREAKAGE, on page 206.

The laws applicable to your particular severance pay situation will depend on whether your employer has a severance plan that falls under the federal Employee Retirement Income Security Act (ERISA). If your employer's severance pay plan is funded, in other words, funds are allocated and set aside for the anticipated severance payment, rather than simply paid out of ordinary cash assets as the need arises, then the plan is probably governed by ERISA rules. The rules governing ERISA plans are beyond the scope of this book. However, you should know that, under ERISA, your employer is entitled to amend or eliminate a severance plan without considering the interests of the employees.

If you think you have been improperly denied severance pay and you do not have a written agreement setting forth your right to severance pay, you may need to establish that the employer had a policy of providing severance pay and that the policy was applicable to you. If the policy was not clearly applicable to you, then you will argue that the policy should have been rightfully applicable to you. If you do not have evidence of a written severance pay policy, you may be able to establish a severance pay policy set forth by the company's personnel policy that becomes part of the employment agreement as applicable to you. Your third option is even more difficult to establish, and that is this—although the company had no regular policy of providing severance pay, severance pay was promised to you in a verbal agreement. Of course, lack of evidence is a problem in this situation.

NOTE: You cannot go to the DLSE if you have a problem being paid your severance pay. The Labor Commissioner's Office is legally prohibited from helping you in this matter. You must go to the courts, either small claims or other civil court.

Severance pay is not related to unemployment benefits and you need not qualify or collect unemployment benefits in order to receive severance pay. In addition, the receipt of severance pay does not disqualify you for unemployment benefits.

STOCK OPTIONS OR STOCK BONUSES

It has become common in recent years for many companies to provide stock purchase agreements for employees. This means that the employee is entitled to purchase stock at some pre-determined price (meaning a low price below the current market value of the stock) at some pre-determined date in the future.

I mention stock options in order to warn you about two things.

1) Stock options are generally not guaranteed until the date of "vesting." This means that even though the employer promises you stock as though it is a guaranteed thing, it generally is not! If you are an at-will employee, and you are relying on

promises of stock to compensate for a lower-than-deserved salary, or as an inducement for you to work your butt off for many years, beware that you may be terminated before that final "vesting" date and all the promises of that stock will vanish in thin air. Gone.

2) Be careful about clauses in stock option agreements that waive any of your rights or take away any other promises that have been made to you and which have not been written down. Be nervous about any promises that are made to you that are not written down on paper, and retained by you.

If you feel that you have been cheated on stock that was promised you but never delivered, or if you were terminated just before the stock was to vest, you may have a lawsuit for a violation of the covenant of good faith and fair dealing. Consult with an attorney knowledgeable in employment law.

MEALS

Your employer may not reduce your hourly wage below minimum wage by deducting for meals or lodging without a voluntary written agreement to do so between you and the employer. If you and your employer agree that you will be paid with a combination of money and food, or money, lodging and food, the most that the employer can charge is as follows:

**$2.05 for a breakfast
$2.85 for a lunch or
$3.80 for dinner.**

Your employer can reduce your wage for meals or lodging but only if the agreement is in writing and the reduction does not put you below the minimum wage in terms of money received.

HOUSING

Any agreement to reduce your wage for lodging must be in writing. If the agreement is verbal, your employer cannot reduce your wages.

The employer can only charge you $27.05 per week to rent

you a room. If you share the room with another person or more, you can only be charged $22.30 per week. If your employer rents you an apartment, he can only charge you two-thirds of what the normal rental would be for that apartment. In other words, if your employer has an apartment that he will rent to you, and similar apartments rent in the area for say, $200.00 a month, your employer can only charge you $133.33 per month for the apartment. He cannot charge you as much as he could normally get for the apartment if he were to rent it to someone who did not work for him.

No matter what, your employer cannot ever charge you more than $324.70 per month for an apartment. If you and your spouse both work for the employer and you both share an apartment that your employer rents to you, he cannot ever charge more than $355.00 per month for the apartment.

Any lodging provided by the employer must be adequate, decent, and sanitary according to usual housing standards. No employee can be required to share a bed. Every landlord, including your employer, has an obligation to provide housing that is "habitable" or livable. Lack of heat, water, or electricity, faulty plumbing, or the presence of vermin can cause living quarters to be unlivable.

What are your rights if the housing provided by the landlord lacks one or more of the items necessary to a "livable" dwelling? You are entitled to stop paying your rent until the landlord fixes the problem. You do not have to fix the problem yourself, or even attempt to do so. You can already be behind in your rent and still stop paying rent until the problem is corrected. If the landlord fixes the problem you are only required to pay the back rent that is determined to be reasonable under the circumstances.

Who determines what is reasonable? Practically speaking, when you stop paying rent your landlord will serve you with a three-day notice to pay the rent or get out. Since you won't do either one, the landlord will sue to have you evicted. You will defend the eviction complaint by saying that the rent wasn't owed because the housing was not "habitable." If it is determined that the housing was not habitable, the judge will determine what is reasonable under the circumstances. Remember that your landlord-employer is not permitted to take your wages to get the rent money. For a complete discussion of tenant's rights find one of the *Nolo Press* books or other books on the subject. See SETOFFS on page 208.

HOURS WORKED

You are entitled to be paid for all your hours worked. "Hours worked" means the time that you are under the control of an employer and includes the time that you may be sitting around or even sleeping under the direction of your employer. "Hours worked" can include time spent working at home if your employer knows or has reason to know that the work is being done. "Hours worked" includes the time your employer requires you to work, as well as the time he allows you to work or knows (or should have known) that you were working.

In order to clarify the concept of when work begins and ends, Congress passed the "Portal to Portal" Act in 1947. A "portal" is an entrance and in this context refers to the employee working after he enters the employers shop (portal) until he exits the employer's shop. Therefore, to be paid "portal to portal" is to be paid from the time of entering the employer's place of business to the time of exiting. The "Portal Act" entitles the employee to be paid for all time at the job site, except for activities deemed "preliminary" or "postliminary." In other words, you must be paid for all your time on the job except for things you do before your work begins and after your work ends.

Under normal circumstances activities that are regarded as "preliminary" or "postliminary" and are not compensable "include, checking in and out and waiting in line to do so, changing clothes, washing up or showering, and waiting in line to receive pay checks." Bear in mind that the same activities that are "preliminary" in some circumstances may be compensable in others if the activities are directly related to the principal duties of the employee.

"If an employee in a chemical plant, for example, cannot perform his principal activities without putting on certain clothes, changing clothes on the employer's premises at the beginning and the end of the workday would be an integral part of the employee's principal activity." If the activity is necessary for the job, and not merely a convenience for the employee, such activity is compensable.

"Preliminary" and "postliminary" activities are also compensable if there is a "custom or practice" for the employer in question to pay for such activities. "Customs" or "practices" common to the industry in general are not adequate, you must show that your employer engaged in the "custom."

STANDBY TIME AND CALLBACK TIME

You must be paid for all time spend on the job site, even if you are standing around and doing nothing. Doing nothing is often an indication that you are ready to serve the employer, and idleness is part of any job. The question becomes more complex if you are standing by away from the job.

Are you working when you are "on call" away from the job site? Making yourself available on an "on call" basis may entitle you to compensation for the "on call" time depending on,

1) The degree to which you are free to engage in personal activities while "on call" and

2) The agreement that exists between you and your employer.

The court uses a catch phrase to illustrate the concept involved. If you are "engaged to wait," your time is compensable and you must be paid for it, but if you are "waiting to be engaged," it is not compensable. The phrase illustrates the court's attempt to determine whether your "on call" activities benefit the employer or yourself. In other words, are you "employed to wait," or are you "waiting to be employed?"

You will be entitled to be paid for your standby time away from work if your activities are regarded as "controlled" during that period of time. You are regarded as spending "controlled" time if your activities and freedom are limited. If, for example, you must carry a beeper that has a limited range, and you must respond to any call, your standby time may be compensable. If you have discretion not to respond, or you have few other restrictions on your activities, you probably will not be entitled to payment. The question is whether the employee does or does not have the freedom to engage in private and personal pursuits during that time.

As in most areas of the law, each case is analyzed individually, and each court (or Labor Commissioner's Office) will differ in how restricted your activities must be before you qualify for on-call overtime. For a complete discussion of this issue see TWENTY FOUR HOUR (0R LONGER) SHIFTS on page 181.

If you are called back to work during a period of standby time, you must be paid for all time spend coming back to the job site. This includes a reasonable time for travel from where you were summoned back to the job site. You must be paid your regular rate of pay for callback time.

If you have an agreement where you are to be paid for "on call" time while remaining free to pursue personal interests, payment for this "free" standby time is not included in computation of the regular rate of pay. What difference does that make? Possibly a big difference in determining your overtime wages. You want to include as much money as you can in the computation of your regular rate of pay because doing so will increase what may be owed to you when you work overtime. Remember, overtime is 1½ times your *regular rate of pay*! If you can increase what is considered your "regular rate of pay," you will increase your overtime.

Secondly, hours worked for purposes of computing overtime, or overtime thresholds, do not include hours paid for "free" standby time. This means that you cannot add your "free" standby time to your regular work time in order to get overtime. Note that in this discussion "free" standby time does not mean unpaid, it simply refers to paid standby or on call time in which you are still permitted to pursue personal interests. If you are not free to pursue personal interests, such as being required to remain on the premises under the control of the employer, this time is then included in the computation of hours worked for purposes of computing overtime. See also TWENTY FOUR HOUR (OR LONGER) SHIFTS on page 181.

ATTENDING LECTURES, MEETINGS & TRAINING SESSIONS
Generally, if you attend lectures, meetings or training sessions at the request of you employer you must be paid for your time. Your employer need not pay you for your time if the following four factors are satisfied:

1) Your attendance is outside your regular working hours.
2) Your attendance is voluntary.
3) The course, lecture, or meeting is not directly related to your job.
4) You are not required to perform any productive work during your attendance.

Your attendance is not voluntary if your employer somehow gives you the impression that your present working conditions may be changed, or the security of your job may be placed at risk if you fail to attend. If there is any suggestion that negative consequences may result from a failure to attend, the attendance is not voluntary.

The course, lecture, or meeting is directly related to your job if it is designed to help you perform your job more effectively. In that case you must be paid for your attendance. The course or meeting is not directly related if it is designed to teach you a new skill or train you for a new job, even if the training happens to make you more efficient, or greatly improves your skills at your current job.

If the course is designed to prepare you for advancement to a better position, rather than just improving your skills in your regular work, you are not entitled to be paid for your attendance. If you voluntarily attend job-related courses after-hours at an independent school, college or trade school, you are not entitled to be paid for your attendance. This is true even if the course is established, paid for, and run by your employer and is job-related.

If you attend an apprenticeship training program you are not entitled to be paid for your attendance if,

1) You are employed under a written apprenticeship agree

ment or U.S. Department of Labor approved program which does not set forth attendance as hours worked,
2) Attendance does not require you to do productive work or perform your regular duties.

ROUNDING OFF

Employers will sometimes "round off" an employee's time to the nearest even number or quarter hour in order to simplify math or bookkeeping duties. It is illegal to "round off" an employee's time card if it deprives the employee of any time actually worked. "Rounding off" is only permitted if the employer "rounds up" and credits the employee with additional time worked.

TRAVEL TIME

You are not entitled to be paid for time spent traveling to and from work. The only situations where you can get paid for time on the road are when driving is an integral part of performing the job duties, or when you are called to work on your off hours for an emergency and it requires you to make an extra trip to and from work that would otherwise not have been made. In those circumstances you should be paid for your driving time. I can't give you any clear cut rule other than that. The analysis must be made on a case by case basis.

If driving is required by the employer as one of your job duties your employer is permitted to establish a separate rate of pay for travel time. He or she may pay you less than your regular rate of pay, not never less than minimum wage. If the addition of your travel time places you into overtime, you must be paid at the regular overtime rate.

SHOW UP TIME

If the employer calls you in to work, or you are required to show up for work on a regular basis, and you report to work, you are entitled to be paid for at least ½ of your regular day's work schedule, even if you are sent home as soon as you arrive. If your regular day's work shift is less than 4 hours, you are still entitled to be paid a minimum of 2 hours, even if you are sent home as soon as you arrive. If you normally work more than 8 hours on a shift, you are only entitled to a maximum of 4 hours pay. In other words, if your shift is normally 10 hours and you come in to work and you only work 3 hours, or if you don't work at all, you are entitled to 4 hours pay, not 5 hours. You must be paid at your normal hourly rate, and it must be at least equal to the minimum wage of $5.75 per hour.

If you are called to work a second time in any one workday, you are entitled to a minimum of 2 hours pay, even if you end up working less than that. Hours that you are entitled to be paid merely for reporting to work are not included in your total hours for purposes of computing overtime. The hours you are awarded are regarded as a penalty against the employer, and are not considered hours worked.

MOTION PICTURE EMPLOYEES

If you work as an "extra" and you are fitted for a costume, you are entitled to one day's wages if you are not given work in the production for which you were fitted. An "extra" includes such work as general stand-in, photographic double, sports player, silent bit, dress extra, or as a dancer, skater, swimmer, diver, rider, singer, or one who does facial expressions, pantomime or other gestures.

If you are called up to work, the employer must tell you at that time if the work involves night work, wet work, or work that is rough or dangerous. If the employer doesn't inform you at the "call up," then you have the option of refusing to work and are entitled to be paid for your time spent.

If you are required to work after midnight your employer is required to provide you with hot meals and hot drinks. This rule does not apply if you are an off-production employee, regularly scheduled to work after midnight.

If you are required to work at night and your duty ends too late to have access to public transportation, your employer is required to provide transportation to take you home.

If the personal clothing or property of the employee is damaged as a result of the nature of the work, the employer must reimburse the employee for the damages.

Extras who attend interviews or auditions which last longer than one and one-half hours, are entitled to be paid minimum wage for their time.

The rules described in this section do not apply to professional actors of either sex.

SPLIT SHIFT

A split shift means that your work schedule is interrupted by non-paid, non-working periods established by your employer. For example, it is a split shift if you work in the morning and then come back to work in the afternoon, after a break in work that is not for rest or for meals. If you work a split shift, you are entitled to one extra hour of pay at minimum wage per day, except when you live where you work.

The additional hour of minimum wage granted for split shift scheduling is not included in the computation of the regular rate of pay for purposes of overtime. Nor is the additional hour added to your regular work hours for purposes of overtime.

The "split shift" rule generally only helps employees who work at the minimum wage. Here is the reason why: If you work for more than minimum wage, any money you make in excess of minimum wage is applied towards the hour of minimum wage that you are entitled to for the split shift. For example, if you work for $6.00 an hour on an 8 hour shift, your employer can apply 25¢ an hour towards the $5.75 that you are owed for split shift time. Therefore, since you are paid 25¢ an hour more than the minimum wage, for 8 hours, your employer can apply $2 (25¢ x 8) towards the $5.75 that he owes you, and so he only owes you an additional $3.75. As you can see, if you work for $6.50 an hour for 8 hours a day your employer doesn't owe you anything. $6.50—$5.75= 75¢ an hour. 75¢ x 8= $6. $6 is more than the $5.75 he would have owed you, and so you are not entitled to any additional money. If you work an 8 hour shift you will not get any additional money from the "split shift" rule if you earn $6.47 or more per hour.

PAID REST PERIODS

When you work a shift that is longer than 3½ hours you are entitled to a rest break of at least 10 minutes for every 4 hours of the shift. For example, if you work a shift of 8 hours, you are entitled to a total rest time of 20 minutes. If you work 10 hours or more you are entitled to another 10 minutes. Authorized rest periods are to be counted as hours worked for which there shall be no deduction from your wages. The rest period is supposed to be given in the middle of each work period, if possible. The paid rest periods are not broken down into portions smaller than 10 minutes.

Paid rest periods must be provided equally for employees of both sexes.

MEAL BREAK

If you work a shift of more than 5 hours you are entitled to a 30 minute meal break. Generally, the meal break is not paid and you are relieved of all work duties. If you are not relieved of all work duties, your meal is "on duty" and you must be paid, or if you are provided with less than a 30 minute break from work for the meal, you must be paid. If your employer does not permit you to leave the premises during the meal break, you are regarded as being under the employer's control and you must be paid for that time. You are regarded as still being under the control of the employer and are therefore, entitled to be paid for your rest time.

See below for employees in the broadcasting or motion picture industries.

Your employer is not permitted to deprive you of your "no duty" 30 minute meal break unless,

    a) the nature of the work prevents an employee from being relieved of all duty and,

    b) there is a written agreement between the parties that the employee will be provided with a paid "on duty" meal break, instead of the required non-paid no-duty break.

Under the new overtime rules, if you work over 8 hours in a shift you are entitled to waive your right to a second 30 minute meal break. This means that you can choose to work an extra 30 minutes (beyond your normal, say 10, or 11 hour shift) and receive a 30 minute meal break, or you can simply leave 30 minutes earlier, and miss the second mandatory 30 minute meal break.

If you work in the lumber industry, you are entitled to receive your meal break between the third and fifth hours after start of the shift. The lumber industry includes sawmills, logging camps, plywood plants, or any other plants or mills that processes or manufactures lumber or lumber products. If you do not work in the lumber industry, the law does not say when you must receive your meal break. It is between you and the employer.

If you work in the broadcasting industry or the motion picture industry you may not work more than six hours without a meal break of at least 30 minutes. In addition, the meal break cannot exceed one hour. If you work in excess of 12 hours, you must be provided with a second meal break of at least 30 minutes.

If you work a night shift, any time between 10 P.M. and 6 A.M., your employer has to provide facilities for buying hot food or drink, or for heating food or drink. You also have to be provided with a sheltered place to eat your meal.

Are You Entitled to Overtime?

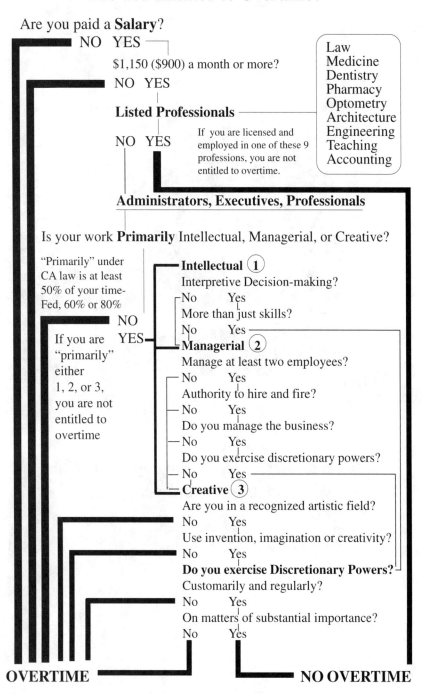

Are you paid a **Salary**?

NO   YES

$1,150 ($900) a month or more?

NO   YES

Listed Professionals

NO   YES

If you are licensed and employed in one of these 9 professions, you are not entitled to overtime.

Law
Medicine
Dentistry
Pharmacy
Optometry
Architecture
Engineering
Teaching
Accounting

Administrators, Executives, Professionals

Is your work **Primarily** Intellectual, Managerial, or Creative?

"Primarily" under CA law is at least 50% of your time—Fed, 60% or 80%

NO

YES

If you are "primarily" either 1, 2, or 3, you are not entitled to overtime

Intellectual ①
Interpretive Decision-making?
No   Yes
More than just skills?
No   Yes

Managerial ②
Manage at least two employees?
No   Yes
Authority to hire and fire?
No   Yes
Do you manage the business?
No   Yes
Do you exercise discretionary powers?
No   Yes

Creative ③
Are you in a recognized artistic field?
No   Yes
Use invention, imagination or creativity?
No   Yes
Do you exercise Discretionary Powers?
Customarily and regularly?
No   Yes
On matters of substantial importance?
No   Yes

OVERTIME   **NO OVERTIME**

"Overtime?! Aw, comm'on boys, you're all salaried executives!"

OVERTIME

OVERTIME PAY

Beginning January 1, 1998, California changed the laws governing overtime for most employees. Prior to 1998 California required overtime for hours over eight (8) in one day, over forty (40) in a week, or for the seventh (7) day of work in a row. Now for most employees, overtime is only required if you work over forth (40) hours in a week. This is the now the same as the federal rules applied in most of the states.

Employees in California are covered under fifteen (15) "wage orders." issued by the Industrial Welfare Commission. Although the new laws eliminating daily overtime, and seventh day overtime apply only to five (5) of the fifteen (15) "wage orders," or categories of employees, the five orders selected cover most employees.

Keep in mind that if you have a claim for overtime, you may want to contact a private lawyer, California law provides for the payment of reasonable attorneys fees by the employer for the private attorney of the employee, if the employee wins in a claim for unpaid overtime. I predict that a private attorney will work harder for your overtime, claim than the burdened (salaried!) employee at the Office of the Labor Commissioner. Nothing prompts serious devotion to your case like the profit motive.

If you work in any of the following industries or occupations, the new overtime rules apply to you: In other words, you are now entitled to overtime only for hours worked over 40 in one week.

Everyone should remember that all employees are entitled to file a claim for overtime for work done up to three years earlier. Here listed are the five labor categories that earn overtime only for working over 40 hours in a week:

1) **Manufacturing Industry**. "Manufacturing Industry" means any industry, business, or establishment operated for the purpose of preparing, producing, making, altering, repairing, finishing, processing, inspecting, handling, assembling, wrapping, bottling, or packaging goods, articles, or commodities, in whole or in part; EXCEPT

when such activities are covered by Orders in the: Canning, Preserving, and Freezing Industry; Industries Handling Products After Harvest; Industries Preparing Agricultural Products for Market, on the Farm; or Motion Picture Industry.

4) **Professional, Technical, Clerical, Mechanical and Similar Occupations**. This classification includes professional, semiprofessional, managerial, supervisorial, laboratory, research, technical, clerical, office work, and mechanical occupations. Said occupations shall include, but not be limited to the following: accountants; agents; appraisers; artists; attendants; audio-visual technicians; bookkeepers; bundlers; billposters; canvassers; carriers; cashiers; checkers; clerks; collectors; communications and sound technicians; compilers; copy holders; copy readers; copy writers; computer programmers and operators; demonstrators and display representatives; dispatchers; distributors; door-keepers; drafters; elevator operators; estimators; editors; graphic arts technicians; guards; guides; hosts; inspectors; installers; instructors; interviewers; investigators; librarians; laboratory workers; machine operators; mechanics; mailers; messengers; medical and dental technicians and technologists; models; nurses; packagers; photographers; porters and cleaners; process servers; printers; proofreaders; salespersons and sales agents; secretaries; sign erectors; sign painters; social workers; solicitors; statisticians; stenographers; teachers; telephone, radio telephone, telegraph and call-out operators; tellers; ticket agents; tracers; typists; vehicle operators; x-ray technicians; their assistants and other related occupations listed as professional, semiprofessional, technical, clerical, mechanical, and kindred occupations.

5) **Public Housekeeping Industry, including Restaurants, Hotels, and Hospitals**. Public Housekeeping Industry" means any industry, business, or establishment which provides meals, housing, or maintenance services whether operated as a primary business or when incidental to other operations in an establishment not covered by an industry order of the Commission, and includes, but is not limited to the following:

(1) Restaurants, night clubs, taverns, bars, cocktail lounges, lunch

counters, cafeterias, boarding houses, clubs, and all similar establishments where food in either solid or liquid form is prepared and served to be consumed on the premises; (2) Catering, banquet, box lunch service, and similar establishments which prepare food for consumption on or off the premises; (3) Hotels, motels, apartment houses, rooming houses, camps, clubs, trailer parks, office or loft buildings, and similar establishments offering rental of living, business, or commercial quarters; (4) Hospitals, sanitariums, rest homes, child nurseries, child care institutions, homes for the aged, and similar establishments offering board or lodging in addition to medical, surgical, nursing, convalescent, aged, or child care; (5) Private schools, colleges, or universities, and similar establishments which provide board or lodging in addition to educational facilities; (6) Establishments contracting for development, maintenance or cleaning of grounds; maintenance or cleaning of facilities and/or quarters of commercial units and living units; and (7) Establishments providing veterinary or other animal care services.

7) **Mercantile Industry**. Mercantile Industry" means any industry, business, or establishment operated for the purpose of purchasing, selling, or distributing goods or commodities at wholesale or retail; or for the purpose of renting goods or commodities.

9) **Transportation Industry**. "Transportation Industry" means any industry, business, or establishment operated for the purpose of conveying persons or property from one place to another whether by rail, highway, air, or water, and all operations and services in connection therewith; and also includes storing or warehousing of goods or property, and the repairing, parking, rental, maintenance, or cleaning of vehicles.

The result of the new laws means that you can be scheduled to work longer than eight (8) hours per day, and you will not be entitled to overtime, unless you work over forty (40) hours during the work week. You will no longer be entitled to double time over twelve (12) hours per day. You will not be entitled to overtime for working on the seventh (7th) day in the week. However, it is still illegal to require you to work seven days in a row on a regular basis, except under certain circumstances. See below.

You are now entitled to work extra hours on any day to make up for short hours on another day, and you will not be entitled to overtime unless the total hours exceed 40 for the week. This also means, for example, that if you miss a couple of days of work, and then decide to work three 12 hour days, you are permitted to do so. Your employer will not have to pay you overtime, since your total hours for the week are 36 hours.

The new overtime laws do not apply to you if you are a member of a union covered by overtime provisions in a collective bargaining agreement and you earn at least $6.75 an hour or more. Nor do the new laws apply to governmental employees.

I have intentionally left in the overtime analysis under the old law. I have done so for two reasons. First, even though the overtime laws have changed, if you worked overtime and were not properly paid for the overtime worked, you are entitled to file a claim for overtime worked up to three (3) years earlier. This means that you can claim overtime under the old law for work done in late 1997, for example, as far in the future as late 2000.

As you can see, there may be many of you who will be able to take advantage of the discussion about the old overtime laws, in order to collect overtime that you may be owed for up to three (3) years ago.

THE FOLLOWING SECTIONS DISCUSS THE OVERTIME RULES UNDER THE PRIOR LAW. THE FOLLOWING RULES APPLY TO ALL OVERTIME CLAIMS FOR WORK PERFORMED BEFORE JANUARY 1, 1998. THESE FOL-LOWING RULES DO NOT APPLY TO OVERTIME CLAIMS FOR LABOR PERFORMED AFTER JANUARY 1, 1998, IF YOU WORK IN AN OCCUPATION DESCRIBED ON PAGES 167.

Under the old law, the computation of overtime could become very complicated and confusing. Remember, these old laws still apply to you if you work in any of the following industries or occupations listed below:

2) **"Personal Service Industry"** means any industry, business, or establishment operated for the purpose of rendering directly or indirectly, any service, operation, or process used or useful in the care, cleansing, or beautification of the body, skin, nails, or hair, or in the enhancement of personal appearance or health, including but not limited to, beauty salons, schools of beauty culture offering beauty care to the public for a fee, barber shops, bath and massage parlors, physical conditioning, weight control salons, health clubs, and mortuaries.

3) **"Canning, Freezing, and Preserving Industry"** means any industry, business, or establishment operated for the purpose of canning soups, or of cooking, canning, curing, freezing, pickling, salting, bottling, preserving, or otherwise processing any fruits or vegetables, seafood, meat, poultry or rabbit product, when the purpose of such processing is the preservation of the product and includes all operations incidental thereto.

6) **"Laundry, Linen Supply, Dry Cleaning, and Dyeing Industry"** means any industry, business, or establishment operated for the purpose of washing, ironing, cleaning, refreshing, restoring, pressing, dyeing, storing, fumigating, mothproofing, waterproofing, or other processes incidental thereto, on articles or fabrics of any kind, including but not limited to clothing, hats, drapery, rugs, curtains, linens, household furnishings, textiles, furs, or leather goods; and includes self-service laundries, self-service dry cleaning establishments, and the collection, distribution, storage, sale, or resale at retail or wholesale of the foregoing services.

8) **"Industries Handling Products After Harvest"** means any industry, business, or establishment operated for the purpose of grading, sorting, cleaning, drying, cooling, icing, packing, dehydrating, cracking, shelling, candling, separating, slaughtering, picking, plucking, shucking, pasteurizing, fermenting, ripening, molding, or otherwise preparing any agricultural, horticultural, egg, poultry, meat, seafood, rabbit, or dairy product for distribution, and includes all the operations incidental thereto.

10) **"Amusement and Recreation Industry"** means any industry, business, or establishment operated for the purpose of furnishing entertainment or recreation to the public, including but not limited to theatres, dance halls, bowling alleys, billiard parlors, skating rinks, riding academies, race tracks, amusement parks, athletic fields, swimming pools, gymnasiums, golf courses, tennis courts, carnivals, and wired music studios.

11) **"Broadcasting Industry"** means any industry, business, or establishment operated for the purpose of broadcasting or taping and broadcasting programs through the medium of radio or television.

12) **"Motion Picture Industry"** means any industry, business, or establishment operated for the purpose of motion picture or television film production, or primarily allied with theatrical or television, motion picture productions, including but not limited to motion pictures for entertainment, commercial, religious, or educational purposes, whether made by film, tape, or otherwise.

13) **"Industries Preparing Agricultural Products for Market, on the Farm"** means any operation performed in a permanently fixed structure or establishment on the farm or on a moving packing plant on the farm for the purpose of preparing agricultural, horticultural, egg, poultry, meat, seafood, rabbit, or dairy products for market when such operations are done on the premises owned or operated by the same employer who produced the products referred to herein and includes all operations incidental thereto.

14) **"Employed in an agricultural occupation"** means any of the following described occupations:
(1) The preparation, care, and treatment of farm land, pipeline, or ditches, including leveling for agricultural purposes, plowing, discing, and fertilizing the soil; (2) The sowing and planting of any agricultural or horticultural commodity; (3) The care of any agricultural or horticultural commodity. As used in this subdivision, "care" includes, but is not limited to, cultivation, irrigation, weed control, thinning, heating, pruning, or tieing, fumigating, spraying,

and dusting; (4) The harvesting of any agricultural or horticultural commodity, including but not limited to, picking, cutting, threshing, mowing, knocking off, field chopping, bunching, baling, balling, field packing, and placing in field containers or in the vehicle in which the commodity will be hauled, and transportation on the farm or to the place of first processing or distribution; (5) The assembly and storage of any agricultural or horticultural commodity, including but not limited to, loading, roadsiding, banking, stacking, binning, and piling;
(6) The raising, feeding and management of livestock, fur bearing animals, poultry, fish, mollusks, and insects, including but not limited to herding, housing, hatching, milking, shearing, handling eggs, and extracting honey;
(7) The conservation, improvement or maintenance of such farm and its tools and equipment.

15) **"Household Occupations"** means all services related to the care of persons or maintenance of a private household or its premises by an employee of a private householder. Said occupations shall include, but not be limited to, the following: butlers, chauffeurs, companions, cooks, day workers, gardeners, graduate nurses, grooms, house-cleaners, housekeepers, maids, practical nurses, tutors, valets, and other similar occupations.

There are three separate situations (described as thresholds) where you are entitled to overtime under the old law and under certain occupations.
You are entitled to overtime if you work more than 40 hours per week, **or** you work more than 8 hours in a day, **or** if you work more than 6 days in the work week (this threshold has additional requirements). Overtime pay is 1½ times your regular rate of pay. Therefore, if you normally get paid the minimum wage of $5.75 an hour, you are entitled to $8.63 an hour if you have worked longer than 8 hours that day, or if you have worked more than 40 hours that week, or if you have worked seven days that workweek. Computing overtime becomes complicated when hours worked exceed both the daily and weekly overtime thresholds. Overtime may also require the inclusion of bonus payments in determining your regular rate of

pay.

You cannot agree to give up your rights to overtime. Any such agreement will not be enforced against you, the employee.

Let's go over the general rules once again. You are entitled to be paid 1½ times your normal hourly wage when:

1) You have worked more than 40 hours during the workweek you are entitled to overtime for any hours in excess of 40. This is described as the weekly threshold. For example, if you work 50 hours during the workweek, you are entitled to 10 hours of overtime. The hours in excess of 40 are paid at the overtime rate, not all 50 hours total. Or

2) You have worked more than 8 hours in any one workday. When you work between 8 and 12 hours per workday you are entitled to overtime for hours 9, 10, 11, and 12. When you work in excess of 12 hours in any one workday you are entitled to double-time. Or

3) You are entitled to overtime if you work 7 days in a row if your hours for the workweek exceed 30 hours, or you worked more than 6 hours in any one day. Thus, if you work 6 days in a row, 5½ hours a day, you have only 33 hours for the week, but if you work the seventh day you are entitled to be paid at 1½ times your regular rate of pay. If you work 6 days in a row, ranging from 4 hours a day to 7 hours a day and your total is only 29 hours for the week, you are still entitled to overtime if you work the seventh day. If you work more than 8 hours on the seventh day you are entitled to double time for any time over 8 hours.

To repeat, in order to get overtime by working 7 days straight, you must have worked *either,* 30 hours or more during the workweek, *or* you must have worked for more than 6 hours at least one day that week. If you have done either one of these two things you are entitled to overtime on your seventh day of work that week.

Don't confuse workweek with "week." Your workweek is not the same as "week" if you begin your workweek on some day other than Monday morning.

If you and your employer agree that you shall work 4 days a week for 10 hours a day, you can do so and overtime will not be owed for the ninth and tenth hour each day. However, for this type of agreement to be enforceable, the agreement must be in writing, and filed with California Industrial Welfare Commission.

OVERTIME AND THE REGULAR RATE OF PAY

Overtime is computed at 1½ times your regular rate of pay. Your regular rate of pay is all the pay you receive from your employment, including salary, hourly wages, piece rate wages, commissions, bonuses (see BONUSES on page 149), and the value of meals and lodging. If you are on salary your pay should be based on no more than 40 hours of work per week, as set forth above. To determine your weekly regular rate of pay, take your monthly salary, multiply by 12 (months), and divide by 52 weeks, then divide the weekly pay by 40 hours (or less, if there is an agreement to that effect). You now have your regular hourly rate of pay for purposes of computing overtime.

Note: You want to include everything you can in computing your regular rate of pay, because doing so will increase your overtime rate of pay.

OVERTIME AND PIECE RATE

If you are an employee earning piece rate wages, your overtime is computed as either,

1) 1½ times the normal piece rate for all overtime hours, or
2) Compute the average wage for the week by dividing the total wages for the week by the total hours worked and pay 1½ the average wage for all overtime hours worked.

Under both alternatives the regular piece rate wage used to

compute overtime has to be at least the minimum wage. Understand that overtime pay is only the extra ½ time in addition to your regular rate of pay.

Different methods may be appropriate for making the overtime computation, such as increasing the piece rate by 50% for overtime hours, or by totaling the hours worked and increasing the average wage earned by 50% for the overtime portion, if you are working on a piece rate or incentive plan system. Either method of computing piece rate overtime is proper so long as it genuinely reflects one and one-half times your regular rate of pay.

COMMISSIONS AND OVERTIME

Under the federal rules you are entitled to overtime when you work for a combination of commissions and hourly wages, and the following occurs:

1) You work in a retail or service establishment.
2) Your regular rate of pay is $8.63 an hour or less.
3) No more than ½ of your total pay comes from commissions.

If all three of these factors exist in your situation, you are entitled to overtime. In order to understand this rule we need to define each of the terms being used.

A retail or service establishment is a branch or retail outlet of a business. You would think of it as a store. A retail store is one that gets a least 75% of it's income from selling retail goods to the public, the ultimate consumer (not for resale).

A service store is one that sells retail service such as restaurants, hotels, barber shops, and repair shops. In the service store the consumer is not buying a "good," but rather, a personal service. For example, if you work selling televisions to the public and you are paid a combination of minimum wage, plus commissions, you would be entitled to overtime if your regular rate of pay was less than $8.63. Anytime you work in a retail or service establishment and you are paid minimum wage and commissions and your regular rate of pay is less than $8.63, you qualify for overtime.

The California rule is the same as the federal rule in terms of how much you can be paid and what percentage of the total can be received from commissions. California differs in terms of what businesses are affected. The California rule applies to wholesale and retail businesses that sell, distribute, or rent goods or commodities.

The federal rule does not include wholesale operations—California does; California does not include service businesses—the federal does. Therefore, applying the principle that the law which provides the greatest benefit to the employee governs, you will apply the California rule for wholesale operations and the federal rule for service businesses.

MULTIPLE EMPLOYERS

The wage and hour provisions apply to each employer individually. If you work two or more jobs, you cannot combine the hours worked for all employers in order to claim overtime based on the total. You are only permitted to combine the hours worked for separate employers if they are somehow business related.

MOTION PICTURE EMPLOYEES

If you are employed in the motion picture industry, you may work up to a maximum of 16 hours a day, including meals, if you are paid overtime. Overtime is computed as 1½ times your regular rate of pay for the first 12 hours. Time and one-half extends to 14 hours if you are at a location and transportation is provided by the employer, or if you are at an overnight location. Therefore, you normally earn double-time for any hours over 12 a day, and if you stay overnight, or are provided with transportation, double-time for any hours over 14 a day.

All employees earn time and one-half for the first 8 hours of the seventh straight day, and double-time for any hours over 8. This overtime rule does not apply to professional actors of either sex.

TIME OFF INSTEAD OF OVERTIME

This occurs when the employee takes regular employment time off instead of receiving pay for overtime. The Division of Labor Standards Enforcement will only permit this type of arrangement when the following conditions are met:

1) The employee must clearly request in writing that he be granted compensatory time off from work instead of overtime pay.
2) The written request must be made before working the overtime.
3) The time off must be given at a rate that equals an overtime rate.
4) The time off must be given by the end of the pay period immediately after the pay period in which the time off was earned.
5) The time off must be given to the employees during normal work time.
6) Records must be kept accurately reflecting overtime earned and taken.

HOLIDAYS AND OVERTIME

Absent any agreement with your employer to the contrary, private employees are not entitled to receive holidays off, or to receive overtime as a result of working on a legal holiday. See also GOOD CAUSE AND UNEMPLOYMENT COMPENSATION on page 225.

LIMITING OVERTIME

Your employer is entitled to establish a policy of no overtime allowed unless specifically okayed by the employer. However, this is enforceable only as a general policy and cannot be used to avoid paying overtime if the employee is actually permitted or required to work overtime in violation of the policy. Generally, the employee's activities must take place with the employer's knowledge and consent. However, the employee's knowledge and consent can be implied if the employer has reason to believe that the employee is working and permits him or her to continue to do so. From your perspective, you need to be able to establish that the employer knew or should have known that you were working the overtime. Make a record, even a note to your boss (that you keep a copy of) stating how pleased you were to complete a project, even though it took until late hours to complete.

If an employee signs an agreement stating that he or she will not work overtime, that agreement cannot be used to avoid paying the employee overtime, if in fact, the employer permitted the employee to work more than agreed to, or was aware, or should have been aware, that the employee was working additional hours.

REQUIRING OVERTIME

Your employer can require your to work overtime in most industries up to a maximum of a total of 72 total hours worked per week in most industries.

I have discussed under MAXIMUM WORKDAYS the occupations in which the employer is restricted from requiring you to work overtime. In all other occupations the wage orders generally prohibit employees from being forced to work in excess of 72 hours a week. Not much protection when you consider that employers can only require you to work six days out of seven. This means that your employer cannot legally work you (in most occupations) more than 12 hours a day!

If your employer insists that you work overtime and you find the demands burdensome you may be entitled to quit for cause. Conversely, if you refuse to work the overtime requested and you are terminated, the termination may be determined to be involuntary and not for misconduct. See UNEMPLOYMENT COMPENSATION for discussions on these issues. The problem remains that if you do not agree to work the overtime you may find yourself out of work, and merely entitled to unemployment benefits as your sole consolation.

You are not protected from termination in refusing to work overtime. See also the discussion on EMPLOYER PERSONNEL POLICIES on page 104.

COMPUTING OVERTIME—WAGE ORDERS 2, 3, 6, 8, 10-15

The following discussion regarding how you compute overtime for the weekly threshold now only applies if you work in an occupation that still includes the three different thresholds for overtime, in other words, the old rules. Look to pages 171. If you work in any of those occupations, then the following discussion still applies to you. However, if you work in any of the occupations listed under wage orders 1, 4, 5, 7 or 9, (see pages 167) then overtime is simply hours worked over 40 on a weekly basis. Confusing?

You need to be aware that, in computing overtime, daily overtime is not included in calculating the weekly overtime threshold of 40 hours. The weekly overtime threshold is reached after the employee works 40 hours of regular time, not the first 40 hours worked. For example, let's say you work three days at 12 hours a day and one day for 4 hours, for a total of 40 hours. If you stopped right now would you be entitled to overtime for the week? You have only worked 40 hours, so you are not entitled to overtime based on the weekly overtime threshold, but you have worked 12 hours for three days, which would entitle you to 4 hours per day of daily overtime, for a total of 12 hours.

Now let's say you come to work and work 8 hours the fifth day and quit for the week. By working the fifth day you now have 48 hours for the week. Have you crossed the weekly threshold of 40 hours? You've worked 40 hours, you say. The answer is no! Look to the first sentence in this paragraph. Daily overtime is not included in calculating the weekly threshold of 40 hours. Why? Because if you count all 12 hours, you count 8 hours of regular time, plus 4 hours of overtime, in order to compute the second situation in which you may be entitled to overtime. If you counted all 12 hours you would be double counting overtime in order to compute overtime.

Therefore, in computing the 40 hour threshold you add up 8 hours of regular time per day for the first 3 days, 4 hours on the fourth day, and 8 hours on the fifth day, for a total of 36 hours. You are not entitled to overtime based on the weekly threshold, but you have earned 12 hours of overtime based on the daily threshold requirement. It is not as though you haven't been paid your overtime, you have. It is just that you have been paid your overtime on the daily threshold basis and not the weekly. **Remember this rule: If you have earned overtime on the daily threshold basis *and* overtime on the weekly threshold basis, you are entitled to receive the greater of the two.**

In our first example the daily overtime was greater. Let's show you an example of where the opposite is true. Suppose you work six days a week for 10 hours each day. How much overtime are you entitled to? First, compute overtime based on the daily threshold basis. Remember, you are entitled to overtime in excess of 8 hours worked per day. You worked 10 hours a day for six days. On the daily threshold basis you are entitled to 2 hours of overtime each day for six days, for a total of 12 hours total overtime. Now, compute your overtime on the weekly threshold basis. Under that rule you are entitled to overtime for all work in excess of 40 regular hours per week. Under this rule you are entitled to 20 hours of overtime. Now how much overtime are you entitled to? 12 hours or 20 hours? You are entitled to the greater of the two! You are entitled to receive 20 hours of overtime.

Notice that you cannot add the two possibilities together to get 32 hours of overtime. You are entitled to choose the greater of the two, and that's all.

California is one of only five states in the country that compute overtime on a daily basis, and now this is true for only some of the covered occupations in this state.

TWENTY-FOUR HOUR (OR LONGER) SHIFTS

If you work for an ambulance company or other organization that requires that you man 24 hour shifts, are you entitled to overtime? The answer really depends on any agreements between you and your employer, whether verbal or written.

Do you and your employer have an agreement to exclude your sleep time from payable time? It is permissible for an employer and employee to enter into an agreement to exclude up to 8 hours from work or payable time for sleep if:

1) Adequate facilities are provided for sleeping and

2) The employee has the opportunity to get at least 5 hours of uninterrupted sleep.

If the employee is not permitted at least 5 hours of uninterrupted sleep, then the entire time must be included as hours worked. The burden is on the employer to provide records establishing that the employees got the required sleep time. If the evidence is inconclusive, the consequences of the failure falls on the employer, not the employee. In those instances the employer will probably end up having to pay the employee for the time. If you and your employer do not have an agreement that excludes up to 8 hours for sleep time, then the sleep time is included in hours worked, and must be paid to you.

If you work less than a 24 hour shift, then all of your time must be paid to you, including sleep time. For example, if you work a 23 hour shift, you must be paid for 23 hours, even if you sleep during the shift. The employer must establish a 24 hour shift as a minimum in order to exclude up to 8 hours for sleep and 3 hours for meals.

If you are on-call 24 hours a day during your work week, as with some plumbers or mechanics, are you entitled to be paid overtime for the hours that you were obligated to be potentially available by phone? The courts use a catch phrase to illustrate the problem. If the employee is "engaged to wait," the time is compensable, in other words, you must be paid. On the other hand, if the employee is "waiting to be engaged," the time is not compensable. The rule is, the employee is entitled to overtime compensation only for idle time when "the employee is unable to use the time effectively for his own purposes." The courts have developed a list of factors to take into consideration in determining whether the employee is so restricted in his activities as to be "engaged to wait," and therefore entitled to be paid for doing so. The factors are as follows:

1) whether there was an on-premises living arrangement.
2) whether there were excessive geographical restrictions on employee's movements.
3) whether the frequency of calls was unduly restrictive.

4) whether a fixed time limit for response was unduly restrictive.
5) whether the on-call employee could easily trade on-call responsibilities.
6) whether use of a pager could ease restrictions and,
7) whether the employee had actually engaged in personal activities during call-in time.

The courts look to the employee's activities during the on-call time to determine whether the activities were for the benefit of the employer. If the activities are not, the likelihood is that the time is not properly compensable, even if the on-call status makes the employee's job "highly undesirable and arguably somewhat oppressive."

OVERTIME AND THE TEN HOUR-DAY WORKWEEK

If you work for a manufacturing firm where there is a written agreement to work four days a week, 10 hours a day instead of the usual five day workweek, you are not entitled to overtime for the ninth and tenth hour every day. You are entitled to daily overtime if you work in excess of 10 hours a day and double-time in excess of 12 hours a day. If you work beyond the fourth day you are entitled to overtime based on the weekly threshold rule. You are entitled to time and a half for the first 8 hours of the fifth day and double-time for anything in excess of 8 hours on the fifth day of work.

The written schedule agreement must be agreed to by at least two-thirds of the affected employees and the agreement must provide for at least four hours of work in any workday.

The employer must provide at least two days off from work each week.

The 10 hour four-day workweek may be adopted by employees in the following industries; personal service industry, canning, freezing and preserving industry, laundry, linen supply, dry cleaning and dyeing industry, mercantile industry, broadcasting industry, motion picture industry, and industries handling products after harvest, and industries preparing agricultural products for market.

...AND THE TWELVE HOUR- DAY WORKWEEK

If you work in the following occupations you may elect to work a 12 hour workday; professional, technical , clerical, mechanical and similar occupations, public housekeeping industry, transportation industry, and the amusement and recreation industry.

The 12 hour schedule is paid at the regular rate, but overtime applies to all hours over 40 in the week and double-time applies to all hours over 12 on the first three workdays of the week and double-time for all hours over 8 for days worked that are not included in the written agreement. For example, if you agree in writing to work three 12 hour days and one 4 hour day, any time worked on the fifth day must be paid at the overtime rate for the first 8 hours, and double-time thereafter.

If two-thirds of the employees agree to the alternative weekly work schedule, the employer is permitted to force all employees to work the same schedule, although the employer may allow up to one-third of the employees to work an 8 hour schedule.

If your employer is a manufacturer who operates a manufacturing facility 24 hours a day, seven days a week, the employer may schedule a three day, 12 hour-a-day workweek, if two thirds of the employees approve of the schedule in writing and if the employer had a preexisting 12 hour day workweek in effect before November 1980. The pre-1980 requirement makes this exception very limited. If the employer does manage to comply, the employer is permitted to adopt a 12 hour three-day-one-week, 12 hour four-day-the-next-week schedule. This averages out to 42 hours each week.

Hospitals are permitted to establish a three day, 12 hour day workweek upon a written agreement. If an employee works more than three days a week the employee must be paid at the overtime rate. Hospitals may also adopt by two-thirds written agreement, a 9 hour, 5 day workweek, with no overtime obligations within that work schedule.

EXCEPTION FOR COLLECTIVE BARGAINING
AGREEMENTS (UNION EMPLOYEES)
If you are a member of a union and you are covered by a
collective bargaining agreement, you are not entitled to overtime if
the following two conditions exist:
1) You are paid some sort of hourly premium for hours
worked in excess of 40 hours each week and,
2) You are paid a wage rate of at least one ($1) an hour
above the minimum wage. (The current minimum wage is $5.75 per
hour)

EXCEPTION FOR MOTION PICTURE PROJECTIONISTS
Employees who work exclusively as motion picture projectionists are not entitled to overtime.

EXCEPTION FOR TAXICAB DRIVERS
Taxicab drivers are not entitled to overtime protection.

EXCEPTION FOR SKI RESORTS
Due to the political influence of ski resort owners, they are
permitted to establish a regular-time workweek of 56 hours a week
during the ski season for their employees. Overtime is only required
for hours worked in excess of 56 hours a week. Therefore, the regular daily and weekly overtime thresholds do not apply to ski resort
employees.

MISCELLANEOUS EXCEPTIONS
You may not be entitled to overtime if you work as a camp
counselor, as a personal attendant, or in a home that cares for the
aged, or if you care for children under age 18 years old and you
provide 24 hour care, or if you work as a ride operator in a traveling carnival.

BONUSES AND OVERTIME
Bonuses are added to your regular rate of pay in computing
your overtime when the bonuses are based on hours worked, production or efficiency. From the employee's point of view, you want

to include bonuses in your regular rate of pay, because doing so will increase the overtime money that you are entitled to. Bonuses are added as a separate component of the regular rate of pay. In other words, bonuses that are based on hours worked, production, or efficiency, are regarded as a form of wages and are included within the computation of overtime, just like your regular hourly wage.

To compute the hourly bonus component to your overtime wage, you divide your weekly bonus amount by the total number of hours worked in achieving the bonus. If you worked overtime to get a bonus, then the overtime is included in computing your "hourly bonus wage rate," however, see the next paragraph for "flat sum" bonuses.

Here is an example; Suppose you worked 40 hours regular time and 10 hours overtime for the week and received a $20 bonus at the end of the week. Your total hours worked were 50 hours. Divide 50 hours into your $20 bonus for an hourly bonus figure of 40¢ an hour. 40¢ an hour is what you earned in bonuses computed on an hourly basis for all your hours worked. Now, what is the overtime due on a "bonus wage" of 40¢ an hour? Remembering that overtime is 1½ times your regular rate of pay, the overtime due on your "bonus pay" is ½ the "bonus wage," or 20¢ an hour for your 10 hours of overtime. Your bonus overtime due is $2 (20¢ x 10 hours).

If the bonus is not based on a percentage of production or some formula, but is instead, a flat sum, such as $200 for working to the end of the vegetable season, or $5 for every week worked, then you do not add in your overtime hours to compute the bonus hourly wage rate. This is better for you, as an employee, because it increases your bonus wage rate, and therefore, increases your bonus overtime. In our example above, your bonus wage is $20 divided by 40, not 50, and becomes 50¢ an hour. The overtime rate becomes 25¢ an hour, and your bonus overtime becomes $2.50 (25¢ x 10).

Bonuses are also added to your regular rate of pay if the promised bonus is, or becomes enforceable against, the employer. If the employer promises a bonus based on a condition, where the fact of the bonus is non-discretionary (the employer obligated himself to pay, although the sum to be paid is undetermined) and the condition occurs, the bonus becomes part of the regular rate of pay when the bonus is paid.

If a bonus is discretionary (not enforceable against the employer) or if the bonus is paid strictly as a gift, such as Christmas or New Years gifts, the bonuses are not includable in the rate of pay in order to be added to the computation of overtime. If the employer promises in advance that he will be providing Christmas bonuses, the employer loses his discretion over the bonus and obligates himself to pay the bonus. Review the section entitled BONUSES on page 149.

OVERTIME AND THE SALARIED EMPLOYEE

If you are a salaried employee you are not entitled to overtime, right? Wrong! It is a common misconception that when you accept a salaried position you are no longer covered by the laws regulating overtime. The California Code of Regulations states that the order governing wages and overtime applies whether you are paid on a time, piece rate, commission, or other basis. In other words, even salaried employees may be entitled to wage and hour protection.

The misconception regarding salary helps create the biggest problem for the salaried employee—proving your overtime hours. The burden is on the employee alleging overtime to substantiate his claim by showing the hours of overtime worked. Generally, salaried employees fail to keep track of their hours for obvious reasons. That's a big mistake! If you are denied overtime, lack of proof may be the reason why. Maintain a diary of your daily work schedule. Keep it simple and be consistent. For further discussion of this issue see EMPLOYEE RECORDS on page 275. You may be entitled to overtime even if you have not kept records.

Your employer is not permitted to avoid the overtime laws by placing you on salary and then working you on a workweek schedule that averages more than 40 hours per week. If your work schedule averages more than 40 hours, your employer is still obligated to pay you overtime.

The issue of overtime for the salaried employee is often confused with the exception for administrative, executive and professional employees, who are not entitled to overtime. To make it even more confusing, the exception is not really for administrative, executive or professional employees as is commonly described. "Administrators, executives, and professionals" is the commonly used phrase, but it happens to be incorrect. Those really excluded from protection are certain intellectuals, managers and creative employees.

The exception from protection really affects two separate groups or types of employees. The first group excluded from protection are known as "named professionals"—people who work in any of nine specified occupations, described below. The second group of employees are those who work in any field in "intellectual, managerial, or creative capacities." In other words, certain intellectual, managerial and creative employees are not protected under the wage and hour provisions—not administrators, executives, and professionals. Remember, you do not want to be excluded under the provisions— you want to be included.

The rules concerning coverage for managers and professionals may be confusing. I suggest that you read the next section several times over until you have an overall understanding of the general type of employee excluded from protection, always remembering that there are always numerous factors considered in every determination of excluded status which make it virtually impossible to predict with certainty whether you would or would not be excluded from coverage in your particular situation.

You must also remember that each case is analyzed by a trier of fact, whether judge, jury or deputy commissioner, that brings with him or her biases, personal and political perspectives, and psychic baggage that may influence the decision in your case to unknown and unknowable degrees. I have found that there is an inclination to favor the employee over the employer. After all, the employee is always the underdog. But do not think that you do not need to prepare and present your case with the utmost care just because those in the Office of the Labor Commissioner seek to help you and may be on your side.

NAMED PROFESSIONALS

There are two categories of professionals that face exclusion under the wage and hour laws. The first is the professional employed in a named occupation. That category is discussed under this heading. The second type of professional is the person employed in a professional capacity in an occupation that is not named under this heading. Confused? I don't blame you. Much of the confusion stems from a juggling in terminology between the federal and state laws on this matter. Don't worry about terminology for the moment and simply follow my lead into the maze. I will try to guide you safely through. Follow the discussion with the flow chart on page 165. Let's begin.

Look to the occupations listed below. If you fall into any of the employment categories listed below and you are employed *in that capacity* then you are exempt from the rules and you are not protected. I emphasize *in that capacity* because you may find yourself in the tough spot of being in one of the groups listed below, but the work you do may differ from the norm for that profession. If so, you may be entitled to protection.

Regarding the matter of being excluded as a named professional, I presume you will be making in excess of minimum wage anyway. The crux of the matter is that you will not be entitled to overtime. If you do not fall within the occupations listed below, then investigate whether you fall within the second general category of excluded employees—certain intellectuals, managers, and creative employees.

There are nine professions not entitled to wage and hour protection.

The excluded categories of named professionals are as follows:

Accounting, architecture, dentistry, engineering, law, medicine, optometry, pharmacy, or teaching, or if you are engaged in an occupation commonly recognized as a learned or artistic profession.

To repeat, if you are licensed or certified in one of the above-named professions and you are employed in that capacity, then you are not covered. What about that last "catch-all" phrase, "...a learned or artistic profession?" This language was borrowed form the federal rules, and under the federal definition "learned professions" refers to the nine professions listed above. In other words, the California legislators unknowingly repeated themselves by adding the "learned" phrase from the federal terminology. The phrase does not add another category of excluded employee. It is just the short way of referring to the same nine professions listed directly above it! So, ignore it.

The second part of the phrase "artistic profession" refers to those jobs that require creative output. This is the same test that is covered elsewhere under California law and known as the "creative exclusion." This phrase doesn't add anything new either. The "artistic professions" require creative output and includes such occupations as creative writers. Journalists generally are regarded as being creative or members of an "artistic profession." However, remember when analyzing the "artistic profession" exemption that the courts commonly interpret the laws against the employer and for the employee. This is known in the legal manner of speech as a form of "strict construction."

As a result of this inclination to interpret the law to protect employees, many occupations that you might think as being "artistic or creative" are not so regarded for purposes of the employment laws. For example, television station directors and television assignment editors have both been determined to be entitled to protection. Producers and editors have been granted protection. Courts have held that journalists create while editors merely rewrite, therefore, journalists are not afforded protection and editors are. For a complete discussion of this exclusion see **(c) Your work must be primarily creative** on page 204.

NURSES; As something of a footnote to the listing of professions that are excluded, nurses are explicitly removed from the list of omitted professions and are therefore permitted protection of the wage and hour laws. A nurse is not entitled to wage and hour pro-

tection only if she or he is determined to be employed in an intellectual, managerial, or creative capacity, as set forth below.

ADMINISTRATORS, EXECUTIVES, OR PROFESSIONALS

Among the ranks of the white collar workers there is one
other group of employees, in addition to the named professionals in
the nine occupations set forth above, that are not afforded the protection of sections 3 through 12 of the wage and hour laws. Sections
3 through 12 cover minimum wage, overtime, breaks, meals, and
related matters. This second group of unprotected employees are
described as anyone employed in an administrative, executive or
professional capacity. Of course, as you and I have already seen,
this is a misstatement.

The second group of excluded employees are really those
that perform in capacities that are primarily intellectual, managerial, or creative. Why then don't we describe the exception as 'IN-
TELLECTUALS, MANAGERS, OR CREATIVE EMPLOYEES?"
We should, but the phrase in use is taken from the federal laws that
the California laws are supposed to be derived from. The phrase
needs to be translated to make sense in California, but we use it
because it is the common terminology. For a clue to this see the
Special Notation below. Hopefully, some of this is becoming clearer
for you. No? Let's continue on anyway.

The rule excluding intellectual, managers, and creative employees may appear to exclude nearly everyone but don't throw your
hands up in despair. This exclusion is not as bad as it seems. In
order to untangle this matter we will look to section 11040 of the
Code of California Regulations which speaks to this very issue.
Remember that when the code speaks of administrators, executives,
and professionals, that the code really means employees that perform work as intellectuals, managers, and as creative artists.

Section 11040 is titled as follows;

**§11040. Order Regulating Wages, Hours, and
Working Conditions in Professional, Technical,**

Clerical, Mechanical, and Similar Occupations.
1. Applicability of Order. This Order shall apply to all persons employed in professional, technical, clerical, mechanical, and similar occupations whether paid on a time, piece rate, commission, or other basis...except that:

(A) Provisions of Sections 3 through 12 [the overtime provisions] shall not apply to persons employed in administrative, executive, or professional capacities...

What does this title and paragraph mean? It really means that all employees (including those in professional occupations) are entitled to minimum wage and overtime protection (that's sections 3 through 12) unless they are administrative, executive or professional employees. Is this a riddle? A professional is covered unless he is a professional? That's what it seems to sound like, doesn't it? I realize that this is confusing, but again, all employees, including those in professional occupations, are covered unless the employee in the professional occupation (or any other) is an "administrator, executive, or professional."

What we can now see is that the word "professional," in conjunction with "administrator and executive" is a word of art in this context. The word has a special meaning in the context of the wage and hour laws.

These three classes of employees; administrators, executives, and professionals (intellectuals, managers, and creative artists!), within most **any** occupation, are specifically **not** entitled to minimum wage and overtime protection. What protection are they entitled to? They are entitled to legal protection for storage lockers, or change rooms, suitable seating facilities, maintenance of room temperature, and provision of elevator facilities! In other words, they are left with no worthwhile protection at all.

All of this brings us back to the rules to remember: The method of computing your pay, whether salary, hourly, piece rate or any other method, is irrelevant to your coverage under California law regulating wage and hours. You are not covered if you are working as a licensed member of a named profession (the list of nine occupations) explicitly excluded from coverage, or if you are working in an administrative, executive or professional *capacity*. The California Law which exempts those three categories of employees from coverage is derived directly from the federal law, but differs in several aspects from the federal definition of those within the three categories.

How do you determine whether you are working in an administrative, executive, or professional capacity and therefore not entitled to protection under the wage and hour provisions? The California Code of Regulations give the following answer:

> (1) The employee is engaged in work which is primarily intellectual, managerial, or creative, and which requires exercise of discretion and independent judgment, and for which the remuneration is not less than $1,150 per month...
> ($900 per month if you work in agricultural or personal service occupations)

Again, we restate the California Code of Regulations, which says that you are an administrator, executive, or professional if,

1) **Your work is primarily intellectual, managerial, or creative, and**

2) **You work requires exercise of discretion and independent judgment, and**

3) **You receive at least $1,150 (or $900) a month.**

Here for the first time, you can see that administrators, executives and professionals are really employees whose work is—primarily intellectual, managerial, or creative! Why didn't they say that in the first place?

In order for the employer to exclude you from coverage

you must meet all three of the conditions. These conditions can be analyzed by looking at the federal laws from which they were derived.

SPECIAL NOTATION: In applying federal law to California, the California lawmakers managed a very subtle change to the federal laws. Under the federal laws, the classes of employees exempt from protection were; executives, administrators and professionals, and the federal rules defined each of the three categories separately, using a combination of criteria special to each category.

California appears to follow the federal law in naming the same three categories for exemption, but California defines each of the categories under the same test. The federal laws do not. California draws elements of the definitions of each separate category found in the federal laws and then applies this single definition to all three of the categories, administrative, managerial, and professional. By changing the definitions, California eliminated the administrative employee exemption altogether, much to the benefit of employees who may have been so categorized under the federal definitions.

Since the California changes benefit the employee, the changes are permissible. The definitional change has no effect on the other two categories, except for the percentage of exempt labor time required. See "PRIMARILY UNDER CALIFORNIA AND FEDERAL LAW, below.

Let's look at the third requirement first. It's the easiest one to analyze. If you qualify for coverage under this requirement we don't have to go any further.

You must receive a monthly pay of at least $1,150, (or $900, if you are in the personal service industry or agriculturally related industries.) This is pretty straight forward, and most employees who may face exclusion under the intellectual, managerial, or creative exemption make more than the minimum wage. You will have to make the initial determination of whether you work in the agricultural, agricultural products, or canning industry, or the household help industry. If you do, then you need only make $900 per month before you satisfy the third of the three conditions necessary to exclude you from coverage.

Making more money than the minimums is bad for purposes of being protected. Don't worry, if you make more than you are permitted to under the third condition. The vast majority of you will (hopefully) make more than you are permitted to guarantee coverage based on the third criteria. Your best opportunity to be covered under the wage and hour regulations is in not satisfying one or both of the first two conditions.

Always remember that all three conditions must be satisfied before you are excluded from protection. If you fail to satisfy any one of the three conditions, you will be covered by the wage and hour provisions.

Federal law requires an employee to be paid on a "salary basis" before that employee may be excluded from wage and hour protection. California state law does not require employees to be paid a salary to be excluded under the wage and hour provisions. This difference is potentially detrimental to the hourly-paid executive employee under California law. Hourly employees are always entitled to protection under federal law. It might be a rare situation, but if I found myself in the position of being an hourly-paid employee-manager, I would argue that federal law prevails over California law in this area since it provides greater protection to employees.

"PRIMARILY" UNDER CALIFORNIA AND FEDERAL LAW

The first requirement under California law states that your work must be *primarily* intellectual, managerial, or creative for you to be excluded from protection. "Primarily" means that more than 50% of your actual working time is spent doing activities that are either intellectual, managerial, or creative. If less than 50% of your work time is devoted to activities other than these three, then you are entitled to protection.

The first thing you need to do is look at your daily schedule and determine where your hours are devoted. If it is obvious that less than one-half of your time is devoted to performing services that fall, or may fall, within any one of those three categories, then you qualify for protection and you need not proceed with the analysis any further.

If it appears that you may be spending more than one-half of your time performing duties that are intellectual, managerial, or creative, then you are at risk of being classified as an executive, etc., and you need to proceed to the second part of the analysis—Is your work intellectual, managerial, or creative?

The second part of this test provides you with three different ways to lose, but remember, even if you are excluded under the "primary" percentage test, *and* under one of the following three categories, this is still less than half the battle for the employer. There is still another requirement that must be met before you lose your protection: The "exercise of discretion and independent judgment" requirement, so don't despair.

California law differs from federal law in the "primary" test. As we have seen, California requires that the exempt employee devote more than 50% of his time performing "exempt" duties (intellectual, managerial, creative). The California "primary" rule is a more-than-50% test.

The federal law requires that the exempt employee must devote 60% of his or her time to "exempt" duties if the employee works in the retail or service industries, and 80% of his or her time to "exempt" duties if he or she works in other industries. These percentages are much more favorable to protecting the employee than the California rules.

Under the federal rules, retail and service establishments are defined as businesses open to the general public, which are engaged in making retail sales of goods or services. The business must receive at least 75% of its income from sales that are not for resale and are recognized as being retail. Examples of retail and service businesses are retail stores selling consumer goods, hotels, motels, restaurants, recreational businesses, (except those offering gambling), hospitals, convalescent homes, public parking lots and garages, auto repair shops, service stations (but not truck stops), and funeral homes.

Businesses that require 80% of the employee's time to be devoted to "exempt" duties to exclude him from coverage are manufacturing, public and private elementary schools and colleges, laundering, cleaning, dry cleaning, or repairing of fabrics, or businesses that sell for resale (wholesalers).

Clearly, the vast majority of all employees fall under the first categories requiring a 60% test under the federal rules. This differs only slightly from the California test and for all practical purposes, is the same under conditions of real life analysis.

If you work in manufacturing or wholesale, or one of the listed occupations which require 80% of your time to be devoted to "exempt" activities, then the differences between the California and federal rules can be significant. You will want to convince the hearing officer than the 80% test should be employed. This can be a delicate matter. You do not want the hearing officer to perceive you as arrogant or presumptuous. Technically, the federal rules are controlling, but practically speaking, you are before a state department that follows California law, not federal.

You may want to tactfully mention your humble understanding of the federal position on the matter as a point to be taken under consideration by the hearing officer and leave it at that. Don't push it. Read carefully the section below on how to win your case.

Now, setting aside the differences in the definition of "primary," let's take a look at each of the three possibilities under the first part of the "executive" test. The first possibility states that,

(a) **Your work must be primarily intellectual.**

This means that more than 50% of your time on the job must be engaged in intellectual pursuits. Intellectual work involves the thinking process. Doesn't any job involve the thinking process? You could argue that taking an order at the hamburger stand involves the "thinking process," and would therefore exempt you as an "intellectual" employee. This is not the case. "Intellectual" has been interpreted to mean utilizing your intellectual capacities beyond what is required to perform manual or repetitive duties and beyond what is required of any person of average mental ability to perform any ordinary job.

The term "intellectual" involves more than just thinking in order to perform your work. After all, everyone thinks when performing work of any sort. The "primarily intellectual" exemption evolved from the exemption under the FLSA regarding professional employees, and we need to look at the "intellectual" exemption in that context in order to fully understand what is meant by the term, and how it fits into the overall picture.

Under the FLSA, "intellectual work" is one component of the exemption for "professional" employees. Work that is "primarily intellectual" refers to the type of thinking required by the job. We most often come across the "intellectual exemption" in cases involving professional occupations. Examples of professional occupations are chemists, pharmacists, designers, engineers, scientists, and the like.

Under the federal cases, in determining what constitutes "intellectual" work the district courts have required that the work be both "intellectual and varied" and of a type that requires a broad application of individual creativity. In addition, the determination of what constitutes "intellectual" work is always made within a broader context of other aspects of the job, such as the degree of independence that the employee enjoys as well as how routine the tasks are, and how much independent decision making is required by the job.

For example, a chemist may be engaged in performing numerous tests to analyze a newly developed chemical. Clearly, the type of thinking required in selecting, analyzing, and interpreting data from these tests is work of an intellectual nature and would seem to be exempt, particularly if the chemist determines what tests are to be conducted, or otherwise exercises control and authority over the framework of the tests. On the other hand, if the chemist performs tests that are routine, simple and preliminary— tests that are commonly performed by laboratory assistants or technicians, then the nature of the work is much less "intellectual" because several components of the "intellectual nature" of the work have been removed.

Under the second scenario, the performance of the tests does not require decision-making interpretive skills of a highly unique and non-standard nature, nor does performance rely upon a highly individualistic thought process.

The nature of "intellectual" work requires more than the

thought processes involved in even highly skilled procedures that are conducted in accordance with strict methods. A distinguishing quality of intellectual labor is the inherently varied signature that such labor produces.

Jobs that require skills necessary to produce a standardized output or product are normally not "intellectual" in nature. Production line output from your work is not "intellectual."

Let's look at another example, that of an X-ray technician. In our example the X-ray technician is responsible for taking a patient, setting them in the proper position, preparing the X-ray for exposure, taking the X-ray, and developing the X-ray for analysis. Obviously, this is a job that requires a high degree of skill, one that requires specialized training and demands an alert and perceptive mental attitude. Is this "intellectual" labor sufficient to exclude our technician from coverage under the law? Looking at what is demanded of the technician, is the intellectual effort of a nature beyond what is required for the performance of repetitive duties? Probably not. In fact, the mental effort required of the technician is precisely that necessary to produce a repetitive and standardized product in a given period of time— the completed X-ray. I would say the technician is not exempted from coverage as a result of performing work of an "intellectual" nature.

On the other hand, the physician who views and interprets the completed X-ray performs work of an "intellectual" nature, for the physician, as he views each different X-ray, is called upon to interpret information contained in the X-ray photographs, draw conclusions from that data and recommend a course of action based on those conclusions. In each analysis of an X-ray photograph the physician is called upon to make creative mental decisions, taken from a constantly changing body of photographic evidence that is, by its nature, not amenable to a standardized diagnosis. The physician will also find himself exempted as a result of working in one of the nine excluded occupations.

If your job requires that you perform manual labor, of even a highly skilled variety, such labor is not "intellectual" in nature.

(b) **Your work must be primarily managerial.**

A manager is someone who spends more than 50% of his or her time performing duties that relate to the management of the business enterprise. Of course, this definition merely begs the question, what constitutes "management of the business enterprise?" As with the "intellectual" exemption, a clue to this exemption is to be found in the federal exemption from which it was created. The California managerial exemption flows from the federal "executive" exemption, thus the California "manager" borrows its analysis from the federal "executive" exemption. Under the federal rules, before you are regarded as an exempt "executive" you must;

a) direct the work of at least two full-time employees on a regular basis.

b) you must have the authority to hire and fire other employees, or your suggestions regarding hiring, firing, and promotions must be given particular weight.

c) you must have as your primary duty the management of the business enterprise.

d) you must customarily and regularly exercise discretionary powers.

Under the California framework of analysis, the exercise of discretionary powers is the second part of the three part test applicable to all three types of exempt work; intellectual, managerial, and creative work. Because of that, the issue of discretionary powers will be discussed below, under the managerial exemption, and again later, under the professional, and creative exemptions. Let's take a closer look at the three components necessary to be regarded as an exempt manager or executive.

The core quality of the executive employee is active engagement in the management of the business operation, and management of the business operation is distinct from production line labor.

To determine whether you are a manager, look at your particular business or company and decide what it is your company "produces."

For example, if you work for a shoe manufacturer, your company produces shoes. If you work for a restaurant, your company produces prepared food products. If you work for a television station, your company produces television programs and so on. The important thing is this: If you perform services that directly relate to producing your businesses product(s), then you are not engaged in managerial labor. You are engaged in production labor.

The courts have found that "executives" who spend their time doing the same type of production labor as regular employees are entitled to the protections provided by the wage and hour provisions. This type of employee is sometimes referred to as a "working foreman." It is not uncommon to have occupations where there are no exempt managers in the business at all! All managerial employees perform duties similar to all other employees and are therefore covered, including the owner of the business himself!

For example, you are a "manager" of a restaurant and if, during the course of your duties you respond to customer requests, help with the preparation of the meals, or monitor the consistency or quality of the meals, you are engaged in activities that directly relate to producing the product, rather than managing other employees who produce the product. Such services are entitled to wage and hour protection and therefore, so are you.

Examples of exempt managerial labor as set forth in the federal regulations involve interviewing, selecting and training employees; setting and adjusting their rates of pay and hours of work; directing their work; maintaining their production or sales records for use in supervision or control; appraising their productivity and efficiency for the purpose of recommending promotions or other changes in their status; handling their complaints and grievances and disciplining them when necessary; planning the work; determining the techniques to be used; apportioning the work among the workers; determining the type of materials, supplies, machinery or tools to be used or merchandise to be bought, stocked and sold; controlling the flow and distribution of materials or merchandise and supplies; approving advertising, authorizing payment of bills; providing for the safety of the employees and the property, and handling customer complaints.

Other factors that the courts consider in determining whether the employee is a manager are; the employee's relative freedom from supervision, the relationship between his salary and other employees for the same kind of nonexempt work, and the frequency of the employee's exercise of discretionary authority.

i) Two or more other employees.

We have seen a sampling of common managerial duties. In addition to such duties, the exempt manager must regularly supervise at least two other full-time employees. Supervising four other half-time employees also satisfies this requirement. An employee who assists the manager in his duties and supervises two other employees only in the absence of the manager, does not satisfy this requirement. A shared responsibility of regularly and customarily supervising two other employees does not satisfy the requirement.

The federal regulations take the position that an employee that customarily manages the minimum of two other employees, usually performs too much protected work to qualify as an exempt executive.

ii) Authority to hire or fire.

It does not matter how high you are up in the hierarchy of management, you are not exempt from protection if, in addition to the other requirements, you are not directly involved in the hiring or firing or promotion or demotion of other employees, either by your direct actions, or by your recommendations that are carried out by other personnel.

iii) Discretionary powers.

Lastly, to be regarded as an exempt manager, you must customarily and regularly exercise discretionary powers. If your work is so completely routine, or regimented that you have no real decision making authority or discretion, then you are not an exempt manager. According to the federal regulations,

The phrase 'customarily and regularly' signifies a frequency which must be greater than occasional but which, of course, may be less than constant. The requirement will be met by the employee who normally and recurrently is called upon to exercise discretionary powers in the day-to-day performance of his duties. The requirement is not met by the occasional exercise of discretionary powers.

According to the federal regulations,

> ... the exercise of discretion and independent judgment involves the comparison and the evaluation of possible courses of conduct and acting or making a decision after the various possibilities have been considered. The term...implies that the person has the authority or power to make an independent choice, free from immediate direction or supervision and with respect to matters of significance.

The federal rules emphasize that the use of authority must be distinguished from the exercise of skill in applying techniques, procedures or standards, or the exercise of decision making in matters of little real importance.

Employees that decide whether a person is a good or a poor insurance or loan risk make decisions based on well defined guidelines or criteria. Their decisions are limited to determining whether there is conformance with the prescribed standards. The employee making the insurance or loan risk decision is exercising skill, rather than discretion and independent judgment. Their decisions do not determine the standards or guidelines to be applied, rather, they only determine whether the pre-determined standards are complied with. A typical example of utilizing skills, rather than real decision making authority, is inspection work. Employees that grade lumber or precious stones, or inspect manufactured products for quality, are exercising skill, not discretionary authority.

Every employee makes decisions in the performance of even the lowest level job. In our prior example we saw that the application of skills involves decision making that doesn't rise to the level of discretionary authority. Such decision making relates only to the performance of skilled routine. As a general proposition we can state that decision making that concerns relatively unimportant matters does not satisfy the statute's requirement for the exercise of discretionary authority. The judgment exercised must be real and substantial and must involve matters of consequence.

In order for the duties of the employee to be truly "managerial," the duties must involve matters of substantial importance to the business. The fact that the duties may involve matters of potentially large economic loss to the business does not necessarily make them of substantial importance. For example, a messenger boy may be entrusted with carrying large sums of money, the loss of which could be catastrophic to the business, yet the messenger boy is not performing work of substantial importance to the business. Another employee may operate machinery that, if misused, could cause serious economic repercussions. That too, is not of substantial importance to the operations of the business enterprise.

Be sure to distinguish between ordinary behavior, the neglect of which could cause serious economic or business consequences, but which is not managerial, and decision-making behavior that goes to the core of the business enterprise, which is managerial.

(c) **Your work must be primarily creative.**

The third general category of exempt employee is the "creative or artistic" employee. Under the federal regulations, work of this type must be original and creative in character in a recognized field of artistic endeavor, and the result must depend primarily on the invention, imagination, or talent of the employee. The work must be in a recognized field of artistic endeavor such as music, writing, the theater, or the plastic and graphic arts. The regulations state:

> (c)(1) The work must be original and creative in character, as opposed to work which can be produced by a person endowed with general manual or intellectual ability and training. In the field of music there should be little difficulty in ascertaining the application of the requirement. Musicians, composers, conductors, soloists, all are engaged in original and creative work within the sense of this definition. In the plastic and graphic arts the require-

ment is, generally speaking, met by painters who at most are given the subject matter of their painting. It is similarly met by cartoonists who are merely told the title or underlying concept of a cartoon and then must rely on their own creative powers to express the concept. It would not normally be met by a person who is employed as a copyist, or as an "animator" of motion-picture cartoons, or as one who retouches photographs since it is not believed that such work is properly described as creative in character.

(2) In the field of writing the distinction is perhaps more difficult to draw. Obviously the requirement is met by essayists or novelists or scenario writers who choose their own subjects and hand in a finished piece of work to their employers (the majority of such persons are, of course, not employees but self-employed). The requirement would also be met, generally speaking, by persons holding the more responsible writing positions in advertising agencies.

(d) Another requirement is that the employee be engaged in work "the result of which depends primarily on the invention, imagination, or talent of the employee." This requirement is easily met by a person employed as an actor, singer, or a violinist, or a short-story writer. In the case of newspaper employees the distinction here is similar to the distinction observed above in connection with the requirement that the work be "original and creative in character." Obviously the majority of reporters do work which depends primarily on intelligence, diligence, and accuracy. It is the minority whose work depends primarily on "invention, imaging, or talent." On the other hand, this requirement will normally be met by actors, musicians, painters, and other artists.

PAYCHECKS

PAYROLL WITHHOLDING
CHILD SUPPORT, TAX LIENS, GARNISHMENT ORDERS

The three listed headings are occasions where your employer is not only entitled to make withholding deductions from your pay, he or she is required to do so. If your employer is making deductions pursuant to a child support order, or a tax withholding order from the State or federal authorities, or a garnishment order in compliance with a court decree, your only chance for correcting the situation is to contact the agency that initiated the action. Your employer has no discretion in the matter.

CASH SHORTAGE OR EQUIPMENT BREAKAGE

It is illegal for your employer to deduct from your wages or require reimbursement from you for any cash shortage, breakage or loss of equipment, unless it can be shown that you were responsible for the cash shortage, breakage or loss of equipment, either through your dishonest or willful act or through your gross negligence. What is important to you about this passage is that the burden is on your employer to establish that the loss occurred either as a result of your dishonesty or through your gross negligence.

You have a very good chance of prevailing if you can show that the possibility existed that someone else could have had access to the money or goods that are missing, and that the access was not a result of your negligence. Perhaps another manager could have accessed the items, or maybe there are inadequate precautionary procedures in place to ensure that no one, not even the owner, could have taken the items. Be aggressive in your defense. No one should be above suspicion, not even the owner. Don't let yourself be the person held responsible for the employer's sloppy business procedures. If the nature of the operation makes it impossible to completely isolate responsibility for a loss to you, then great! That's the employer's problem, not yours.

If your employer alleges that you were responsible for the

loss or destruction of equipment, he or she has the responsibility to show that the loss or destruction occurred, not because of your negligence, but because of your *gross* negligence, or dishonest or willful act. This is a tough requirement. You, as the employee, are in the position of being entitled to go to the DLSE hearing, state that you were not responsible for the loss in question and insist that the employer prove that you did what he or she is alleging. The burden is on the employer.

UNIFORMS AND EQUIPMENT

If the wearing of a uniform or special clothing is required by the employer as a condition of employment, such as the uniform at any fast food restaurant, the employer must provide and maintain the clothing free of charge.

Is it permissible for the employer to require the payment of a security deposit to ensure the return of clothing or equipment when the employee terminates employment? No. This is illegal.

The employee is obligated to return clothing or equipment at the end of his or her employment but if the apparel or equipment is lost, stolen or destroyed through no fault of the employee, the employer cannot make the employee pay. The employer cannot require the employee to be the guarantor of the employer's goods.

As a practical matter, if the employee tells a hearing officer that he has the employer's items, the hearing officer will insist that the employee return the items. But if the employee denies having the items, even though the employer contends that the employee has the items, the employer cannot withhold the employee's wages. The employer should have protected himself by taking out a bond for the clothing or equipment. The employee cannot be held liable.

What if the employee provides prior written authorization for the employer to deduct the cost of the item from the employee's last check if the item is not returned? This type of agreement is not enforceable against the employee if the employee states that he or she doesn't have the items, or that the items were lost or destroyed through no fault of theirs.

Deductions which are expressly made in writing by the employee to cover insurance premiums, hospital or medical dues, or where the item is provided for the benefit of the employee, not the employer, are authorized. Obviously, deductions made for the return of clothing and equipment are for the benefit of the employer, not the employee, and are not enforceable against the employee.

If tools or equipment are required of the position, the employer is responsible for supplying the tools or equipment free of charge. The employee is only required to supply his or her own common tools of the trade if the employee makes at least $11.50 an hour (twice the minimum wage) and it is customary in the trade or profession for the employee to provide his or her own tools, or there is a collective bargaining agreement that provides for the employees to provide their own tools.

If you are paid any less than $11.50 an hour, the employer must supply the tools or equipment.

SETOFFS

It is improper for your employer to deduct money from your paycheck for money that you owe the employer, except through a lawful garnishment order. The employer has to obtain a court's permission before he or she can deduct money from your wages. For example, suppose you borrow money from your employer and you fail to pay him back. Your employer is not permitted to deduct that money owed from your paychecks, which is referred to as "self help." He or she must give you your paycheck and then ask you for the money back.

For example, what happens if your employer allows you to take vacation time before you have earned it and thereafter you are terminated or you quit employment before your rights to the vacation time are earned? The vacation given is regarded as an advance on wages and may be recovered from the employee at the time of termination. The money is not regarded as a "debt" that is owed to the employer but simply wages that have been paid in advance.

The money or vacation time is only regarded as an advance on wages if the employee was told beforehand that the vacation time was an advance and would be subject to repayment at the time of termination. This rule is true for any wage advance, not just vacation time. The rule applies to business expenses, or any other item advanced to the employee.

GAMBLING OR LIQUOR DEBTS OF SEASONAL LABORERS
It is improper to make any deductions for gambling or liquor debts from the paycheck of any seasonal laborer, as defined on page 222.

ELECTRONIC TRANSFERS (DIRECT DEPOSIT)
If you have provided written authorization for your employer to deposit your payroll checks electronically to your bank account your employer is prohibited from either; using that authority to attempt to make withdrawals, or access your account when you employment has ended. If your employment ends the employer is no longer authorized to make electronic transfers. This means that it is normally not proper to pay you your last paycheck by direct deposit.

PAY DOCKING
Pay docking is a reduction in pay made for arriving late to work. The employer is entitled to dock your pay a minimum of 30 minutes if you arrive late for work 30 minutes or less. For example, if you are late 5 minutes, or 10 minutes, or anything less than 30 minutes, your employer can reduce your pay by 30 minutes worth. If you are late more than 30 minutes, your employer can only deduct the wages that would have been earned for the actual time that you were late. For example, if you were 41 minutes late, your employer can only deduct 41 minutes from your earnings. There is one unusual twist to the 30 minute docking rule.

If you are docked 30 minutes for being late, you are not required to work for that time either. Your employer is not permitted to dock you the 30 minutes and force you to begin working prior to the expiration of the 30 minutes. You are entitled to a non-paid break for the time remaining of the 30 minute period for which you are being docked. However, if your employer expects you to begin work, I recommend doing so. You are entitled to the time remaining, however, refusal could prompt a confrontation and I have been advised by at least one Labor Commissioner's office that your refusal would not be protected by that office if the employer alleged that you were insubordinate. Act with caution in this area.

REDUCING WAGES

It is improper for an employer to reduce a "for cause" employee's agreed-to wage rate without notice to the employee of his or her intention to do so in advance. Substantial reduction of a "for cause" employee's wage may constitute a discharge of the employee. Substantial reduction is anything over a 20% reduction in pay, but it may be less. See DISCHARGE OF EMPLOYEE on page75, and WORK RELATED REASONS TO QUIT on page 228.

ASSIGNMENT OF WAGES

An agreement to assign your wages transfers your wages directly from the employer to a third party. In other words, your employer pays your paycheck directly to someone else. Wage garnishments, and tax liens are forms of assignment, though not voluntary. Assignment agreements are usually drafted to pay off monies owed by the employee to a third party. Assignment agreements are only enforceable against the employee making the agreement if all of the following requirements are satisfied;

1) The agreement is written in a separate "assignment agreement".
2) The agreement is signed by the employee being obligated.
3) The agreement describes the loan or other transaction that the assignment agreement relates to.
4) If the employee is married you must obtain the written consent of the spouse.
5) If the employee is a minor you must have the written consent of the parent or guardian.
6) The assignment must contain a statement declaring the marital status of the employee, and the employee's

legal status—whether a minor or an adult.

7) There can only be one assignment agreement per transaction or set of related transactions, and the agreement must contain a statement confirming that fact.

8) A notarized copy of the agreement and accompanying statements must be filed with the employer which is,

9) Accompanied by a statement of the amount owed by the employee to the third party.

10) The assignment is not valid if the employee is subject to any other assignment or earnings withholding order.

11) An assignment cannot exceed 50% of the employee's wages or salary.

The Office of the Labor Commissioner has is not bound by the rules of assignments. The Labor Commissioner is authorized to receive or collect monies on behalf of an employee without an assignment agreement signed by the employee. The Labor Commissioner has the authority to impose fines on employers who may refuse to comply with a Commissioner order.

ASSIGNMENT OF FUTURE EARNINGS

An employee cannot obligate himself to assign wages not yet earned. An assignment of future earnings is revocable at any time by the employee. In order to revoke, the employee must notify the employer in writing. The assignment stays in effect until then. EXCEPTION: An assignment of future earnings is valid if the assignment is for necessities of life, and only for the amount needed to furnish such necessities.

WHEN MUST YOU BE PAID YOUR FINAL PAYCHECK?

IF YOU ARE FIRED OR LAID OFF!

If you are in the unfortunate position of being laid off (and who hasn't been?) you are entitled to your final paycheck immediately.

The only exceptions to the rule are if you are among a group of employees that work in the seasonal curing, canning, or drying of

perishable fruit, fish, or vegetables. If you work in one of those occupations **and** you are all terminated as a group as a result of the ending of the season, then you all must be paid within 72 hours (3 days).

If you are laid off individually, and your termination is not a result of the ending of the season, then you must be paid immediately. This means that if you are terminated before the normal seasonal termination date you are entitled to be paid immediately.

If you work in the motion picture industry and you are laid off in a group, the employer has 24 hours to give you your check, excluding Saturdays, Sundays, and holidays. The payment may be mailed to you if you so request and the date of mailing is the date of payment for purposes of timeliness. If you are not laid off in a group, you must be paid immediately.

If you work in the business of oil drilling and you are laid off, the employer has 24 hours to give you your check, excluding Saturdays, Sundays, and holidays. Notice that here the employer has 24 hours, whether you are laid off in a group or by yourself. The payment may be mailed and the date of mailing is the date of payment.

If you are fired or laid off you are entitled to be paid at the place of firing.

If you are paid on a commission basis, you are entitled to your commissions, if they are capable of being calculated at that time, when you are terminated.

You must first make a demand for the wages owed you.

You do not need to make your demand in writing in order for your demand to be effective. Just a statement to your employer or the manager in charge will do. You do not have to state the amount owed you in your demand. If you make a demand for more money than is really owed you, the demand is still good for the amount that is actually owed.

IF YOU QUIT

If you quit your job you are entitled to receive your final paycheck within 72 hours (3 days). If you provide 72 hours (3 days) notice that you are going to quit, you are entitled to be paid immediately upon your resignation taking effect.

What if you provide less than 72 hours notice, such as 48 hours? Are you entitled to receive your check 24 hours after that? Maybe yes, maybe no. I have found a split of opinion among offices of the Labor Commissioner (although there shouldn't be). Some offices hold that there is no apportionment under the notice requirement. It is all or nothing. Therefore, if you provide your employer with 71 hours notice, you will still not be entitled to receive your final check until 72 hours after your employment ends. To get your check immediately upon quitting you must provide at least 72 hours notice, no less. The notice need not be in writing. You can tell your employer verbally or by any other method that conveys the message.

Some offices will accept less than 72 hours notice and reduce your waiting time accordingly. Under this application if you provided 24 hours notice and you were not paid within 48 hours after that, penalties against your employer will be levied.

If you are in doubt as to what the office of the Labor Commissioner in your area will do, you may want to contact your local office in advance and discuss the situation with them.

You are entitled to have your final check mailed to you if you request it and you provide your employer with a mailing address. The date of mailing constitutes the date of payment for purposes of the requirement that you must be paid within 72 hours of quitting.

YOUR REMEDY IF YOU ARE NOT PAID ON TIME

A right doesn't do you much good if you don't have effective remedies available to you if the right is violated. What is your remedy if you are not paid on time? Perhaps you were fired by a manager on a Friday and the owner wasn't available to pay you until the following Monday? If the employer willfully fails to pay you immediately, he or she will be liable for your full wages for every day that you have to wait, up to a maximum of thirty days wages. Therefore, if you were fired on Friday and you weren't paid until Monday, you are entitled to an additional three days pay according to your regular full schedule and at the same wage. If you quit on Friday, your employer was not obligated to pay you until Monday anyway and so you are not entitled to receive damages.

For you to be entitled to receive damages, your employer must "willfully" fail to pay you. Your employer does not need to possess a malicious or evil attitude towards you in order to willfully deprive you of your pay. In fact, his or her mental attitude is not at all relevant. Your employer is regarded as having acted "willfully" for purposes of the statute if he intended the result that occurred. In common language, you can say that willful is the same as intentional. It doesn't matter that your employer doesn't have the money to pay you, or that he thinks you are a great guy or gal, but doesn't want to pay you until he confirms that your work was adequate— You are entitled to be paid no matter what!

What if you are paid by check and the check bounces? Your employer will be penalized for the delay in payment caused by the bounced check. What if the check bounced unintentionally? It would appear that the employer would still be liable. This is supported by the fact that there is an exception to the general rule of employer liability for unintentional non-payment; If you work in the building and construction industry your employer is permitted to avoid the penalty if he can show that the bad check was given to you unintentionally. This explicit exception implies that other employers are not so fortunate! If you do not work in the building and construction industry, your employer is liable for the delays caused by a bounced check, even if it was unintentional.

Your employer will not be penalized if you made yourself scarce, hoping that your employer would make a mistake and pay you late. You have an obligation to make yourself available during normal business hours to receive your final paycheck at the place that you normally receive your paychecks. If you make a request for payment at the proper place and you are refused, you've satisfied your obligations and your employer is in violation. Again, make sure you make a request for payment. It is critically important.

If the employer is insured by a bonding company to guarantee payment of wages, the bonding company will be liable to you for the wages that were due. The bonding company will not be liable for any penalties that may be due for the delay in payment. However, the employer will still be liable to you for the full amount, wages and penalties, even if he or she is bonded. A bonded employer simply provides you with a second party that you can look to for payment of the wages due.

The labor code section that imposes the penalty of a day's wages for every day that your final paycheck is not paid to you also states that the penalty shall accrue (increase) until an action is commenced, or until paid, whichever comes first. If by chance you've read this code section, don't be concerned that your claim for late payment before the labor commissioner is "the commencement of an action" terminating the accrual of penalties. It isn't. Proceed with your claim, the penalties will increase for every day that you do not receive your pay—up to the maximum of 30 days. These penalties are important because **you** receive the penalty money—not the government. This civil penalty is mandatory, the labor commissioner must impose the penalty.

Due to the importance of this issue, Labor Code Section 203 is reproduced below.

Section 203. Failure to make payment within required time; penalty; employee avoiding payment; limitations of actions

If an employer willfully fails to pay, without abatement or reduction, in accordance with Sections 201, 201.5, and 202, any wages of an employee who is discharged or who quits, the wages of such employee shall continue as a penalty from the due date thereof at the same rate until paid or until an action therefor is commenced; but such wages shall not continue for more than 30 days. No employee who secretes or absents himself to avoid payment to him, or who refuses to receive the payment when fully tendered to him, including any penalty then accrued under this section, shall be entitled to any benefit under this section for the time during which he so avoids payment.

Problems sometimes arise when an employee is governed by a union collective bargaining agreement that provides for different remedies than provided by California law. One such case arose when a Safeway employee was terminated and demanded immediate payment of her final paycheck as provided for under California law.

The collective bargaining agreement (the union agreement) required that the employee first seek binding arbitration. The employee did not receive her check for 3 days. The employee filed a claim with the office of the Labor Commissioner (DLSE). The DLSE refused to collect the paycheck from the employer or give the employee her 3 day penalty, stating that to do so would be to improperly "interpret" a collective bargaining agreement. The DLSE is barred from "interpreting" collective bargaining agreements. The case went all the way to the United States Supreme Court.

The Court held that the DLSE did not need to interpret the labor agreement in order to determine that the employee had not been paid on time according to California law. The Court said you only had to look at a calendar to determine whether or not the employee had been paid on time. Since the state law requires immediate payment upon termination, no union agreement can remove that right.

The basic rule seems to be, if the terms of the union agreement are not the basis of the wage dispute, the DLSE can accept employee wage claims even though the employees are covered by a collective bargaining agreement.

You may file a lawsuit to recover the penalties owed to you for an improper delay in payment of your wages. You may file a lawsuit to recover penalties during the same period of time afterwards that you would be entitled to sue for the recovery of the wages. See HOW SOON MUST YOU ACT on page 220.
LATE PAYMENT, REGULAR PAYCHECKS

What are your rights if your employer is late paying your regular paycheck? So far our conversation has only dealt with last paychecks. Recently the Ninth Circuit court has held that an employer violates the FLSA if the employer fails to pay regular paychecks on time. The employer will be subject to late payment penalties for delinquent payments. This rule applies to both private employers as well as the State of California as employer.

EMPLOYER BANKRUPTCY

What do you do if your employer files for bankruptcy before you are paid? This is a tough situation. First of all, be wary if your employer starts being late in paying you though there's not much that you can do about it. If your employer does file for bankruptcy and you are owed money file a claim with the bankruptcy court where the employer filed for bankruptcy protection. The court will provide you with a *proof of claim* form, or you can acquire a *proof of claim* form at most local office supply stores.

Under the regularly used section of the bankruptcy code you are entitled to what is called a third priority for all wages, severance pay, sick leave pay, or vacation pay due you within ninety days prior to the filing of the bankruptcy petition by your employer. You are entitled to file a claim for up to a maximum of $2,000. Wage claims older than 90 days pre-filing are much worse off in priority.

Third priority means that you fall within the third group of creditors to be paid under a plan of reorganization or liquidation, and you will be paid only after all the creditors in groups one and two are paid. This isn't great because in bankruptcy the only group of creditors that is assured of getting some money are the lawyers and the private trustee (if there is one) and, you guessed it, they are always in the first group of people to be paid anything. They are "class one." You want to get into the same class as those folks.

If your claim for is wages earned after the filing you are normally entitled to first priority by claiming what is called a section 503(b) Administrative expense priority for services rendered for the benefit of the estate (your employer). If your section 503(b)(1)(A) claim is accepted by the judge, you will be paid as a first priority claim. In addition, there is no $2,000 limit to what you may be paid if you happen to be owed more than that.

Don't worry that you don't have the slightest idea what I am talking about. You don't need to know what all this means in order to get your money. Just follow the instructions. On the claim form under the classification of claims section where it states UNSE-CURED PRIORITY CLAIM and follows with the appropriate boxes to check, mark your claim under **Wages, salaries, etc.** and also mark either a box that says OTHER and fill in the following statement just as it is written here,

Administrative Expense under section 503(b)(1)(A)

or, check the box (if there is one) indicating administrative expense priority. The key phrase here is "administrative expense." Claiming an "administrative expense" priority means that you are claiming that the labor you provided helped keep the business operating. The bankruptcy trustee is required to analyze your claim and establish the proper priority. I suggest you file your claim as a first priority as set forth above and let the trustee worry about the rest.

HOW SOON MUST YOU ACT?

Nearly all legal proceedings to enforce a right or privilege should be started within a particular period of time after the alleged violation or injury occurred. The laws requiring you to file your complaint within a certain period of time after the injury or the vio-lation of the agreement or whatever occurs, are called "Statutes of Limitation." The time periods will vary depending on the legal basis for your particular claim.

Your employment rights that you allege have been violated were created for you either by statute or by an agreement (contract) between you and your employer. If your claim arose under a right created under the FLSA you should commence legal proceedings within two years after the employer's first act that prompted the proceedings. If the employer acted "willfully," you are given three years to file your claim. If your action is based on the employer's breach of a verbal agreement, you are given two years after the day the contract is broken. If the contract is written, you are given four years after the day the contract is broken.

The safe rule to remember is: Contact an attorney immediately. Begin your action within one year after the day your rights were first violated. It is always advisable to consult with an employment attorney if you feel that you may have suffered any type of injury in your job. There may be procedures that you are required to follow that you do not even know about. It sometimes happens that people wait to seek the advice of a lawyer, only to find out that they waited too long.

WARNING: You are only permitted 30 days to file a complaint with the DLSE based on illegal discrimination or retaliation which falls under the authority of the Office of the Labor Commissioner. In order to determine whether you only have 30 days from the time of the illegal act see the listing on page 62. If your employment complaint deals with a rule that has a "DLSE" after it, you only have 30 days to file a complaint with the DLSE for a violation of that rule. The 30 day limitation does not apply if you plan to pursue your case in civil court or before some other department.

What if you have waited too long and the time period for bringing a legal action has passed? If your claim is small, and you are considering proceeding before the labor board, or small claims, begin a legal proceeding even though your time to do so is officially "expired." You will generally be permitted to do so, and there is a chance that you may still collect what you are owed. The requirement that you begin a legal proceeding within a particular period of time does not bar or prevent your claim unless the defendant actively alleges it as a defense that your claim is "too late." Lawyers call these types of defenses "affirmative defenses." If the employer is not aware that your claim is late and fails to cry "late" as a defense, or cries "late" too late in the course of the proceedings, the employer loses "lateness" as a defense. You will be permitted to proceed against the employer as though you acted within the proper period of time.

If your claim involves substantial sums of money, or the possibility of serious liability, and the other side is represented by an attorney, (or likely to be) it is unlikely that you will get very far filing an outdated claim.

FREQUENCY OF PAYMENT—REGULAR PAYCHECKS

The general rule is that you are entitled to be paid at least twice a month on days designated in advance by the employer to be regular paydays. See EMPLOYEES OF VEHICLE DEALERS on page 223. How soon after the termination of the pay period must you be paid?

If your first pay period of the month covers from the first through the fifteenth, you must be paid no later than the twenty-sixth. If your second pay period extends from the sixteenth through the last day of the month, your must be paid no later than the tenth day of the following month.

SALARIES OF EXECUTIVE, ADMINISTRATIVE, OR PROFESSIONAL EMPLOYEES may be paid only once per month. Your employer must pay you by the twenty-sixth day of the month for which the labor was performed, and the payment must include the unearned portion between the date of the payment and the last day of the month. In other words, your employer must pay you for the entire month on or before the twenty-sixth of the month. For a complete discussion of salaried executives see OVERTIME AND THE SALARIED EMPLOYEE beginning on page 186.

If you are entitled to overtime, in addition to your regular wages, the overtime must be paid to you no later than the payday for the next regular payroll period. In this case, overtime earned in month one must be paid by payday near the end of month two.

WEEKLY PAYMENT

You can be paid weekly or biweekly (every two weeks) if the wages are paid no more than seven calendar days after the close of the payroll period.

AGRICULTURAL EMPLOYEES

All regular wages, other than final wages, are due and payable twice a month on regularly scheduled paydays and within seven days of the close of the payroll period. If you are paid from the first through the fifteenth you are entitled to receive your pay by the twenty-second. If you are then paid from the sixteenth through the end of the month you are entitled to receive your pay by the seventh of the next month.

SEASONAL LABORERS

Wages earned from seasonal labor, as defined in the beginning of this book, must be paid in the presence of the Labor Commissioner or his deputy or his agent, if so requested by either the employee or the employer.

CERTAIN EMPLOYEES HOUSED BY THE EMPLOYER

If you are boarded and lodged by your employer, you are only entitled to be paid once a month. This applies to employees in agricultural, viticultural, and horticultural employment, stock or poultry raising, and in household domestic service.

EMPLOYEES OF FARM LABOR CONTRACTORS

If you are an agricultural worker and you work for a farm labor contractor you are entitled to be paid at least once a week and the payday must be on a business day during business hours.

EMPLOYEES OF VEHICLE DEALERS

If you work for a licensed car dealer and you are paid on a commission basis, your employer may pay you once a month on a regularly scheduled payday. This rule also protects salesmen and mechanics of car dealers.

Chapter Three

UNEMPLOYMENT COMPENSATION

Unemployment compensation is money paid by state government to eligible unemployed individuals. In order to be eligible to receive benefits you must be unemployed through no fault of your own, you must register for work and be willing and able to work. You must also make a claim for benefits for the week for which you seek benefits, and you must have attempted to secure work for the week (or weeks) that you are unemployed. There is also a one week waiting period before you can begin receiving benefits.

AVAILABLE FOR WORK

In order to qualify to receive unemployment compensation the individual must be "available for work."

Are you eligible for work if you are not able to work because you have been arrested? You are still eligible for work if you are arrested and held in custody for up to two days if the charges are later dropped. If you are lawfully arrested, and held for more than two days you are not "available for work" for that week and you are ineligible to receive unemployment benefits.

If you are unable to work as a result of a physical or mental disability, you are not entitled to receive unemployment benefits for each day that you were unable to seek employment. However, you are still entitled to receive benefits for each day that you are able to work.

If you are unable to seek employment because you are a full-time student, you are not entitled to receive unemployment benefits. You may be entitled to benefits if you are a part-time student and you have supported yourself for at least two years as a part-time student.

Illegal aliens are not entitled to unemployment compensation. Undocumented workers do not have authorization to work and are therefore not regarded as being "available for work" as required.

If you suffer the death of an immediate family member you are allowed two work days off from the seeking of employment without losing your eligibility by being "unavailable for work." You are allowed four work days off if the relative was out of state at the time of death.

GOOD CAUSE AND UNEMPLOYMENT COMPENSATION

You do not qualify to receive unemployment compensation if you were either terminated for work-related misconduct, or you voluntarily quit your last employment without good cause. You will be entitled to unemployment compensation if you voluntarily quit with good cause for doing so.

I will provide a broad overview of various situations that you may encounter in quitting or being terminated from employment which involve the concept of good cause.

When analyzing any situation to determine whether good cause existed for you to quit your job, or whether good cause existed for your employer to terminate you from your job, the law expects the parties to act reasonably under the circumstances. If you quit your job the law expects you to have first done all that a reasonable person would have done under the circumstances to either correct the problems that you found intolerable if that was possible for you, or inform your employer and request that he or she correct the problems. For example, you may be expected to request a job transfer to a different department if you have conflicts with a supervisor, or seek alternative child day-care accommodations if you are faced with a schedule change that you find burdensome.

Furthermore, the law expects you to minimize your injuries afterwards as best you can.

QUITTING VS. TERMINATION

The first issue that you may face in seeking unemployment is whether you voluntarily left your job or were terminated. Often it is not clear.

What if you are laid off due to a slow down in the job? Are you entitled to unemployment? If the layoff is temporary and for a stated period of time if you quit during that period you are regarded as having left voluntarily and you are not entitled to unemployment. If the layoff is indefinite and the employer does not tell you how long you can expect to be off work, and you terminate your employment during that period of time, you have not voluntarily left your job. You are entitled to unemployment.

If you are laid off during a trade dispute that you are not involved in, your leaving is not voluntary. You are entitled to unemployment.

What if you are suspended for a definite period of time? May you receive unemployment during that period? If your suspension was a disciplinary measure as a result of employee work-related misconduct, you will not be entitled to unemployment. If the suspension was due to lack of work or other non-disciplinary cause, you are entitled. If, at the end of the suspension period you fail to return to work, your failure is a voluntary leaving of work.

What if you and your employer voluntarily agree to give you a leave of absence from your work? A leave of absence merely suspends your employment relationship and you are not entitled to unemployment during the leave period. If at the end of the leave, the employer cannot provide work for you and the failure was unanticipated by the employee, you have not left voluntarily and you are entitled to unemployment. If, at the end of the leave period you do not or cannot return to work for personal reasons, your leaving is voluntary. This is true even if you request an extension of the leave of absence and your employer refuses.

If you agree at the beginning of your employment, to work

for an employer for a pre-determined period of time, and at the expiration of that period you decline not to accept an offer to continue your employment, your refusal to renew is not a voluntary leaving of employment and you are entitled to unemployment. For example, you sign a one year employment agreement and you leave after the year is up even though your employer has offered to renew your contract—your are entitled to unemployment.

If your employer gives you the option of either quitting or being fired, your quitting is not voluntary. If your employer gives you the option of either quitting now or being terminated in a few days and you choose to quit now, your quitting is not voluntary. However, if you quit in anticipation of being laid off in the near future but the employer has not taken any definite action, your quitting is voluntary. The determining issue is whether you or your employer causes your unemployment. If you act before your employer has a chance to, you have terminated your employment voluntarily. It is always safe advice to let your employer make the first move.

If you are given the choice to "bump" another employee, but you choose not to and permit yourself to be terminated instead, your termination is voluntary.

QUITTING YOUR JOB AND GOOD CAUSE

If you quit your job without good cause you are not entitled to collect unemployment benefits.

There may be circumstances where you quit your job and still be entitled to receive unemployment benefits. We will discuss a number of such situations.

For example, if your employer "forces" you to quit, you will be entitled to receive unemployment benefits. See also CONSTRUCTIVE DISCHARGE on page 78. This may occur under any number of circumstances which would prompt a reasonable person faced with the same situation to quit. You may have numerous reasons for quitting work and not all of them need to provide good cause for quitting if even one of your reasons provides good cause and is a substantial motivating factor in your decision to quit, or if taken together, they provide good cause.

If you are subjected to unfair and unreasonable disciplinary actions by your employer, you may be entitled to unemployment benefits if you quit.

If you suffer an increased hardship in your means of transportation to and from work, not a result of your own fault, you may be entitled to quit and receive compensation. For example, your employer changes the location of your worksite, or your employer changes your hours of work, or you move to a distant location due to family obligations. If you have a serious illness in the family, or a change in marital status, or a change in parental obligations, any such change may be good cause to terminate your employment. Remember that each situation will be analyzed in terms of the reasonableness of your response under the circumstances. The obligations imposed on you by the change in family or marital circumstances must be serious enough to compel a reasonable person to respond to them in a like manner.

WORK RELATED REASONS TO QUIT

There are numerous situations that may entitle you to quit with good cause that we will be discussing including; complaints with tools and equipment, religious or moral objections, transportation problems, family problems, change in marital status, reduction in wages or change in job duties, undue risk of physical injury, forced retirement, other job prospects, too many or too few work hours offered, union problems, or problems with working conditions.

If your employer has an obligation to provide you with tools or equipment necessary for you to perform your job, and fails to do so after being notified of his or her obligation, your quitting employment is with good cause. You have an obligation to inform your employer of the lack of proper equipment, and the employer must fail to acquire or repair the tools or equipment before you can quit for cause.

It is not good cause to quit employment for lack of tools when you make at least $11.50 an hour or more and it is customary in your trade or profession for the employee to provide his or her own tools.

If the employer's failure to provide proper tools or equipment increases your risk of injury, you have good cause to quit your employment.

"Risk of injury" can include any injury that requires the services of a physician. You are not entitled to quit out of concern for your safety unless the risk to your safety is beyond that normally assumed by the nature of the work. The risk must be beyond what a reasonable person would be expected to tolerate. You cannot quit simply because you may wish to rest, unless it is on the advice of a physician.

You are also expected to avail yourself of all grievance procedures before you resort to quitting.

Not only may you sometimes quit to protect your physical health, you may sometimes quit to avoid compromising your morals or religious beliefs. The determination of what constitutes a "moral risk" is decided on the grounds of accepted social standards, such as being asked to do something that is illegal, or discriminatory, or dishonest or unethical.

You may quit with good cause if you have sincere religious objections to any of your job duties. For example, suppose you work in a restaurant that does not serve alcoholic beverages, but in the course of your employment the restaurant obtains an on-sale license and starts selling alcohol. Quitting may be with good cause if you have religious objections to alcohol and no accommodation can be made to your religious objection. As in other discussions of religious belief, the sincerity of your religious beliefs may be subject to inquiry.

You may have good cause to quit if you suffer an unexpected hardship in transporting yourself to or from work. It is impossible to state a hard and fast rule in these matters. Much depends on your distance to work, the nature of your work schedule, your family obligations, the cost of transportation in relation to what you earn, etc. Just be aware that if you are forced to quit your job due to unexpected transportation problems, you may be entitled to unemployment benefits.

Leaving your job is with good cause if you are compelled to do so to attend to any number of personal or family matters that require your presence. This may include such things as attending to the health of a sick family member, or providing supervision of a child under your care, or increased obligations that may result from a change in your marital status. Family members include your spouse, children, adopted children, parent, grandparent, brother or sister, grandchild, son-in-law, daughter-in-law, or any person over whom you have assumed responsibilities of a parent-child, parental, or grandparental relationship. The family member need not live in your household. For example, if you were raised by your aunt and uncle, and one or both of them becomes ill, requiring your care, you would be entitled to regard your relationship to them as between a parent and child.

If you marry, or plan to marry and your spouse requires you to relocate to a new geographical area too distant for commuting, your leaving is with good cause. This also includes circumstances where you are attempting to reconcile with your current or former spouse and your spouse lives out of the area.

If you are a minor under parental control, and your family moves to a new geographical area, your leaving is beyond your control and for good cause.

There may be numerous reasons to leave your work which fall under the general category of "personal affairs" and which provide good cause. Be careful to remember that you must first do everything that you reasonably can to avoid having to quit your employment. You must be in a situation where you face compelling circumstances.

What if you quit because you feel that your skills are not being properly put to use in your job? Is quitting under those circumstances with good cause? Generally, no. Quitting can be for good cause when you are hired on the understanding that you would perform certain duties that require your skills and, after being hired, your job duties are changed and your skills are no longer utilized. It is not good cause to quit if you do so merely because you felt that the job did not provide enough potential to develop new skills that you wish to acquire.

It is not good cause to quit simply because you fear that you are not competent to perform your job duties.

It is good cause to quit of your employer is erratic in paying your wages on time and in the proper amounts, or intentionally refuses to pay your full wages when due.

If your employer reduces your wages by 20% or more, this is regarded as providing good cause to quit. It is unclear exactly how small the reduction may be before you have good cause to quit. It may be as little as 10% but it cannot be said with certainty. Be careful. What may be considered "good cause" for purposes of obtaining unemployment benefits is definitely not the same "good cause" needed to quit and then sue the employer for wrongful termination. See also CONSTRUCTIVE DISCHARGE on page 78.

It is not good cause to quit if you were aware of the wages to be paid at the time of your employment, but you became dissatisfied with the wages at a later date. Nor is it good cause to quit if you request and are denied a pay increase or an advance on wages.

Is it good cause to quit if you don't like the working conditions or job duties that you are subjected to? Generally, mere dissatisfaction with working conditions or job duties is not sufficient to quit with good cause. The working conditions must be so bad that they would not be tolerated by a reasonable working person. Again, have you taken steps to try to correct the situation if such efforts are not pointless?

If you are singled out for discriminatory treatment or offensive job duties, you would have good cause to quit. You are not required to submit to illegal discrimination.

There may be situations where good cause exists to quit resulting from the manner that you are required to perform your work.

What if you object to one or more of your employer's rules or requirements? An employer's rule or requirement is unreasonable **under any one** of the following circumstances:

1) It is impossible for you to physically comply with the rule.
2) The rule imposes a new and unreasonable burden on you.
3) The rule is not designed to further or protect the employer's business.
4) You reasonable believe that the rule is illegal, you object

or try to object, and the employer makes no attempt to explain the reason for the rule. It is not important whether or not the rule is actually against the law.

5) You reasonably believe that complying with the rule could result in an undue risk of injury or illness to you.

Work requirements are unreasonable if any one of the following occurs:

1) The duties would impose an undue risk of injury or illness for you if you complied.
2) The duties are demeaning to you considering the nature of the job position that you hold.
3) The duties are intended to harass, abuse or discriminate against you.
4) The duties that you are assigned entitle you to a higher wage than the employer is paying you.
5) The employer assigns you to duties that are inferior in skill and status than your usual duties.
6) The work duties are objectionable on moral grounds and you object to the employer.
7) The duties or work requirements will substantially increase your workload.
8) The duties assigned to you will cause you to lose proficiency in the skills that you were hired for.

Is it good cause to quit in order to take another job? Again, this depends on what the trier of fact determines to be the "reasonableness" of your actions under the circumstances of your case. Would a reasonable person do the same thing in your situation? Quitting a permanent job to accept a temporary job is usually not regarded as good cause. However, you can quit a temporary job for a permanent job even if the permanent job pays less, since in the long run, it may provide better prospects for you. If you quit your job to accept a better one, you may be entitled to quit a few days early in order to prepare for the new job, or move, or even take a few days to rest if you had not had a vacation.

Quitting a long term permanent job in order to begin your own business is not good cause.

Good cause to quit can exist when the employer makes unreasonable demands to work on holidays or the number of days during the week, or requires you to work too much overtime, or provides too few hours of work, or otherwise changes your work schedule so as to cause you an undue and unreasonable hardship in your particular situation. For example, you may be solely responsible for minor children and being forced to work six days a week may exceed your abilities to secure adequate child care. Under these circumstances, if your employer cannot accommodate your need to work only five days, and you cannot, after best efforts, obtain child care services, good cause would exist to quit.

DISCHARGE OF EMPLOYEE AND UNEMPLOYMENT COMPENSATION

The situation may arise where you are terminated from employment. Under what circumstances may you be entitled to receive unemployment benefits?

In general, if you are terminated for work-related misconduct you are not entitled to receive unemployment benefits.

It is misconduct if you willfully or wantonly (with knowing indifference to the consequences) cause an injury to your employer's interests. In order to be guilty of misconduct you must also have a duty to act or refrain from acting in some way as a result of the employment relationship, and your failure must be the cause of the injury to your employer.

It is not misconduct to merely do a poor job, or act negligently in the performance of your job obligations. It is not misconduct if you made a mistake that injured your employer without intending to do so, unless the mistake is so outrageous as to be regarded as wanton disregard. Mistakes due to inability to do the job properly, or lack of skill, or inefficiency, or poor judgment is not misconduct unless you had received prior warnings about the very same activity (or activities) and failed to perform better when you have to ability and capacity to do so. If it is simply beyond your abilities to do your work any better than you have, your continuing failure is not misconduct.

Misconduct must be connected with work or affect the employer's business interests. Misconduct can involve actions by an employee away from the job if the actions injure to tend to injure the employer's interests. Injuring the employer's interests can involve acts which cause a loss of customers, or disruption in the workplace, or loss of discipline, or injury to the employer's public image, or loss of property or equipment, or any financial loss

If you have committed some act of misconduct against your employer and your employer doesn't terminate you immediately afterwards, your employer has condoned or accepted the improper activity and cannot later change his mind and terminate you for that misconduct. Any delay by the employer of more than a few days implies an acceptance of the misconduct, and a subsequent discharge by the employer would not be for misconduct. You would be entitled to unemployment benefits.

The following are common situations involving misconduct as it relates to receiving unemployment benefits.

ABSENCE FROM WORK

If you have notified your employer that you will be absent from work, and you are given approval, your employer cannot terminated you for work-related misconduct. However, if you stay over your period of excused Absence from work and engage in unauthorized conduct without notifying your employer, you may be terminated for misconduct. It is not misconduct if you had compelling reasons for the continued absence and you were unable to notify your employer.

If you give your employer a false reason for your need to be absent from work, and you knew or should have known that your absence would not be permitted for those reasons, you have engaged in misconduct and may be terminated. Your discharge would be for dishonesty. I will discuss dishonesty in more detail below.

What if you absence is unexcused? It is not misconduct the first time you are absent without prior excuse. If your unexcused absence is not the first such occurrence it is misconduct if you did not have a real, compelling and substantial reason for being absent without prior notice to the employer. It is misconduct if you failed to give notice of the absence and you did not have a real, compelling and substantial reason for failing to give notice. As you can see, there are two components to unexcused absence as misconduct.

1) Absence without a compelling reason and
2) Failing to provide the employer with notice.

You may be liable for misconduct if you do either one of the two items listed above. For example, you may be terminated for misconduct if you notify your employer that you need to be absent from work if your reasons given are not compelling, or you may be terminated if you had a compelling and legitimate reason to be absent from work but you failed to provide prompt and timely notice to your employer.

There is no law requiring a doctors excuse if you are absent from work over a certain number of days. Such requirements are only a result of employer policy. However, a policy requiring a doctors excuse will be upheld if it is determined to be reasonable, in furtherance of a legitimate business interest, and is not intended to harass the employees, and it is not applied unfairly.

There are special rules if you are absent from work against your will because you have been arrested or jailed.

If you are absent from work for more than 24 hours because of an arrest and you are subsequently convicted of the charges (or you plead guilty), you are regarded as having voluntarily left your employment without cause. You are not entitled to unemployment benefits if your employer thinks that you walked away from the job and terminates you

If the court gives you the option of paying a fine or serving jail time and you remain in jail because you have no funds with which to pay the fine, you are not regarded as having voluntarily left your job. Your failure to give timely notice to your employer is also excused. If you are terminated, you are entitled to unemployment benefits.

If you are determined to be not guilty of the offense or any lessor included offenses for which you were jailed, you are entitled to unemployment benefits if you are terminated as a result of your unexcused Absence from work. This is also true if you enter a drug diversion or rehabilitation program resulting from certain drug arrests.

If you have been jailed you are generally excused from giving notice to your employer unless, under the circumstances, it would have been convenient and reasonable for you to do so.

Even though it may be improper to terminate you for reasons of unexcused absence if you miss work as a result of being arrested or jailed, you may still be terminated for the commission of the illegal act itself in certain circumstances. See ILLEGAL ACTIVITIES below.

VIOLATING A DUTY TO YOUR EMPLOYER

An employer owes his or her employer a duty not to willfully or recklessly harm the employer's interests. This can involve either acts or statements by the employer which demonstrates a lack of regard for the employer's interests. Normally, the first incident committed by an employee is not enough to permit discharge of the employee. Employees are permitted an error of judgment. However, be very careful if you have been reprimanded even once, any repetition of the prohibited conduct or language may be sufficient to have you terminated, especially if it occurs within a short period of time.

What kinds of acts or statements demonstrate willful and wanton disregard for your employer's interests? This could include such things as deliberately talking bad about the boss or a supervisor, or the employer's product, or aiding a competitor, or diverting the employer's business to yourself, or inciting or encouraging the destruction of equipment or the work premises by other employees.

It is not misconduct to gripe about the job if the employee makes use of the proper channels in doing so. Griping to the owner without first complaining to your supervisor may be misconduct.

Violating a duty to your employer must normally involve doing something that has a direct connection with your employer's business interests.

OFF-THE-JOB ACTIVITIES

Generally, activities performed away from your place of employment on your own time do not involve your employer's business interests. An intrusion into your off-duty activities may be an invasion of your privacy. There are exceptions to the general rule, particularly if the off-duty behavior involves criminal or morally reprehensible activities. For example, if you work in a pharmacy and you are convicted of selling or manufacturing illegal drugs, such behavior would directly affect your employer's interests and you could be terminated for misconduct.

Your off-duty activities need not be criminal to provide cause to terminate you for misconduct. For example, if you work at a youth center and you have a reputation for going to pornographic bookstores, or topless bars, such conduct may injure your employer's public image and discharge would be appropriate.

Generally, you cannot be discharged for activities you did before you began work at your current place of employment, but if you conceal the activities from your employer, that may be enough to get you discharged under the "BAD ACTS" doctrine, below.

DISHONESTY

You can be discharged for cause for any act of dishonesty such as lying, stealing or pilfering or anything indicating a lack of trustworthiness. This includes falsifying time or work records, misusing employer property or equipment, making false statements about co-workers, or submitting false expense records, etc.

You may be discharged even though the employer does not have a specific rule prohibiting dishonesty.

You may be discharged if you witness another employee commit a dishonest act or statement and you fail to report the incident to the employer. You do not have a duty to report minor acts of dishonesty, unless you are specifically hired in that capacity. You are required to report anything that may cause substantial economic injury to the employer, or threaten the employer's health or safety.

You may be discharged if you encourage other employees to commit acts of dishonesty.

INSUBORDINATION

Insubordination is the refusal by an employee to submit to reasonable and lawful orders, regulations, or rules of the employer or supervisor. Insubordination generally involves a series of acts or statements by the employee that have resulted in prior warnings or reprimands. If the incident is serious enough the employee may be discharged for insubordination without giving the employee a second chance. See the previous section WORK RELATED REASONS TO QUIT for a discussion of employer rules and regulations that may be unreasonable. See also VIOLATING EMPLOYER RULES below.

Insubordination can also involve remarks by the employee which damage or tend to damage the employer's interests. Therefore, you may willingly follow the employer's order, but if you make statements that are injurious, you may still be guilty of insubordination. Be careful what you say. Be careful how you say it. Insubordination can result from vulgar, obscene, profane, insulting, derogatory, or offensive language of a vile nature spoken toward the employer or supervisor.

ALCOHOL OR DRUG USE

It is misconduct to show up for work while intoxicated, or to be intoxicated when you return to work from lunch or a break.

It is misconduct to drink anything intoxicating during work hours.

It is misconduct to return to work with offensive physical affects resulting from earlier intoxication while off-duty if you have received one previous warning or reprimand. You do not need to be intoxicated when you arrive at work if your previous drinking causes you to be impaired in your ability to do your job properly. This can include such things as showing up for work with liquor on your breath, or looking sloppy and bloodshot.

You have a defense to being discharged for misconduct if you can establish either;

1) Your employer permitted or condoned the behavior
2) You had an irresistible compulsion or inability to stop yourself from you behavior. You may have a

defense if you can show that you are a chronic alcoholic and could not help yourself. However, remember that current alcohol use is not a protected disability and you may find yourself terminated for alcohol-related reasons other than intoxication-misconduct

If you have been terminated for alcohol use and denied unemployment because your termination was for misconduct in order to utilize the irresistible compulsion defense you must complete an alcohol rehabilitation program. The program must either be;

1) A program certified by the State Department of Alcohol and Drug Programs (ADP) or the State Department of Health Services (DHS) or licensed by the state within which it is located.
2) A reputable non-licensed program such as Alcoholics Anonymous (AA) or Narcotics Anonymous (NA).

The proof of your completion must in writing by either a physician or a treatment program administrator.

Misconduct involving intoxicants includes illegal drug use.

POOR WORK PERFORMANCE

Poor work performance due to simple negligence or inability to do the job properly is not misconduct. Intentionally or deliberately failing to do your job properly is misconduct.

Intentionally failing to correct a physical or mental limitation or impairment that may prevent you from doing your job properly is misconduct. For example, you know your hearing is failing but you refuse to have your hearing tested or take corrective action. Your failure to correct your hearing (assuming you could do something about the condition) would be misconduct if your hearing loss impaired your ability to do your job.

Misconduct can include deliberate work "slow-downs" where your quality of work does not worsen but the quantity of your work output is reduced.

Your employer has the right to raise the work output requirements placed on you so long as the increase is not unreasonable or done to harass or discriminate against you.

It is misconduct to repeatedly act rude or discourteous to the public after receiving warnings or reprimands about such behavior.

It is misconduct to be grossly negligent in performing your job. What is gross negligence? Generally speaking, gross negligence occurs when you do something in violation of your employers rules and regulations knowing that to do so could result in substantial losses or liability to the employer, and you have no logical and reasonable explanation for your behavior.

Negligent behavior may be misconduct if the employee persists in the behavior in disregard of repeated reprimands or requests to alter the behavior.

It is not misconduct if you do something that turns out to be detrimental to your employer if you were acting in good faith. Your error in judgment must be forgiven if you acted with reasonable diligence, even though your decision was wrong.

RELATIONS WITH CO-WORKERS

Bad relations with co-workers is misconduct if it is brought on by you with deliberate disregard for your employer's business interests.

It is misconduct to intentionally cause fights with or among co-workers, cheat them, lie to them, or steal from them. It is misconduct to intentionally disrupt the workplace or harass other employees, either verbally or physically.

It can be misconduct to swear at or verbally abuse another employee, but the issue of misconduct must be determined in the context of the situation. Language which would be inappropriate in an office complex may be acceptable in a lumberyard or steel mill. The rule against foul language is not intended to prohibit banter between employees. A certain degree of accommodation is expected among employees.

TARDINESS

It is an implied duty of any employment that you show up to

work on time. Tardiness, or being late for work, can be misconduct under any of these situations;

1) Being continuously late for work, after having been warned that continued tardiness would result in termination.

2) Inexcusable tardiness combined with other violations of rules and regulations by the employee.

3) A single act of tardiness that foreseeably causes substantial injury to the employer's interests.

It is not misconduct if you have a compelling reason for being late, even though you may have a history of being late. However, oversleeping, not allowing enough time to make your commute, or missing your public transportation are not compelling reasons for being late.

It is not misconduct if there was no substantial injury to the employer's interests as a result of your tardiness and your tardiness was minor (several minutes late).

VIOLATING EMPLOYER RULES

As we discussed in the earlier section dealing with good cause to quit, employer rules must be reasonable and must relate to protecting some legitimate employer interest in order for you to have to abide by them.

Employers are entitled to enforce rules regulating clothing and appearance. See also GROOMING AND CLOTHING on page 130.

If an employee refuses to abide by an employer's grooming or clothing rules it is misconduct if the following three conditions are all met.

1) The rule is reasonable and rationally relates to enhancing the employer's business interests.

2) The benefit to the employer from the rule is greater than the imposition on the employee's constitutional right to freedom of expression.

3) The employer's rules are the least invasive alternative

available to secure the necessary business objective.

Employers are entitled to prohibit gambling or game playing by employees on the business premises during work hours. Generally, it is not misconduct if the employees engage in gambling or game playing on the business premises during off-duty hours. Like other activities conducted by employees on their own time away from the job, such activities are normally their private business, unless their activities negatively affects the interests of the employer, particularly in relation to public perception of the employer's interests.

Any activities engaged in, or condoned by the employer are not misconduct.

Employers have the right to enact and enforce safety rules in the workplace. In fact, such rules are nearly always regarded as reasonable. Intentional or wanton violation of such rules is misconduct.

Employers are entitled to establish and enforce rules relating to both customer purchases and employee purchases of goods and services. Employee violations of rules relating to customer purchases generally are minor, unless the employee acts in knowing disregard for the rules after repeated warnings. Intentional violations relating to employee purchases are generally more serious and are misconduct.

Employers are entitled to require employees to record their compensable time on a time clock. Knowing refusal is misconduct. Falsification of time clock records is misconduct.

ILLEGAL ACTIVITIES

Criminal convictions for activities conducted away from work do not normally establish employee misconduct. Illegal activities by employees may be misconduct if;

1) The employee uses information obtained from work to carry out the criminal enterprise, or
2) There is a substantial connection between the criminal activities and the employer's business enterprise.

PERIOD OF INELIGIBILITY

If you voluntarily left your employment without cause you are ineligible to receive unemployment benefits. If you were terminated for misconduct you are ineligible to receive benefits.

How long are you ineligible? You are ineligible until you regain employment and earn at least five times your weekly benefit amount. This means that you are ineligible so long as you remain unemployed from the job for which you were disqualified!

How much is five times your weekly benefit amount? It depends on how much money you made during the prior year of continuous employment (described as your "base period"). Your benefit amount could range from $40 a week to $230 a week, depending on how much money you earned in the prior year. Therefore, you need to earn anywhere from $200 to $1,150 in order to purge your ineligibility. In addition, you must have earned at least $1,300 during one quarter of your base period to become eligible for a new claim. You may become eligible, in the alternative, by making at least $900 in one quarter and at least $1,1250 for the base period (one year). These are minimum figures, and in all likelihood you will need to make more to qualify for a new claim. The computation can be complex. These figures illustrate the basics. The local unemployment office will provide a complete analysis of your particular situation.

If you are disqualified because you have refused to accept employment you are ineligible for a minimum of anywhere from two weeks, up to ten weeks.

If you are disqualified for making a false statement or withholding information in order to collect unemployment benefits, you are ineligible for up to 15 weeks. The 15 weeks of disqualification may be imposed up to 3 years later. If you are disqualified for false statements or withholding of information more than once, your period of disqualification can be extended another 8 weeks. If you are convicted in a criminal proceeding of making a false statement or withholding information you will be disqualified for up to one year.

Chapter Four
Presenting Your Wage Case at the Office of the Labor Commissioner

HOW TO WIN YOUR WAGE CASE

The first step in winning your case is determining whether you have one. It is extremely important for you to understand that the determination of whether or not you "have a case" is much more than deciding whether you are owed money or were mistreated. It involves the broader questions of whether you have evidence to prove your position, and whether pressing your case at the present time is in your own best interest. Naturally, I cannot guarantee that this book will ensure that you will win your case, but I can provide you with suggestions that will help keep you from sabotaging your case.

WHERE TO GO FOR HELP

Let's look at the first item—you have been treated badly. You have either been shorted hours, or overtime, or you have suffered from harassment, or you have been improperly terminated or passed up for promotion, or whatever.

You have three basic options; consult an attorney, go to your nearest Department of Labor Relations Office as set forth on pages 333 and file a claim, or file a claim in small claims court. You could also proceed in superior court on your own without a lawyer, but I don't recommend it.

You may also have the option of filing your claim with the nearest Equal Employment Opportunity Commission (EEOC) office or the Department of Fair employment and Housing (DFEH). However, the unbelievable delays that you will probably experience are such that I do not recommend the EEOC as an effective course of action, nor can I recommend the DFEH. Recent studies reported in the *Sacramento Bee* newspaper indicate that out of 300,000 inquiries received by the DFEH in 1992, only 3.2% were investigated and a little over .5% were settled! You may wait months just to get an interview that ultimately leads you nowhere. However, if I were faced with a situation where my other options appeared to be foreclosed for whatever reason, then I would certainly pursue the remaining avenues available to me. Consider all possible options open to you.

I recommend that you first consult an attorney in the following types of cases; sexual harassment, wrongful termination or demotion, discrimination based on race, skin color, age if you are least 40 years old, religious beliefs, national origin, or sexual orientation, or any claim that may involve substantial sums of money, or where attorneys fees for a private attorney are permitted, such as non-payment of wages, or overtime, or fringe benefits. I believe that in most instances you should first consult an employment attorney. It should not cost you anything to do so. They can help guide you.

If your claim is based on sexual orientation discrimination, you may also file a complaint directly with the Department of Labor Relations, which is the Office of the Labor Commissioner, rather than civil court. I cannot recommend one course of action over another. If you feel more comfortable handling the matter yourself, then file a claim with the DLSE yourself, but again, only after first consulting with a private attorney.

Decisions relating to wage and hour law rendered by the DLSE are appealable to civil court. In other words, assuming you have brought a case before the DLSE and you have won, the losing party has the right to appeal the decision within 10 days of receipt of the decision, order or award. Your employer can then force you to begin again in civil court as though the proceedings before the office of the labor commissioner did not take place. The trial in civil court is said to be "de novo," which means anew or afresh for the second time. Although this may sound frightening there is no reason to be nervous or fearful. The fact is, very few of the cases brought before the DLSE are ever appealed. Only about 8% are ever appealed and the majority of the remaining 8% that are appealed are upheld or settled.

There is no right to a "de novo" appeal in non-wage and hour matters. For example, if you file a claim against your employer for sexual orientation discrimination before the DLSE and you win, the employer is not entitled to appeal to the civil court on a "de novo" basis.

If the DLSE awards a decision in the employee's favor, and the employer chooses to appeal, the DLSE provides legal representation for the employee. The attorney from the DLSE handles the case and all related matters for the employee. The DLSE does not like to see people "spend wages to chase wages." The DLSE will not provide you with legal help if you do not completely agree with the decision. On the other hand, the DLSE does not provide legal counsel for the employer under any circumstances. If the employee loses at the hearing before the DLSE, he or she may appeal but in that instance the DLSE does not provide legal counsel for the employee. The employee is on his own, but then again, so is the employer.

If the employee appeals to civil court and loses in the civil suit, the employee is liable for the judgment, as well as court costs and employer's attorney fees. Interestingly enough, in the more than 70 sexual orientation complaints that were brought before the DLSE through 1992, and determinations made thereon, none were appealed to civil court.

California is the only state that has attorneys on staff within the Office of the Labor Commissioner to aid employees.

Except for hearings before the DLSE, it is not my intent to

focus on matters of legal tactic or procedure which are best handled by your attorney. My objective is to provide you with an overview of the substantive rules so that you become aware of your employment rights. How you should proceed in your particular case is beyond the scope of this book, although I will make some general recommendations for your consideration.

I recommend having most cases, even wage and hour matters, analyzed by an employment attorney. Legal and procedural matters can be very complex and given the potentially enormous judgments that can result from employment related cases, a professional opinion makes sense. In recent years, average judgments for employment related cases have exceeded $1,500,000 per case! — and the judgments have been getting larger!

Labor cases that involve any claims arising out of wrongful termination, discrimination, sexual or political harassment and the like can involve complex issues of law and are likely to be vigorously defended by legal counsel. Competent prosecution of such cases is well beyond the capabilities of the non-lawyer. The down side of all this is that expenses for the plaintiff's attorney can also be enormous. If you have a weak case or a small dollar case, attorneys may be reluctant to handle your case on a contingency basis. This means that you might be forced to pay for legal counsel on an hourly basis, whether you win or lose. The interested attorney will need to be convinced that yours is both a valuable and a winnable case before you will be given the opportunity to have an attorney represent you on a pay-if-you-win basis. Your foresight in collecting evidence becomes crucial!

Despite my cautions, some cases can be best handled by presenting your case yourself before a hearing officer of the Labor Commissioner's Office. The same suggestion applies to sexual orientation complaints. I simply must stress that you have to make the judgment call and it is cheap insurance to obtain a professional opinion before you commit yourself to a course of action.

You may also file a claim or complaint with the Office of the Labor Commissioner if your claim involves overtime, minimum wage, improper payment, late payment, or other wage and hour problems. Remember that if you hire a private attorney on a contingency basis, you may be able to collect reasonable attorneys fees from your employer if you win.

No matter what situation you face I must stress that having the law on your side means nothing without the evidence to prove your position. Often, the difference between a good case and a terrible case is not the facts, but the evidence, or proof available. Rodney King would probably be in jail (rather than a being a millionaire) were it not for the evidence presented by the video tape proving that the cops brutally beat him. It is critical that you make best efforts from the first moment that you are aware that a problem may exist or be developing, to collect and preserve evidence to support your claims. Try to obtain and preserve written records of important occurrences. If you complain about something to your employer or a manager, do so in writing. Keep copies of promotions, performance evaluations, both positive and negative, correspondence, job duty changes or whatever. It is critically important to keep copies of e-mails or other correspondence sent to you from management. Written evidence is very effective and will help you immensely when the time comes. For further browbeating on this topic see BRING YOUR EVIDENCE WITH YOU and DISCHARGE OF EMPLOYEE on pages 260 and 75.

ASK FIRST

Before you confront your employer with what you have learned in this book, or worse yet, file a claim against him or her, attempt to resolve the matter without angering or alienating your employer. The following are tactical suggestions, mental exercises for those of you who are still employed and must consider the impact upon your employer.

CONSIDER YOUR EMPLOYER'S NEEDS

If you are employed and wish to remain that way, view the situation from your employer's perspective. Let's say that you are a salaried employee, you are owed overtime, and you plan to notify your boss of that fact. How will your boss perceive your position? Your boss may feel that your attitude shows a lack of devotion or reflects insubordination or worse, treachery. He or she may feel threatened. Your employer may become angry. From your employer's perspective, he or she probably wishes to keep you happy in order to maximize your productive output but at the least cost.

You need to ask yourself, are you a critical employee or one that may be easily replaced at little cost to the company? If you are in a weak job position you may wish to avoid acting on you rights, choosing instead to document your case as best you can for some time in the future when it is in your best interests to act. Always keep in mind statute of limitations problems. See HOW SOON MUST YOU ACT on page 219. If the situation is one like sexual harassment that may be impossible to contend with, you must face the consequences as they occur.

FOCUS ON BENEFITS, NOT THREATS

If it is possible, tell your employer what you want in a non-confrontational manner. If you are owed overtime, let your employer know that it is as big a surprise to you as it is to he or she and you would like to take care of this matter now so that the difficulty can be minimized and avoided in the future. Present your case from the viewpoint of doing your boss a favor by educating him or her, and thereby avoiding a more costly mistake with some other employee, or groups of employees.

Point out your devotion to your employer. Ask your employer for his or her advise on how to best correct the situation. What would make your employer happy? Place your employer in the position of being the one who is responsible for correcting an injustice, rather than regarding himself or herself as the "victimized" employer. Point out how fortunate it is for your employer that this situation can be corrected now before it becomes unmanageable later on. This type of negotiation with your employer focuses on positive things, rather than threats.

PRESENT A STRONG, PERSUASIVE POSITION

In any negotiating situation, whether you are utilizing the tactic of promising benefits to the other party, or threatening disaster, you are better off if the other party is convinced of the strength of your position. Your employer will be more likely to work with you if your employer is convinced that his or her position is weak, and opposition is risky and likely to result in worse consequences than coming to an agreement.

Consider showing your employer the passage in this book that states your position. Seeing something in black and white is persuasive. There is no sure way to convince your employer to be reasonable. Some people don't get the message until a judge tells them her decision to their face. Your employer may be just stubborn and shortsighted. However, try diplomacy first.

Document your attempts with a written request to your employer. It may not do any good but it prevents your employer from alleging that he or she wasn't given the opportunity to correct the problem, and it shows that you have made good faith efforts to resolve the matter reasonably. Your written request should not be threatening. If diplomacy has no effect, impress upon your employer the seriousness of the situation and most importantly, your seriousness.

RESORT TO THREATS

If your employer cannot be reached through friendly means, or if you no longer work for the employer and you do not have to worry about future dependence on your past employer, consider a different approach—threaten your employer! We're not talking about physical threats, we're referring to legitimate threats of legal action to enforce your rights. We are talking about convincing your employer that you are prepared to take whatever legal efforts are necessary to correct the problem or recover your money. Present your case forcefully and as coherently as you can. If your employer still refuses to be reasonable, then read on...

FILING YOUR CLAIM

Look to the back of this book on page 331 for the Office of the Labor Commissioner nearest you and go there. They will have claim forms in English and Spanish, along with instruction booklets describing the hearing procedures you can expect to encounter. Fill out a claim form. Sample claim forms in English and Spanish are reproduced for you on pages 335, 336. If you have any questions or problems, an experienced employee will help you. If you do not speak English, most offices have staff that speak Spanish. If you speak another language, bring someone with you who can act as an interpreter for you. When you file your claim you can expect a wait of anywhere from thirty to ninety days before you can be scheduled for a conference or a hearing. You will receive written notice from a hearing officer, within thirty days, informing you of the action recommended by the DLSE; either a conference, a hearing or dismissal. Generally, claims are initially scheduled for a conference.

THE CONFERENCE

If your claim is scheduled for a conference you will receive a *Notice of Claim Filed & Conference,* which will describe the claim, and give the date, time, and place of the conference. The notice, which is sent to both parties, will also tell you to attend.

The conference is the first meeting between yourself, your employer and a deputy labor commissioner. The conference takes place in the office of the deputy commissioner and is intended to try to resolve the dispute at the earliest stage, if at all possible. It is usually conducted more informally than the hearing. Statements can be taken on all matters but you are not under oath. In other words, if you lie you cannot be charged with perjury. You should bring all of your evidence with you and be prepared to argue your case as convincingly as you would in a hearing. Your effectiveness in a conference may help you prevail without the necessity of a hearing.

Do not be late for the conference or the hearing. If you are late for your hearing the DLSE will probably permit you 15 minutes leeway, beyond that you can expect the hearing officer to dismiss your case, unless you provide a good reason for your absence. On the other hand, if the defendant is late or fails to show for the conference he doesn't lose, the conference is simply waived and a hearing is set for a later date.

If the defendant pays you in whole or in part, or if you come to an agreement prior to the hearing, notify the deputy labor commissioner as soon as possible. You are entitled to withdraw your claim at any time before a conference or a hearing, or even at the last moment as the hearing commences. If you wish to withdraw your claim, make the request in writing to the deputy labor commissioner.

If you fail to come to any agreement at the conference, the

deputy labor commissioner will either set the matter for a hearing or dismiss your claim altogether.

THE HEARING

If you are scheduled for a hearing you will receive, either by certified mail or personal service, a *Notice of Hearing or Notice of Claim Filed and Hearing*, which will set forth the time, date and place of the hearing.

The hearing is a formal proceeding, which means that the hearing is recorded and all evidence presented is under penalty of perjury. In addition, you are entitled to be represented by an attorney, to present and rebut evidence, to question the opposing party or witnesses by cross-examination, and to have a translator.

The formal rules of evidence do not apply, which means that the presentation of physical evidence and testimony is much more dependent upon the discretion of the hearing officer and, in my experience, more likely to be admitted and listened to than under courtroom procedures. The hearing officer has complete authority over the conduct of the hearing. Because of the latitude accorded the introduction of evidence and testimony it is very important that you pay attention to the suggestions offered below in presenting your case.

If the defendant fails to attend the hearing, the hearing officer will proceed with the hearing based on your evidence and testimony. The hearing will not be rescheduled unless the hearing officer determines that the interests of justice would be served by a rescheduling of the hearing and a removal of the decision based upon the defaulting party's demonstration of mistake, inadvertence, surprise, or excusable neglect.

If you fail to attend the hearing your case will be dismissed.

PREPARING FOR THE CONFERENCE OR HEARING

You cannot prepare for the conference or hearing if you do not know the purpose of the hearing. What is **your** purpose for this hearing? Your objective is to convince the hearing officer of the validity and reasonableness of your claim. You must be believed and consequently, you must be believable. Dress comfortably but try to avoid being outlandish, unless that is how you are most comfortable. A labor hearing is not the best place to demonstrate your pride in your green-studded, mohawk-haired Elvis outfit. Be reasonable. Present yourself politely and—take a bath beforehand! I am serious. Hearing officers are easy going when it comes to what you wear but no one enjoys being offended.

Request to sit in on at least one hearing prior to the day of your own. The public has a right to witness labor hearings. This will familiarize you with the environment and the procedures that you will face at your hearing and will help get rid of any feelings of nervousness that occur in unfamiliar surroundings and proceedings. If you are relaxed, you will think more clearly when presenting your own case. Call the morning that you plan to sit in on a hearing to be sure that hearings are being held, and let them know what your plans are. It will make it easier for the labor personnel to accommodate you.

If you do not speak English, inquire before your hearing to find out if an interpreter will be available. If not, then be sure to bring a friend or relative who can interpret for you. If you bring friends or relatives for emotional support, it is possible that they will not be permitted to remain during the hearing, unless they are called as a witness and not until then, but this is not a hard and fast rule. It is within the discretion of the hearing officer.

Regarding the preparation of evidence and witnesses, see BRING YOUR EVIDENCE WITH YOU on page 260.

THE HEARING OFFICER IS NOT YOUR ATTORNEY

People have a tendency to forget the obvious, that the hearing officer is a public employee, who has duties and responsibilities, other than to help you with presenting your case, or ruling in your favor.

Do not regard the hearing officer as your attorney. Tell yourself that if you want the officer to rule in your favor, you have got to help him or her by providing them with the information they need to do so. They will have to justify their decision to someone in authority over them. Provide the facts and legal arguments necessary to permit the hearing officer to rule in your favor.

TWO PRESENTATIONS

The following are two different examples of presenting the same overtime case. The first example suffers from structural problems and is used to show you what not to do, the second example shows marked improvement.

> I am a manager at Acme Golf Club manufacturing. I work about 55 hours a week, including my driving time. My paychecks , which are $500 every two weeks, don't show any overtime. I told Roger I wasn't being properly paid for overtime and he said "Why do you think you are on salary, anyway?" The law says that if I don't supervise two other employees, I am entitled to overtime. Well, I don't. Sometimes I help Phil set up his job site but otherwise I do all my own work. I've been working for these guys for four years now and I have never made any decision about how to make their clubs or where to sell them or anything like that. Marty in the front office knows how much time I put in. I don't have any time cards because I am on salary, but I wrote down what I think my total hours are for the last couple of years. You can take a look at it if you like. I mentioned it to Marty and he said that he could come in and back me up if you needed it, but otherwise he'd rather not. I could also bring in some other employees who will testify that they often work overtime and don't get paid for it. In conclusion, I want to say that the law says that I am not a manager and I am entitled to all the time I wasn't paid for and so that's what I want and nothing else. Thank you.

The second example:

> My name is Terry Sample. I work for Acme Golf Clubs, a corporation that manufactures golf clubs for wholesale distribution. I am employed un-

der a verbal agreement and I've been employed at Acme for 4 years. I receive a salary, paid once every two weeks. The salary is based on an hourly figure of $12 an hour, excluding what other benefits there might be. I have been promoted 3 times.

I work in a department with one other full-time employee and three part-time employees. My job title is "production manager" but my job duties involve the following: I spend more than one-half of my time at work screwing heads onto golf clubs. I do this from around 8 a.m. to 12:15 P.M.. 5 days a week. I take a lunch break from 12:15 to 1:15 P.M.. When I return in the afternoons I generally spend about an hour filling out production forms. I sometimes help Phil in the packaging of the clubs. If someone doesn't show for work then I may end up filling in for them. That occurs an average of once every 10 working days. I generally spend the last hour doing book work and arranging the next day's production schedule.

I don't hire employees, though I recommended firing Louie Manale last fall when I caught him stealing clubs. I haven't recommended terminating any other employee, nor have I ever been asked about those sort of things. I'm not otherwise involved in the management decisions of the company.

I feel that I am entitled to overtime because in my job with this firm I wasn't an excluded administrator, executive, or professional. First of all, I wasn't employed in a named professional occupation. As you can see, I wasn't employed as an attorney, or a medical doctor, or any of the other excluded occupations. Secondly, it's my feeling that I wasn't employed in a primarily intellectual, managerial, or artistic capacity. My employer will no doubt say that I was a manager but it is my point that I was not employed as a manager according to the wage law for the following reasons;

If I am correct, in order to be a manager excluded from protection I must meet the following requirements; First, I must have management as my primary duty. Second, I must direct the work of a least two other full-time employees. Third, my job must require me to exercise my discretion and judgment, and finally, I must be paid at least $1,150 a month. Of the three requirements, I don't satisfy even the first requirement because as a so-called manager of the golf club production department, I spent more than half of my daily time screwing heads on the clubs. My job was really more like a working foreman I guess, since the majority of my time was spent in actual production of the clubs.

Even if my employer disputes the amount of time I spent working on golf club heads, I never had any real decision making authority. I simply did as I was told. I didn't determine what clubs to produce or in what quantities. I didn't determine what materials to use or who to buy them from. And I certainly wasn't involved in hiring people or setting their pay or other benefits.

I made a written request of the company for my payroll records, but they said that the computers were down and didn't know when they would be fixed. I have here a copy of my written request to Acme on that matter and a second letter showing their response. Marty Jones, an employee of Acme who works in the front office and maintains those records was willing to testify, but wasn't able to attend. Here's his written statement in support of me for whatever persuasive value you may give it.

In these two examples we have two presentations involving the same fact pattern. The first presentation is not totally incorrect, nor is the second totally correct, but each is helpful in highlighting do's and don'ts of an effective presentation. Let's begin with the overview.

PROVIDE A BRIEF, COHERENT, FACTUAL OVERVIEW

The hearing officer does not know your case nearly as well as you do and he or she never will. Nor does he or she have the degree of interest in your case that you do. You must help yourself by helping the officer understand the overall picture of what your claim is all about and through that, generate his or her support for your position.

Provide a brief, factual background of your job, your job duties, the nature of your claim and what it is you seek to correct the situation. The hearing officer would like to help you, but he or she cannot if he or she does not know what is going on. As the plaintiff, you will be given the first opportunity to state your case. It is crucial for success that you begin your presentation in an orderly and understandable fashion, paying close attention to what the issues are. You cannot be persuasive if the hearing officer is forced to spend his or her mental efforts untangling the jumbled facts in your presentation. The hearing officer has an expert's understanding of what information is important and what is not, but the hearing officer cannot always draw forth information out of a confused and undirected presentation.

In the first example the claimant throws the listener into the middle of his problems without first setting the stage. The result is confusion. In the second example, the listener is given a clearer picture of the employment environment, the type of company, and the products that are manufactured. The listener's difficulty in trying to discover your direction has been removed because you are providing guideposts for the listener. A listener is more apt to believe you, to find you persuasive, if he or she is not forced to exert mental efforts trying to figure out what you're trying to say.

KNOW YOUR CLAIM (KNOW THE LAW)

Know the law and know what it is you want from the proceedings but do not lecture the hearing officer. You are not Perry Mason. For example, if you think that you are entitled to overtime, why do you think so? Know the three situations under which you are entitled to overtime—and state the applicable ones in your presentation.

If you are a salaried executive, why are you not excluded from coverage? Know why, in your case, you do not meet all the requirements set forth for the excluded executive. In order to know why you are not an excluded executive, you must know the requirements for exclusion. Study the rules that you believe apply to your claim. Be prepared to name them, one by one.

Try to present statements of fact, and statements of the rules of law applicable to your case, rather than conclusions of law. Let the hearing officer provide the conclusions of law. After all, he or she doesn't want a lecture from you on what the law is, but it is nevertheless important that you set forth the law in your presentation. You want to state the rules of law as you understand them, in order to let the hearing officer know where you are headed in your presentation and why he or she should decide in your favor. You do not want to state broad conclusions of law in order to impress the hearing officer with your vast knowledge. In other words, don't, in effect, tell the hearing officer how he or she must decide the case. You won't impress her, you will only reduce your persuasiveness and strain her patience. I realize that I appear to be giving you conflicting advice but I am really trying to lead you through what is a touchy tactical situation. I am attempting to convey to you the critical importance of presenting the law that supports your position without acting like a lecturing oppressive clod in the process.

In the first example on page 253 the claimant presents his case in a muddled fashion. The listener is left with a feeling that the claimant doesn't know what he wants to prove. In the second example the claimant has detailed his position by the thoughtful presentation of each element of his claim or defense. By breaking down the components of his claim or defense, the claimant has made his presentation more understandable and easier to support.

As a part of knowing and presenting your claim, be sure to present every element of your claim. Do not leave any element or legal rule out, no matter how obvious you may think the rule to be. I have made this mistake in presentations that I have made, omitting in one case, the one (I thought obvious) rule of law that would have

"In case you didn't know, the labor code says..."

forced a decision in my favor. After winning less than I legally should have, I realized that I made a mistake by not telling the judge about the obvious rule for him to consider. Everyone can use a refresher in the rules when it comes to strengthening your position. Make it easy for the hearing officer to feel good about deciding in your favor. Better yet, convince the hearing officer that the law requires that he or she decide in your favor.

MOVE FROM GENERAL TO SPECIFIC

In the second example, the claimant has convincingly moved from the general to the specific. He begins by providing an overview to the hearing officer why he should not be excluded from protection, briefly setting forth the possible categories of excluded executives that he could potentially fall under. He then casts off each category that he obviously does not fall within, finally coming to the more problematic specific requirements that appear to apply directly to him.

The technique of moving from the general to the specific strengthens the persuasiveness of your presentation by making it easier for the listener to follow. Claimants and defendants alike sink in the confusion of presentations that have no beginning, no middle and no end. Give your presentation a structure and a purpose. **Give your presentation a beginning, a middle, and a conclusion.**

DISSECT YOUR ARGUMENT

You must be prepared to disassemble the legal basis for your claim and present it in neatly laid out pieces, rather than as an unanalyzed chunk of assertions. In our first example the claimant asserts legal conclusions, rather than statements of component fact that would lead the officer to the proper conclusion. You are much better off showing how you satisfy each and every requirement of the rules that apply to your case, and letting the hearing officer draw the proper conclusions.

In the first presentation our claimant simply asserts, " ...the law says I am not a manager..." He has asserted a conclusion of law, rather than presented evidence satisfying the elements which make up the rule of law. In the second example the claimant tries to guide the officer by stating what he perceives the rules to be, states the components to the rule that must be met and attempts to deal with each element in turn. The claimant is not without error, his approach may be a little heavy handed and awkward. I don't think that the attempt is offensive, and the claimant lets the hearing officer know where he is going with the argument.

The claimant presents a brief statement of the rule that he thinks applies, then dissects his case into its component parts, which lends understanding to his presentation.

BRING YOUR EVIDENCE WITH YOU

In preparing for your claim you should study the nature or your claim, and the defenses that you would reasonably expect your employer to make in opposition to your claim. The knowledge that you gain from these inquiries will tell you what or who you need to bring with you to the hearing. One of the most common failings that I witness in hearings over and over again, is the plaintiff or defendant who fails to bring his evidence with him and expects the hearing officer to rule in his favor based on assertions like,

> If you want, I can bring in witnesses who will tell you that what I'm saying is the God's truth!

The unavoidable response is always,

> You should have thought about that before. The hearing is here and now, not tomorrow or whenever and I can't base my decision on testimony that you could have presented, or would have presented, but didn't. Sorry.

It is up to you to prepare your case. It is up to you to present your case. You are the one making the claim and you must think the thing through if you expect to convince the hearing officer of the validity and propriety of your position. In analyzing your case you may come to the realization that it is your word against your employer's, and it would be more persuasive if you had additional written or verbal support for your claim. Acquire the support before you walk into the commissioner's office the day of your hearing.

Make sure your witnesses show up by bringing them with you if you have to. If you think that your witness's will fail to attend and yet you still think that they will aid your case if compelled to attend and testify, then you can apply for the issuance of a personal court order (subpoena) compelling the witness's attendance at the hearing. You should apply to the Labor Commissioner for a personal subpoena at least ten days prior to the date of the hearing. You must submit, in writing, the reasons why you think that the witness's attendance is relevant and necessary. You are responsible for serving the subpoena, and you must also pay for the serving of the subpoena.

If your witness cannot show up or refuses to and you think it best not to compel them, try to obtain a written statement from the witness and introduce the statement (known as a declaration) into evidence. It may not be given as much weight by the hearing officer as direct testimony, due to the inability to cross examine the person who made the statement. The declaration will be considered and may even swing the decision in your favor. Type up a statement of the testimony that you wish to introduce and include at the end of the testimony the line,

> I declare under penalty of perjury that the foregoing is true and correct. Executed at ___Your Town___ __, California on __/__, 1994.

Bring all written receipts or pay stubs or employee policy manuals or whatever written support you can gather together for your claim. If you cannot obtain written support, bring copies of written requests that you made to the employer for such written support that he had control of and would not or could not provide for you. Demonstrate that the failure to document the situation is his fault, not yours.

As with witnesses, you can apply to the Labor Commissioner for the issuance of a court order (called a subpoena duces tecum) to compel the production of documents or records that are in the possession of the opposing party. You must apply for the court order at least fifteen business days (3 weeks) before the date of the hearing. As with subpoenaing a witness, you are responsible for paying for serving the subpoena, and you must provide a written statement telling why the introduction of the documents is both relevant and necessary.

In both instances of court orders telling people to show up and court orders compelling the production of papers in the other person's possession, the decision to issue the court order is within the discretion of the hearing officer.

If you bring written evidence that you want the hearing officer to consider, be prepared to leave the written evidence with the officer. Do not bring your only copy. Copy your evidence first and bring the copy(s), retaining the original for your records. See DISCHARGE OF EMPLOYEE on page 78.

AVOID THE IRRELEVANT

A major pitfall of not knowing your case is being led off into the dark forest of the irrelevant. If your claim is for receiving your last paycheck late after being terminated for cause, stick to your claim without embarrassment or distraction. I almost guarantee that after you have made your initial presentation, or during it, your employer will respond by pointing out one or more of the following: you were a thief, you were unreliable, you were negligently responsible for the loss of business or the ruining of equipment, you were an unreliable drug user or heavy drinker, you borrowed money that you failed to repay, you often called in sick, business has been poor, the employer has a new bookkeeper that is just becoming familiar with the business, the employer made a mistake and didn't know that you needed your check, and so on. You avoid the irrelevant by knowing your case, knowing what the issue is and sticking to it. You will remain unbothered because you will anticipate the onslaught of irrelevant personal attacks that will surely arise.

Do not let yourself become engaged in an argument with your employer over irrelevant issues, either theirs or yours! Stop talking to your employer, turn to the hearing officer and let the hearing officer continue the hearing. Arguments outside the scope of the issues that you are attempting to prove may be emotionally compelling but they are distracting, confuse the issues and are to be avoided.

ANTICIPATE YOUR EMPLOYER'S ARGUMENTS

Effective preparation involves placing yourself in the shoes of your employer and anticipating what he will present in defense of his position. Some people find this exercise difficult because it involves mentally tearing down the arguments on your behalf that you have formulated and have strong emotional attachments to. You have convinced yourself of the rightness of your position, and you can't imagine any legitimate opposing arguments. Your mental processes develop a bad case of tunnel vision. Start imagining and be creative. If you do this exercise properly you will strengthen your presentation by making yourself aware of your weak points (there are some).

When the hearing day arrives and you find yourself sitting at a table next to your employer your confidence will soar when you hear arguments against you that do not take you by surprise. You will be prepared because you have already wrestled with the opposing arguments in your own mind and have spent hours analyzing their weaknesses and their relevance. You are now in a good position to dispose of your employer's arguments quickly, thoroughly, and convincingly.

In our second example the claimant anticipated that his employer would respond by arguing that the claimant was a manager excluded from protection. By doing so the claimant has prepared the hearing officer for the weaknesses in the claimant's case and reduced the impact that the testimony would otherwise have had.

PAY ATTENTION AND LISTEN

It is easier than you think to become emotional during an exchange and have your reasoning abilities shut down as you mentally battle with verbal exchanges that continue on in your head. This experience is a form of the
"I should have said that!"
phenomenon. When you are done speaking, mentally let it go and direct your full attention to either the hearing officer or the opposing party. Hear what they are saying. Try to remain calm. It may be

helpful to jot down key words during your employer's presentation to jog your memory when it is time to question him on the statements he has made.

Do not interrupt the hearing officer or argue with him or her under any circumstances.

ANSWERING AND POSING QUESTIONS

After you have made your presentation your employer will be entitled to ask you questions in a manner of cross examination. An effective tip to remember is, if you are asked a question pertaining to something irrelevant or nonsensical or argumentative, do not succumb to a defensive mental posture by answering the question. By answering the question you have just fallen into the trap of the "forest of the irrelevant" and it may be days before you find your way out. Control the need to convince the hearing officer that the employer is a lying jerk. Control the need to defend yourself against the irrelevant attacks that will be made on your character. With this type of question, you are much better off by responding to the hearing officer, rather than the opposing party, and you may frame your response something like,

'I don't see how my membership in the midget doll club has anything to do with my employer sending me my last check."

By directing your answer to the hearing officer you avoid starting a direct confrontation with the opposing party, and you defer to the judgment of the hearing officer to determine whether he or she thinks the question is fair and proper in their mind. Remember, what the hearing officer thinks about the question is important.

Do not address your employer by his or her first name. Address your employer by his or her legal last name. You don't want the hearing officer to think of your employer on a personal basis.

After the opposing party has made his or her presentation you will be given the opportunity to ask questions. Do not feel compelled to ask questions. If you cannot think of a question whose answer will likely clarify an issue, then don't ask. Restrain the urge to ask the opposing party why he or she is such lying, lowdown scum. The answer certainly won't please you and probably will do nothing towards getting you your money. If you decide to ask a question, ask your question and do not lecture or make statements to the opposing party. I often see it in hearings, and it only initiates pointless bickering and irritates the hearing officer. Your objective is to convince the hearing officer of the rightness of your position, not the other party. Save your statements for your presentation.

DON'T REPEAT AND REPEAT AND REPEAT

It is a common error to repeat your arguments in the hopes that by doing so you will better convince the hearing officer. Don't do it. They are intelligent and have a better understanding of the issues than you. If you feel for some reason that the hearing officer is "just not getting it," you will generally be given an opportunity to present a summation at the end of the hearing, providing you with an opportunity to beat it into his or her head one more time.

ENDING YOUR PRESENTATION

End your presentation with a brief restatement in summary form of the main elements of your case. You should tie up the loose ends and present your position as a coherent whole so that it appears logical and proper to support. Touch upon the main legal elements that you have established in support of your position. It is a recap of the highlights.

SUMMATION

You may or may not be given an opportunity to make a short summation at the close of the proceedings. If you have nothing to say that wasn't already said at the end of your presentation, keep yourself from repetition and say something like,

"I conclude my case based on everything that has been entered into the record."

If the final questioning has drawn out something that needs clarification or comment, then do so.

HAND THE HEARING OFFICER A WRITTEN STATEMENT OF FACTS AND LEGAL ARGUMENT

After you have completed your argument, you are in the perfect position to play your secret and perhaps, winning card. Hand the hearing officer a short typewritten statement of your case, setting forth the critical facts and the law that demands judgment in your favor.

A written summary of your case provides you with the perfect opportunity to have something in writing that can be reviewed a month later as the officer is planning to render a final decision. Remember, the decision will probably be delayed for up to 45 days, possibly longer. Although the hearing is generally taped, a written argument has the advantage of being thought out in advance and should reflect that deliberation.

Keep the statement short—no more than 3 double spaced typewritten pages. Feel free to write less. State only the critical, core facts. State the law that applies. State how the core facts support the legal decision you want. Finally, have your paper reviewed by a friend or relative. Does it make sense to them? Do they understand your argument? Is it persuasive? Good, now even if you panic in the oral presentation, your paper will be remembered more than your incoherent rambling.

AFTER THE HEARING

Do not expect the hearing officer to give his or her decision the day of the hearing. At the termination of the hearing the hearing officer will inform you that you will be notified of his or her decision within fifteen to forty five days. You will receive written notification by mail, and the notification will include the reasons for the hearing officer's decision. The notification will also tell you of your appeal rights.

APPEALING THE DECISION

An appeal must be filed in the proper justice, municipal or superior court within ten days after the decision, order, or award is served. Remember, if your employer loses and chooses to appeal the decision, the DLSE will provide you with an attorney to handle the case for you. If you lose and choose to appeal the decision, you will not be provided the help of a lawyer. Win or lose, your employer is not provided with a lawyer from DLSE. The employer must always hire his or her own lawyer.

PROHIBITED RETALIATION

Employers are prohibited from discharging or discriminating against any employee for filing a complaint, instituting a proceeding, testifying or preparing to testify in any such proceeding before the office of the labor commissioner, or for exercising any rights under the law. If the employer attempts to retaliate against you, he will be exposing himself to absolutely horrendous potential legal liabilities, which is not to say that it won't happen (people can be surprisingly stupid). If it does happen contact an attorney immediately. See also ANTI-RETALIATION LAWS on page 100.

ONE LAST THOUGHT—GET A PRO TO ARGUE YOUR CASE FOR YOU

Occasionally, despite our how-to advice and all your diligent preparation, the day arrives, you make your own presentation, and it is terrible! To make matters worse, not only did you ramble incoherently, you forgot to present a written argument! Or worse yet, you write more poorly than you speak.

For some of us the best thing is not to always do it ourselves. This involves some soul-searching and perhaps, feedback from friends or relatives as to their assessment of your skills at presentation and persuasion. If you come to the realization that self help is self destruction, do yourself a favor and spend some of your prospective recoveries in order to have a decent chance of collecting some money. Hire a professional. That is what we are here for. Helping to ensure a win/win situation. Besides, in some situations, if your attorney wins for you, attorneys fees will be awarded. Your attorneys fees may have to be paid by your employer!

Chapter Five

EMPLOYEE RIGHTS ON THE JOB

MEDICAL CARE

As an employee you are not automatically entitled to receive medical coverage from your employer. Medical or dental insurance plans are available at the option of the employer under such terms as both parties may decide upon.

If you are promised benefits in your company's employee handbook, any such benefits will generally not be enforceable against the company if the policy is amended or dropped, and the handbook contains a disclaimer (and most do) stating that changes can be made by the company at any time.

California has a workers' compensation system designed to be the exclusive remedy for employees injured or killed on the job. Under most circumstances, an employee injured or killed on the job is prohibited from suing the employer personally for his injuries. The traditional rules of personal liability are replaced by mandatory participation in the workers' compensation system. An introduction to the workers' compensation system is provided on page 224 and following. For questions regarding your workers' compensation rights I suggest you contact an attorney experienced in that field, or the relevant department of the Industrial Relations Department under the White Pages in the telephone book.

ALCOHOL AND DRUG REHABILITATION

If you are a current employee with an alcohol or drug problem, your employer is obligated to accommodate you if you wish to participate in a rehabilitation program. Your employer may not be required to accommodate you if to do so would impose an unreasonable burden (undue hardship) on the employer. What determines whether your attending a rehabilitation program would be an undue hardship on the employer? Many factors are considered; the size of the company, the financial resources, the nature and cost of the accommodation, and possible alternatives to the requested accommodation.

If you have a medical disability, your employer may be obligation to actively attempt to accommodate you, even if you fail to request an accommodation. For a further discussion, see the section on DISCRIMINATION AND HARASSMENT.

RIGHTS TO PAID VACATION TIME

As an employee you have no automatic legal right to paid vacation time. The right to a paid vacation is only created by agreement between the employer and the employee. Even though your employer is not obligated to provide you with paid vacation time as a job benefit, if your employer does provide for paid vacation time, he or she must abide by certain rules regarding vacations.

The employer has the right to control the scheduling of vacations. The employer may prohibit the taking of vacations during a particular time of year, or conversely, require the taking of vacation time during a particular time of year. The employer may also determine how much vacation time may be taken at any one time. Taking accumulated vacation time all at once could be a hardship for the business. Interestingly enough, even though vacation time is not a right, if your employer provides paid vacation time as a benefit, it is non-forfeitable once your right to it has "vested."

Vacation time is regarded as another form of compensation for work performed. It is not a gift or an unearned gratuity from the employer. Vacation time is regarded as deferred or delayed wages for services performed. Therefore, the right to vacation time "vests" or becomes permanent proportionately as labor is rendered.

For example, suppose your employer has a policy that states that every full time employee is entitled to one week of vacation time after one year's service on the job, or after a stated "anniversary" date. You work full time, but you are laid off after ten months. Are you entitled to any vacation time? According to the employer, your right to vacation did not "vest" or become permanent until you had put in a full years service, and since you were laid off prior to the years end you are not entitled to the vacation time. Is this proper? No. The California courts do not permit this kind of policy. Since vacation time, when offered, is part of your payment for working, your right to the vacation time became permanent on a proportional basis during the year as you worked. When you were terminated after ten months, you were entitled to 10/12ths of your year end vacation time, payable in wages, based on your ten months service. You are entitled to a proportional share based on the percentage of the vacation pay period worked.

If you are terminated from your job, you are entitled to be paid for all accumulated vacation time when you are terminated. You are entitled to be paid within 72 hours if you quit without notice. Make sure you return to your place of employment and ask for your vacation money, then make a written record of your request. I cannot overemphasize the importance of keeping good written records of all your vacation time taken and how much remains. Written documentation of everything relating to your employment rights is very important. See WHERE TO GO FOR HELP on page 244.

Always create a written record whenever possible.

Vacation time that is not used continues to build up for the period of time that you are permitted to commence legal proceedings and cannot be forfeited (taken away) by your employer.

If your employment is based on a verbal agreement, no matter how informal, you are entitled to bring legal actions within two years of the act or occurrence about which you have a complaint. If your employment is based on a written agreement you have up to four years after the occurrence of the act or occurrence. If employer fraud is involved you have five years to begin legal proceedings. You may be aware that these time frames deal with common "statute of limitations" periods for beginning any type of legal proceeding. Remember that the limitation periods presented by statute of limitations only limit you if the defendant (employer in this case) actively argues them at the appropriate time during the proceedings. For example, suppose you have accrued unpaid vacation for seven years and suddenly realize after reading this book that you are entitled to be paid for that time. Let's say you were employed on a verbal agreement. The statute of limitations rule would say that you a only entitled to sue for only the last two years of unpaid vacation. The first five years that you let accumulate unknowingly has grown "stale" and is now too old to begin legal proceedings to collect. Have you lost your right to get any of that first five years of unused vacation pay? Not necessarily. Several possibilities exist. If the employer does not know about the two year limitation and does not raise that matter as an affirmative defense he will have waived the defense. See also HOW SOON MUST YOU ACT on page 220. Secondly, the particular trier of fact may award damages in excess of what the limitations period would provide. Third, your factual situation may involve employer abuse, or continuing violations of a kind that permit you to extend the normal period of recovery.

**A "use it or lose it" vacation policy in
which accrued vacation is lost if not used
within a stated period of time, is illegal.**

Therefore, an employee who voluntarily refrains from taking vacations, knowing that the employer's policy does not allow carryover of unused vacation time, or payment of money instead of vacation time, does not waive his right to be paid for accrued, but unused, vacation time.

The employer may be able to accomplish nearly the same result by having a vacation policy that "suspends" the accrual of additional vacation time beyond a set minimum if not utilized within a certain period of time. In other words, the employer may require that accrued vacation be utilized before "new" vacation time accumulates. Since the employer is theoretically not depriving you of earned vacation time, but merely suspending the accrual of "new" vacation time, it is legal. This is known as a "vacation cap," or "no additional accrual" policy. The determination of which type of policy is in force may well depend on the employer's written employee handbook or other evidence, written or otherwise, of company policy or practice. It is advantageous to you to show evidence of forfeiture-type language in the employer's conversations, or written or verbal policies.

For a discussion of what happens if your employer allows you to take vacation time before your right to it has been earned see SETOFFS on page 208.

Recently a case arose involving school administrators who had one-year contracts and who had earned a right to vacation time. The employer sought to avoid paying the accrued vacation monies by terminating the administrators "early" and paying the administrators the balance of what was owed to them up to the normal termination date out of the accrued vacation. This was ruled illegal. The employer cannot take away an employee benefit and then "pay off" or "make good" that benefit with the employee's vacation pay. This was regarded as just another attempt to get around the requirement to pay accrued vacation wages earned by the employee.

PENSIONS

As an employee you have no automatic legal right to a pension, but if the employer has an established pension plan that is known to the employee and the employee continues to work in the honest belief that he will be covered by the plan, he is then entitled to enforce his right to a pension. The right to receive a pension is also enforceable under the doctrine of promissory estoppel, as described in the section on bonuses.

Employers have the right to establish required periods of service for the vesting and maturing of pension benefits. There is very little state law regarding pensions, due to the passage of the Federal Employee Retirement Income Security Act of 1974 (ERISA). ERISA preempts state law regarding most aspects of pensions. This means that ERISA controls over any applicable state laws. Nearly all private pension or employee retirement plans are governed by ERISA. Due to the complexity of the law in these matters, it is virtually impossible to provide general answers to questions you may have regarding your pension plan.

The most common questions I receive deal with vesting rights, and the legality of vesting time requirements, and percentage limitations. Obtain and read your pension handbook. If you have unanswered questions, contact the company representative. If you need further clarification, or if you have grievances, seek out the advice of an attorney familiar with ERISA, if the company representative is not helpful.

SENIORITY RIGHTS

As an employee you have no automatic legal right to seniority. If your place of employment has a company policy or collective bargaining agreement recognizing seniority and providing benefits for seniority, all of your seniority rights come from the contractual agreement and no where else, and are consequently limited by the agreement or contract. If you have a question or problem regarding seniority, try to get a written statement or written seniority policy memo from your employer. Have the statement or memo looked at by an attorney or staff from the nearest office of the DLSE.

If your employer has a policy favoring employees with seniority, such policy cannot discriminate against women for purposes of obtaining seniority or promotions.

If you don't receive a pay stub when you are paid, you are entitled to at least an additional $100 as a penalty against your employer.

PAY STUBS

When you receive your pay you are entitled to receive a pay stub or piece of paper listing,

1) Your gross wages.

2) Total hours worked if you are paid on an hourly wage.

3) All deductions taken out of your pay.

4) Net wages earned.

5) The inclusive dates of the payroll period.

6) Your name and social security number.

7) The name and address of your employer.

If your employer intentionally fails to provide you with a pay stub or written receipt as required, you are entitled to recover from your employer a minimum penalty of $100, plus costs and reasonable attorney fees. If your injuries exceed $100, you are entitled to your damages in excess of $100. In no event shall you receive less than $100.

Your employer is obligated to keep a written record for a period of three years, of all deductions taken from your wages. The records must be properly dated, showing month, day, and year of the deduction. You are entitled, upon your reasonable request, to inspect or copy the records maintained of payroll deductions. Your employer is entitled to charge you for the cost of photocopying the records, but no more than that. You are entitled to inspect or copy these records even if you no longer work for the employer.

EMPLOYEE RECORDS

Your employer must keep written records on you that include your full name, home address, occupation, social security number, and date of birth. Your employer must keep time records that show when you began and ended each shift, meal periods, total daily hours worked, total wages paid each pay period, including value of room and board, if any, total hours worked in the pay period, and your hourly rate of pay. If you work under piece rate, then the employer must provide an explanation of the incentive plan and keep a written record of your total production.

Your records are to be made available to you for inspection within a reasonable period of time upon your reasonable request. This normally means that the employer can require that you inspect your personnel files during normal business hours. You are entitled to inspect personnel files that are used, or have been used, to determine your qualifications for employment, promotion, raises, or termination, or other disciplinary action.

The records must be kept at the place where you report to work. The employer must keep copies of your employee records for at least two years. Your employer cannot prevent you from reviewing your files, however the employer may place reasonable restrictions on your inspections, such as limiting your inspections to certain hours of the day or requiring your inspection requests to be in writing.

You should request a copy of your complete personnel file even if you have no explicit right to receive copies of the complete file (you only have a right to a copy of the documents that you have signed). If the employer refuses to permit photocopying, you should inspect the file with a witness and completely index the contents of the file to ensure that no improper additions or deletions occur in the file. Make thorough notes. You are not permitted to make "corrections" to documents in your personnel file, even if what is written in the file is incorrect.

You are permitted to make a verbal or written request to see your files. However, as you know, I always recommend doing everything in writing. Of course, keep copies of all your written requests or correspondence. You never know...

You are entitled to inspect your complete file until the statute of limitations period runs out on any potential claims that you might bring, even if you no longer work for the employer. This means that under most circumstances you are entitled to inspect your file for as long as you work at the job, and at least two years after you no longer work for your employer.

You are entitled to receive, on demand, copies of all documents **signed** by you, as an employee, relating to obtaining or holding employment, including applications, contracts, signed performance reviews, and termination agreements.

Are you entitled to inspect the personnel files of other employees? You are not entitled to inspect the personnel files of other employees without showing a "compelling need" for the file(s). Other types of documents, such as records of government bids, proposals, or contracts may be obtainable by showing a "compelling need" for the information in the files and by showing that they are not private business records, or set forth confidential business sources or information.

For all practical purposes, if you need to see the personnel records of other employees, and your employer refuses your requests, you will probably have to employ an attorney or the DLSE to help you.

You are not entitled to see letters of recommendation, or records relating to the investigation of a possible criminal offense. However, you should request letters of reference even though your employer is not obligated to provide them to you. If your employer refuses, request letters of reference with the names removed, or, in the alternative, a comprehensive summary of the contents.

This brings us to a very important point in our discussion. The fact that you have labored overtime long and hard means nothing if you cannot substantiate your hours. You must be able to present legitimate and credible time records to support your claims. As a perceptive reader you know that the employer has an obligation to keep records detailing your total hours worked. Obtain photocopies of your time cards. You are entitled to do so. Be wary of the employer that supports his position with work schedules showing when you were supposed to have worked, rather than your actual time card. Changes requiring unexpected overtime would rarely make it to the official schedule.

What if you are on salary and do not use a time card or other record of your time? You may have a small problem. Your employer will undoubtedly testify that you were hired for a 40 hour work week. Your paychecks will reflect your hourly wage multiplied by 40 hours, and unless you can come up with timely and believable records to the contrary it is possible that you will not prevail. I suggest you maintain a diary of your daily totals. Make short notations that explain why, despite your diligent efforts on behalf of your employer during your normal hours, you were compelled to put in additional hours for his or her benefit. Be diligent and most of all, consistent. You can keep your notes short. This will, at times, seem like a real hassle. Ask yourself, is it more convenient to give up even one hour of overtime? You won't think so when that time comes. This is one of those situations in which you will find it more difficult to win unless you have prepared well in advance. However, failure to document your hours in a timely manner may be correctable if your employer has made the same mistake. See the discussion below.

What happens if the employer fails to keep adequate payroll records? We've said that the employee has the burden of proving that he or she is entitled to the overtime hours claimed, but if the employer has failed to keep adequate and accurate records, then the consequences of the failure fall on the employer. If the employee gives some evidence showing the amount of overtime that he or she has worked, even if the evidence was compiled from memory well after the fact, and the employer has failed to maintain proper records indicating the hours that the employee has actually worked, then the burden of proof shifts to the employer to dispute the employee's claims. Since the employer did not maintain proper records either, the court will side with the reasonable inferences to be concluded from the employee's time records compiled from memory.

If neither the employee nor the employer has kept records of the actual time worked by the salaried employee, the employee will probably be entitled to collect overtime based on his or her own recreated record.

APPLICANT RECORDS

Employers are required to keep all employment applications and other applicant records for a period of two years. Every employer must keep records of every applicants race, sex, and national origin. However, it is also illegal for an employer to base an employment decision on this information or an applicant's failure to provide this information.

You are not regarded as an applicant if you send an unsolicited resume or provide other unsolicited information to a prospective employer.

If you are apply for a job and the prospective employer requires you to sign an employment application, a copy of the application form must filed with the Division of Labor Standards Enforcement. Failure to file the application form with the DLSE is a misdemeanor crime.

MEDICAL RECORDS

Employers who maintain medical records on employees are governed by the California Confidentiality of Medical Information Act, as well as the ADA. California law makes medical records confidential and private.

Medical records must be kept separate from other personnel files and access to medical files must be restricted. The only people entitled to access employee medical records shall be managers that need to determine the physical abilities of the employee whose records are being examined, safety employees to determine whether the employee requires special treatment, or governmental officials.

The employer is not permitted to disclose the contents of medical records to anyone else without a written, signed authorization from the employee, except in cases of court order, governmental order, search warrant, or other authorized legal demand.

A health care provider may disclose medical information in it's possession under certain circumstances, such as, for the treatment of the patient, to the insurer or entity responsible for payment of medical bills, to medical licensing agencies, coroner's office, probate court, or parties to a lawsuit in which the medical condition is at issue.

An employee authorization must be signed and dated by the employee or legal representative. The authorization must state the types of information that are permitted to be disclosed, the name and function of the person entitled to disclose the information, the name and function of the person entitled to receive the information, the use(s) that the information is restricted to, and the cutoff date, after which the employer is no longer permitted to disclose the information. The authorization must advise the person signing the authorization of their right to a copy of the authorization.

An employee is not required to authorize disclosure of medical information. The employer is prohibited from retaliating against an employee for refusing to disclose medical information. But if the employer cannot establish the employee's physical ability to perform the job without the information, the employer is permitted to terminate the employee. In other words, the employer is entitled to have access to information necessary to determine the employee's physical abilities to perform the essential duties of the job.

FEDERAL PLANT CLOSING ACT

The Worker Adjustment and Retraining Notification Act of 1988 (WARN) requires all employers in all industries, including service industries, with 100 or more full-time employees, or with 100 or more employees who together work at least 4,000 hours per week (averaging 40 hours per employee), to give at least 60 days written notice before a plant closing or a mass layoff.

You are permitted to file legal proceedings up to three years after the plant closing that occurred in violation of the law.

A plant closing is a permanent or a temporary shutdown of a single site of employment, or one or more facilities or operating sites within a single site, if the shutdown results in loss of employment by 50 or more full-time employees.

A mass layoff is a reduction in work force at a single site of employment in which either 500 employees lose their jobs or at least 33% of the full-time employees (50 employees or more) lose their jobs.

Employers who fail to give the proper notice are liable for back pay, up to a maximum of sixty days pay, for each affected employee. The employer is liable for lost benefits, civil penalties, and reasonable attorneys fees. The employer has the option of providing severance pay instead of the required notice on an equivalent exchange basis. In other words, the employer must provide either sixty days notice or sixty days of severance pay, or (for example) forty days severance pay and twenty days notice, etc.

Under either option (notice vs. severance pay) the end result is that the law requires severance pay for any period less than sixty days for which notice of the closing is not given in advance.

The notice requirements do not apply if the plant closing is caused by business circumstances that were not reasonably foreseeable, or if the closing was due to natural disasters such as flood, earthquake or drought. Nor is notice required if the mass layoffs are a result of a completion of a particular project known at the time of hiring or if the required notice would place the company in danger of bankruptcy. Finally, notice is not required if the company offers the laid off employees alternative employment at another site within six months after termination within commuting distance, or the employees agree to a transfer to another site at any other location within thirty days of the offer.

The employer is permitted to give less than 60 days notice if the employer is "faltering" or the plant closing or layoffs are due to "unforeseeable business circumstances." If the employer provides less than 60 days notice under these circumstances, the employer is required to provide a short explanation for the shortened notice. This is a very easy requirement to meet and provides little comfort for the employees so affected.

You are permitted to file a claim under WARN for up to one year after the plant closing.

The numerous limiting requirements of the act make the law useless to most employees. However, there is a slight chance that you may be entitled to severance pay.

MANDATORY RETIREMENT

Mandatory retirement is illegal in California.

California Government Code section 12942 states:

Every employer in this state shall permit any employee who indicates in writing a desire, in a reasonable time and can demonstrate the ability to do so, to continue his or her employment beyond any retirement date contained in any private pension or retirement plan.

This employment shall continue so long as the employee demonstrates his or her ability to perform the functions of the job adequately and the employer is satisfied with the quality of work performed.

There are two exceptions to this rule. The first is for physicians who are at least seventy years old and are employed by a professional medical corporation which provides for mandatory retirement. The second is for executives or high policy-making employees at least sixty-five years old, who are entitled to pensions of at least $27,000 a year, and who have held the position for at least the last two years. Federal law states that the executive must be entitled to a pension of at least $44,000 a year. Therefore, if you are in this situation and your pension is greater than $27,000 but less than $44,000, file your complaint in federal court.

LITERACY ASSISTANCE

If your employer has twenty-five or more employees, he or she is required to provide assistance in enrolling any employee who requests it, in an adult literacy education program. The employer is not obligated if it would cause an undue hardship for the employer's business. For a discussion of what constitutes an undue hardship see UNDUE HARDSHIP on page 24.

The employer is not obligated to provide time off with pay.

It is illegal to terminate an employee as a result of a disclosure of illiteracy.

SMOKING

The United States Supreme Court has held that there is no constitutional right to smoke at work, nor is there a constitutional right to have a smoke-free workplace. Consequently, employers are permitted to exclude smokers from employment, or pass onto smokers the additional costs incurred in insuring them.

Employers have the right to prohibit smoking, but are not (yet) required to do so. This may soon change under the Americans With Disabilities Act (ADA) because a California court has held that inability to breath in a smoky workplace is a physical disability. Employers are also entitled to refuse to hire smokers. Employees that have sought a smoke-free workplace, alleging that smoking is injurious and in violation of the Occupational Safety and Health Act (OSHA) have lost their cases. The courts have held that employees do not have the right to sue under OSHA. Only the Department of Labor has the right to do so. Employees have the right to file a complaint based on smoke in the workplace, but the decision to file suit is with the Department of Labor.

Employers that permit smoking in the workplace are required to post a notice stating that the employer permits smoking and that smoking is known to cause cancer. Employer attempts to prohibit or restrict off-duty smoking by employees are invasive of the employee's privacy rights and are probably illegal.

California cases have held that a smoky environment may constitute an oppressive work environment resulting in a constructive discharge. An employee who quits under such conditions will be entitled to unemployment compensation.

This area of the law is changing rapidly. Governor Wilson passed into law a bill prohibiting smoking in all public and private workplaces. Your city or county may also have even stricter ordinances limiting or prohibiting smoking in numerous areas that make this discussion largely irrelevant.

OFF-DUTY ACTIVITIES

Sometimes employers will attempt to curtail or control the off-duty activities of their employees. Any attempts to restrict an employee's off-duty activities, such as, drinking alcoholic beverages, engaging in dangerous sport, or dating other employees, run the risk of being invasive of the employee's constitutional right of privacy.

The employer may be permitted to place restrictions on off-duty behavior where the employer is able to demonstrate that the employee's behavior damages the employer's reputation or product, imperils the safety of other employees, causes disruption at the workplace, demonstrates a conflict of interest harmful to the interests of the employer, threatens confidential business practices, renders the employee incapable of performing his job duties, or threatens any other legitimate business interest.

The employer should be prepared to prove that the off-duty restrictions prevent certain financial losses to the company. Employers should be aware that if the policy infringes on the right to privacy, and the employee is discharged for violating the company policy, the employee may have a wrongful termination, or constructive discharge, or invasion of privacy case that could end up being brutally expensive for the employer.

The question of restricting off-duty behavior becomes one of balancing the intrusiveness of the employer's restrictions, against the character of the employee's behavior that is curtailed by the restrictions.

Since employee privacy is regarded as a fundamental right in California, the employer must be extremely careful about any activity that could be perceived to be an invasion of employee privacy. For example, it is improper for an employer to discipline or discharge an employee who has a personal relationship with a business competitor. Very rarely will the employer be permitted to intrude into the sexual privacy of its employees.

Employers should restrict their regulation of sexual conduct to on-the-job activities. For example, disciplining an employee who received a drunken driving conviction would be proper only if the employer could show a direct relationship between the conviction and job duties. Discipline would be proper, for example, if the employee were a school bus driver. Discipline would not be proper if the employee's duties did not involve driving, and the employer was not somehow uniquely affected by the conviction. If the employer ran an alcohol rehabilitation program, that employer might be uniquely situated so as to justify discipline.

See also SEXUAL ORIENTATION DISCRIMINATION.

MOONLIGHTING

Moonlighting is the term used when individuals hold down more than one job at a time, generally in reference to a full-time job and a second, after-hours job.

May your employer prohibit you from working two jobs? Our answer in typical legal fashion is—maybe! As you should be aware by now, the issue is one of balancing the employer's legitimate concerns for employee loyalty, protecting the security and reputation of the company, etc., against the employee's right to privacy, and the employee's right to pursue making a living as best he or she can.

To determine whether an employer restriction on moonlighting is valid, the court will ask: Is your second job with a competitor? Do you have access to sensitive business secrets? Does the second job sacrifice your ability to properly perform your primary job? Etc.

If the employer does not come forth with a compelling business reason why the activity should be restricted, any such restriction would probably be improper and unenforceable.

SEVEN YEAR CONTRACTUAL LIMITATION

Personal service contracts cannot be enforced beyond seven years from the beginning of the service by the employee or obligated party. This means that you cannot obligate yourself to work for someone for longer than seven years at a time.

This problem most commonly arises for entertainment or sports figures. Someone may sign a contract obligating themselves to perform or produce for long periods of time, only to discover at the peak of their capabilities that they have obligated themselves to a career at low pay, compared to what they could have been receiving as a result of their immense, and unanticipated, popularity. This law prevents them from obligating themselves for longer than seven years at a time.

EMPLOYER LIABILITY FOR THE ACTS OF OTHERS

Is your employer liable to you if you are injured by the negligent or intentional acts of fellow employees? Generally, your employer is liable for injuries caused by the negligent acts of his agents that occurred within the scope of their employment, even if the employer is blameless and received no benefit from the action.

In addition, your employer is liable for the willful, criminal, fraudulent, or felonious acts of agents committed within the scope of their employment. An agent can be a manager, another employee, a volunteer who happens to be helping out, or possibly even a customer or other member of the general public. If the employer hires someone who later causes injury to you, the employer may be liable to you for negligence in the hiring of that employee.

The employer is generally not liable for actions that occur outside of the workplace, and are not reasonably foreseeable within the job duties of the employees.

However, with workplace violence becoming more commonplace, employer liability is expanding also. Recent cases illustrate the danger for employers. Normally an employer is not liable for sexual assaults committed by an employee. It is thought that such behavior is strictly personal and not contemplated as occurring within the expected job duties of the employee. However, a Los Angeles case held the city of Los Angeles liable for the rape of a woman by a police officer. The court held that the conduct was not "so unusual or startling" as to prevent the employer from being liable In another case involving the molestation of a student by a teacher the court held that the victim could not sue the employer for employer liability for the molestation, but the victim could sue the school district for negligent hiring and supervision of the guilty teacher. If you have been a victim of workplace violence by another employee, the first question you will have to answer is whether the violence by that person against you was "reasonably foreseeable" by the employer.

An employer may have a duty to warn an employee about a dangerous fellow employee or a third party (a non-employee) under certain circumstances. There will be a duty by the employer to warn if:

1) The employer has actual knowledge of the known danger. For example, the employer knows of a specific employee, ex-employee, or third party who has made definite threats, or has otherwise evidenced known dangerous behavior.

2) The employer must have actual knowledge of specific threats against a known and specific victim. For example, the dangerous

person has told the employer that he plans to kill Jane Doe, a current employee. or John Doe a customer.

Under these circumstances the employer has an obligation to warn the intended victim. The employer is not responsible for guaranteeing the safety of the intended victim. For example, if the dangerous person, without prior warning, enters the store with an automatic weapon and shoots everyone in the building, the employer will not be held liable. The employer will not be held responsible for actions that are unforeseeable. The critical issue in most cases is whether the acts occurred within the scope of the employment relationship, and whether the acts were reasonably foreseeable by the employer so as to justify placing a duty on the employer to do something to prevent the acts from occurring.

Remember that in most situations involving injuries to an employee within the scope of employment, the employee is forced to seek recoveries from workers' compensation. The employee is not permitted to sue the employer in civil court. The employee will be permitted to sue the employer directly under any of the following situations;

1) If the employee is injured by a willful assault by the employer. The employee is entitled to sue the employer when the employer personally attacks the employee, or the employer was aware of a danger to the employee, failed to warn the employee, and the employer failed to take proper corrective or preventive measures to protect the employee.

2) If the employer knows about a dangerous person, such as the ex-employee threatening Jane Doe, and conceals the information about the danger and an innocent employee is injured as a result.

3) If the employer engages in offensive or injurious conduct that is outside the normal scope of the employment relationship. For example, if the employer engages in sexual harassment against an employee, the employer may be sued in civil court.

4) If the employer is also a landowner or property owner and the employee is injured on the premises. For example, if an employee was injured as a result of a defective stairway in a building owned by the employer, the employee will be entitled to sue the em-

ployer in the capacity or role as a property owner, not as an employer. This is a new theory of liability designed to permit the employee to avoid the restriction of having to file only a workers' compensation claim.

Under a new law, every employer must provide written notice to any employee who is injured as a result of a crime that occurred in the workplace, that the employee is entitled to receive workers' compensation benefits.

EMPLOYER LIABILITY FOR CONCEALED DANGERS

An employer is required to inform, in writing, all affected employees of any concealed dangerous condition within fifteen days of learning of the concealed danger. The employer does not need to inform the employees if the condition is corrected within the fifteen day period. Failure to notify the affected employees, in writing, of a hidden danger that may cause serious injury, is a crime.

The employer or manager has "actual knowledge" of the danger if he or she has information of a concealed danger that would convince a reasonable person of its existence.

NON-COMPETITION AGREEMENTS

A non-competition agreement, generally referred to as a covenant (promise) not to compete, is a contract which prohibits the person making the promise from engaging in a lawful profession, trade, or business. Such contracts are not legally recognized or enforceable, except in a couple of situations.

The first is where the promising party promises not to compete as part of the sale of goodwill from his business, trade, or profession. "Goodwill," in this context, is the value of the business attributable to the name or image of the seller, or the premium on the value of the business resulting from the uniquely personal efforts of the selling party. Selling parties may agree not to compete with the buyer of the business as part of the consideration for selling the business. In other words, part of the sales price received is for the promise not-to-compete with the buyer. Such restrictive promises will be upheld if the promise not to enter into a similar business is limited to a certain geographical area for a stated period of time.

The elements necessary for an enforceable covenant not-to-compete that is made as part of the sale of a business are:

1) The contract must be made in conjunction with the sale of the goodwill of a business.
2) The agreement must be definite. The promise will not be inferred.
3) The person making the promise must have a saleable interest in the business.
4) The agreement must be limited to a promise not to engage in a similar business.
5) The agreement must be limited in territory to a specified county or counties, city, or part thereof, in which the business sold has been carried on.
6) The agreement must be limited in time to the period during which the buyer or successor in interest carries on the business.

If the agreement is too broad it is not totally void and will be upheld within limits imposed by the court.

Employees are not permitted to promise away their right to make a living.

A promise not-to-compete entered into by an employee with his employer, to take effect after termination of their employment relationship, is a restraint on engaging in a lawful business and is generally void. The employee may promise not to enter the same business, or work for someone else after his employment ends, but he is nevertheless entitled to do so, despite the promise. This rule has been the law in this State since 1872.

California law also prohibits even minor penalties for employees who choose to compete with their ex-employers. For example, an employee who signs an agreement that forfeits the employee's pension benefits if the employee competes with the ex-employer, is illegal. Furthermore, employees are prohibited from signing away their rights or agreeing to abide by the laws of another state in order to avoid the California law.

TRADE SECRETS
This brings us to the second situation where promises not to compete are sometimes enforced. They are enforced when it is necessary to protect disclosure of trade secrets and confidential business communications by the departing employee. What is a trade secret? A trade secret is defined under the Uniform Trade Secrets Act as information that is valuable because it is not commonly known by the general public and is kept secret through the reasonable efforts of it's owners. The employer is not required to keep the trade secrets actually secret so long as the employer makes reasonable efforts to do so.

Simply stated, it is either information, a process, a technique, a formula, a specification, specialized data that has been collected, or strategic business information, etc., that is not commonly known to the general public, that gives the possessor of the information a competitive edge or advantage in the business. The employer must be able to show that the protected information, etc., is valuable, not commonly known to everyone else in the industry, and that the employer took serious steps to keep the information secret. For example, if you make off with the customer lists, were these lists available to all employees, or were the lists restricted to the very few? If any employee could obtain this information, it is arguable that the employer did not take proper steps to ensure that the information remained secret.

What happens if a departing employee seeks to contact or solicit business from customers that the employee dealt with in his or her former job? The departing employee is entitled to contact or even attempt to gain the business of his prior employer's customers. The only limitation is the employee must not use the former employer's trade secrets.

Are customer lists trade secrets? Customer lists are usually not regarded as trade secrets. The departing employee has the right to notify customers of his or her change of job, either before or after the job change occurs, and the employee may actively compete with the old employer by trying to take away the old customers from him. The departing employee may even be permitted to copy the customer list off the old employer's Rolodex files in order to compete with him! Be careful. There is always the possibility that a judge will declare the customer list to be a protected trade secret, not subject to removal or use.

There is a statute in California that specifically states that the names, addresses, and identity of customers of a telephone answering service are trade secrets of the service's owner.

What if your employer asks you to sign an agreement where you promise not to solicit the employer's customers? Like non-competition agreements, any such promise is not enforceable against you, except in those situations where the customer list is a protected trade secret. Otherwise, you are permitted to sign the agreement and then violate the agreement.

You are not permitted to solicit your co-workers to work for the competition. It is regarded as a violation of your duty to your employer. If you terminate your employment you may still not solicit or encourage your former co-employees to leave their employment to work for you or anyone else. If you encourage employees to do so you may be liable for damages to your prior employer.

An employee is not permitted to compete with his or her employer while employed, but the employee is permitted to prepare to compete with the employer as soon as the employee is no longer so employed.

If you have left the employment of your prior employer and you have obtained new employment, be aware of any communications from your old employer to your new employer, or anyone else in your industry. It sometimes happens that your old employer makes allegations that you have taken protected trade secrets, or done something else bad or unethical. If your employer has made such statements, and such statements are untrue, you may be able to sue for defamation or "interference with prospective economic advantage." See the section on defamation for a further discussion.

EMPLOYEE INVENTIONS

Employee inventions, referred to as "intellectual property" refers to something created or invented by an employee during the time of employment. Generally, whenever an employee creates something as part of his job duties, or which results from work performed for the employer, the thing created belongs to the employer. This rule does not apply to employee inventions or creations that the employee developed entirely on his or her own time without using the tools, supplies, fixtures, or secret information of the employer.

If the employer asks the employee to sign an employment agreement or a release that gives the employer rights to any employee invention, such an agreement is unenforceable if the item is created on the employee's own time, etc. If an employee is asked to sign such an agreement, the agreement must state that it does not apply to the inventions created by the employee under the circumstances described above.

EMPLOYEE LEAVE

There are both federal and California laws that provide for leave from work for employees facing sickness of a family member or birth of a child. The impact of the laws may not be dramatic since the **leave taken is unpaid** and few people can afford to take extensive time off from work, even if they have the right to do so. In any event, the rules are set forth below.

California enacted legislation early in 1994 which conformed California law to federal law.

FEDERAL FAMILY AND MEDICAL LEAVE ACT (FMLA)

The FMLA is a federal law that became effective August 5, 1993. The FMLA provides up to twelve weeks of unpaid leave each year for the birth or adoption of a child, to care for a seriously ill family member, or for the serious illness of the employee. If both spouses work for the same employer, they are only entitled to twelve weeks leave between the two of them every twelve months, if the leave taken is for the birth or placement of a child or the care of a parent. A "child" includes a disabled adult. That is, someone who cannot care for themselves.

The law provides coverage for most employees that work

for employers of at least fifty people within 75 miles of your job site. If you work for a company that has fewer than fifty full-time, part-time or temporary employees within 75 miles of your job site, your employer is not required to provide the twelve weeks of unpaid leave. An "employer" is defined as any type of business organization, including public agencies, such as state and federal employers. However, certain federal employees are not covered, nor are elected or appointed public officials eligible. There are special rules for the following employees,

a) employees of educational agencies.
b) school employees.
c) civil service employees.
d) some Congressional employees.

To be eligible as an employee you must have been employed by the employer for at least the entire prior twelve month period. You must also have worked at least 1,250 hours in the prior twelve month period (about 24 hours a week). You must also work at a job site that employs at least fifty people, or be within seventy five miles of a job site that employs at least fifty people under the same employer.

You are entitled to take off one day or less at a time to deal with an ongoing condition, such as repeated medical treatments. This means that you are entitled to take employee leave in chunks of time at least as short as [a couple of hours at a time, if that is necessary.] one hour at a time. You may take leave in fractions of an hour if the employer ordinarily accounts for absences from work in fractions of an hour. For example, if the employer customarily docks you 30 minutes for being late for work, you are entitled to take employee leave in blocks as small as 30 minutes also. If the employer were to keep track of your hours in 10 minute increments, you could take leave in 10 minute increments also. The smallest block of time used by the employer is the amount of time you can take for employee leave.

Your supervisor is not entitled to determine when, or how much time you may take off within the 12 week maximum. You are entitled to take the time off in such blocks of time that you find necessary. For example, you may need to take 4 weeks off, then work for a month, then take an additional 8 weeks off. You are entitled to do so. Your employer has no discretion in the matter.

If you need to take leave from work on an intermittent basis, in other words, in small chunks of time on more than one occasion to care for a family member or yourself due to a single incident or illness that causes the leave, you can only do so intermittently if it is medically necessary. If you wish to take intermittent leave for the birth of a child, or the placement of a foster child or adopted child, you can do so in California without the permission of the employer (unlike under the federal law).

You may also be entitled to convert your full-time job to part-time under the same circumstances described above. If it is medically necessary for you to work no more than part-time in order for you to recover from "a serious health condition", you are entitled to do so. You are entitled to work part-time if it is medically necessary to care for a family member. You are also entitled to work part-time to attend to the birth or placement of an adoptive or foster child with or without the permission of your employer. However, you are required to take a minimum of two weeks leave under these circumstances. You can take less than two weeks leave, to as little as one day, but only if your employer agrees to the shorter period of time off.

If both spouses work for the same employer, the employer is entitled to limit the employees' combined leave to 12 weeks during any 12 month period if the leave taken is for the birth or placement of a child or for the care of a parent with a serious health condition.

. If you take time off from work under the California Family Rights Act, which permits 12 weeks off, you cannot claim an additional 12 weeks thereafter under the federal law. The leave time available under the California and federal laws runs at the same time except for leave taken on account of pregnancy, childbirth, or related medical condition. Under those circumstances you are entitled to two periods of leave.

Employees may be entitled to take pregnancy leave under the California Pregnancy Leave Act. The act applies to employers who have at least 5 employees

Under the California Pregnancy Leave Act employees are entitled to take an additional six weeks of leave for a "normal" pregnancy. A "normal" pregnancy is one that, in the opinion of the employee's physician, does not involve high risk or unusual complications.

If the employee suffers a disability on account of pregnancy, childbirth, or related medical condition, the employee is entitled to take up to four months of unpaid leave. The employee is not required to take the four months off all at one time. The employer cannot penalize the returning employee for taking more time (under the 4 month pregnancy rule) than would ordinarily be permitted under the employer's rules. See also PREGNANCY DISCRIMINATION on page 33.

Morning sickness is considered a disability for purposes of taking pregnancy leave.

A pregnancy related disability will qualify the employee to take FMLA leave if the disability involves a "serious health condition. Normal prenatal care is considered a "serious health condition."

If an employee takes pregnancy disability leave, the employer must provide a written guarantee that the employee will be reinstated to her old position or an equivalent one if she so requests.

Under the California Family Rights Act the employee may elect to take paid sick leave time off if the leave is taken for the serious health condition of the employee. If the leave taken is for the serious health condition of the employee. In addition, the employer can require that paid sick leave (or other accrued or collected leave) be utilized during the time off.

If the time taken off by the employee is for the care of a sick family member or for the care or placement of a child, then paid sick or other leave can be used only if both the employer and the employee agree. Neither party can force the other to use up paid leave time.

Under federal law if both **spouses** work at the same job site the employer can limit their combined leave to 12 weeks. Under California law if both **parents** (not spouses) work at the same job site the employer can limit their combined leave for the birth or foster care placement of a child to 12 weeks. Under the rule that employees are entitled to apply the law that provide them with the greater benefits, unmarried parents would both be entitled to 12 weeks of leave. In other words, the California rule would be over-ridden in the case of unmarried parents, since the federal rule limiting leave only applies to spouses.

If you find yourself having to make use of the leave laws, you must be prepared to return to work by the expiration of the 12 week period. If, in week 13 you are not yet recuperated sufficiently to return to work, are not protected, and are at risk of termination.

Your employer cannot require you to return before the 12 week period is up by offering you light duty work or by otherwise easing your job duties. You are still entitled to 12 weeks off.

REASONS FOR LEAVE

You are entitled to take an unpaid leave for:

1) The birth, adoption or foster care placement of a child,
2) To care for the "serious health condition" of a parent, spouse, child or,
3) To care for your own "serious health condition" which renders you unable to perform your job.

DEFINITIONS

Under the leave laws a spouse is either a husband or wife as defined under the state laws recognizing marriages. In some states if you live with someone for a period of years (generally seven years) and set yourself forth as husband and wife even though you have never married that person, you may become entitled to spousal rights under the doctrine of "common law marriage." California does not recognize "common law " marriages. You cannot take leave off work to care for the health of a spouse in California unless you have married that person in a

"Uh, boss I think I'm going to have to use some of my employee leave!"

ceremony recognized by the State of California.

Under the leave laws a child is a biological child, an adopted child, foster child, or stepchild by marriage, and under the age of 18 years. A person who is mentally or physically disabled and unable to care for him or herself is regarded as a child even if that person is over 18 years old.

A parent is someone's biological parent, or foster parent, or any person who acted as the parent to the employee when the employee was under the age of 18. A parent does not include a parent-in-law.

SERIOUS HEALTH CONDITION

Under the federal law a "serious health condition" is defined very liberally. It includes any illness, injury, impairment or physical or mental condition that involves either,

a) in-patient care in a hospital, hospice or other residential facility, or

b) "continuing treatment" by a health care provider.

This means that you are entitled under federal or California law to get unpaid leave if your illness involves the care of a health professional (for example, a doctor, nurse, or psychotherapist) and the illness is expected to keep you away from work for more than three days.

"Serious health condition" includes voluntary cosmetic surgery if it requires at least one nights stay in a hospital or other facility. "Serious health condition" also includes stress disorders or ailments. If you see a psychologist and he or she recommends time off for rest, your employer must oblige you with leave.

You are entitled to take leave for any "continuing treatment' by a health care provider. This means that you can take time off for treatment by a health care provider that requires you to make more than one visit to the provider. For example, this may mean that you are entitled to take up to a total of 12 weeks off for repeated physical therapy for tendonitis or other arthritic condition, physical therapy, or chemotherapy, or any other repeated type of therapy.

NOTICE OF LEAVE

You are obligated to provide thirty days notice of your intended leave when you are able to do so. If the condition is unexpected or sudden, you must provide notice as soon as you can. You are required to make a reasonable effort to minimize any potential disruption to the employer by scheduling the medical treatment at a convenient time, when it is possible to do so. If it is not possible, then you are not required to take your leave at a time convenient for your employer.

If you plan on using leave under the leave laws be sure to notify your employer that you wish to use leave time, and not your company's sick time or accrued time. Be sure to keep a written record of your statement to that effect.

CERTIFICATION OF MEDICAL CONDITION

The employer may require that you provide certification of the medical condition which requires your absence. The employer can require that you provide,

1) The date that the health condition commenced.
2) The relevant medical facts regarding the medical condition.
3) A statement that establishes that the employee seeking the leave is needed to care for the family member in question, or that the employee is unable to perform his job due to the condition.

The employer has the right to require a second or a third medical opinion, chosen and paid for by the employer. If the second opinion is in conflict with the first, the employer may seek a third and binding opinion by a mutually agreed-upon health care provider.

REINSTATEMENT AFTER LEAVE

The employee is entitled to be reinstated to his or her former position (or equivalent) upon return from leave. However, the returning employee is not entitled to collect seniority or other employment benefits during the time off. Nor can the employee forfeit any employment benefit that has been accrued before the employee took the leave, such a vacation time, or sick leave, if not used instead of FMLA leave.

What is an "equivalent" position? It is a position that is virtually identical in terms of pay, privileges, benefits, rank or authority, and working conditions and in the same geographical area as the original position. The new position must have the same daily and weekly shift schedule as the old position.

What if you are unable to perform the essential functions of the job after you return from leave? Are you entitled to your old position or a new "equivalent" position? No. Under the Federal Medical Leave Act, you are not entitled to you old position or an "equivalent" new position if you are now unable to perform the essential functions of the position. However, you may be entitled to receive "reasonable accommodations" to your disability under the Americans with Disabilities Act (ADA). In addition, you may be entitled to receive workers compensation benefits if you are unable to perform your job duties.

Note that if you are paid among the highest 10% of employees within 75 miles of the job site, you are not entitled to be reinstated to the same or equivalent position upon your return if to do so,

1) would cause substantial and grievous economic injury to the employer and,
2) the employer notified the employee in advance that he or she would not be reinstated to his or her old position if the employee insisted on taking leave.

The employer must notify the "key employee" in writing of the employer's intention not to reinstate the employee if the employee takes leave. The written notice must be delivered either in person or by certified mail.

If the employee has already commenced leave when the employer discovers that economic hardship will result if the employee continues the leave, the employee forfeits his old position if he or she continues the leave after being notified by the employer of the change in circumstances. The employee is entitled to ask to be reinstated to his or her old position even if the employee did not return to work when notified by the employer that reinstatement of the employee to his or her old position would cause the employer substantial and grievous economic injury. If the employee requests reinstatement, the employer must then determine if reinstatement would cause substantial and grievous economic injury. If the employer determines that it would, the employer must give the employee written notice of the decision not to reinstate. The notice must be given in person or by certified mail. If the employer fails to provide the proper notice, the employee must be reinstated.

HEALTH BENEFITS

Under state and federal law the employer is obligated to maintain the employee's health benefits during the period of leave taken. If the FMLA leave taken is unpaid, the employee may be required to pay for the employee's share of the health care premiums. If the employer is going to require the employee to pay for the employee's share of the health insurance premiums during the time that the employee is off work and unpaid, the employer must first notify the employee in writing. The notice must include the conditions under which the employee will be required to make the insurance payments. If the employee is over 30 days late in making a premium payment, the employer may terminate coverage. However, the employer must first provide 15 days prior written notice of termination.

If the employee fails to return from leave, the employer can recover the premiums paid for maintaining the health care coverage, unless the failure to return was out of the control of the employee and through no fault of his or her own.

If you feel that your rights under the leave acts have been violated you can bring suit (file a complaint) with the Wage and Hour Division of the U.S. Department of Labor, or file a private lawsuit. You should generally plan on filing the suit or complaint within two years after the violation of your leave rights. If the denial was wilful, you will have three years after the violation to file your complaint. If you win you will be entitled to your damages, including lost wages, benefits, or other compensation, attorneys fees and other costs, and you may be entitled to reinstatement and promotion.

Chapter Six
WORKERS' COMPENSATION

As pointed out in earlier discussions, California has replaced personal lawsuits with the workers' compensation system for injuries suffered by employees at the workplace. If an employee is injured at work, he or she is probably entitled to workers' compensation benefits. The determination of whether you are entitled to benefits will depend on whether the injury arose out of work and occurred in the course of employment. These are legal phrases which are used to determine when an injury falls under the authority of the workers' compensation system. An employee's injury must be related to his or her work in some way in order for the injury to be covered. This would appear to be a simple determination at first glance, but it can become very complex.

The first question we ask when an injury occurs is,

Did the injury happen on the job?

Many injuries occur on the employer's premises and occur directly as a result of the work that the individual was performing. Typical examples would be loading a truck and having some of the load fall on you. However, there are some injuries which are more questionable. Consider an employee who arrives at work early and the business is not open yet. While the employee is waiting he changes the oil in his car and is injured. Would this be an on-the-job injury? The answer is yes! This was an actual case and the Judge found it to be a compensable claim.

Injuries resulting from accidents occurring during normal commuting to and from work are not usually covered but again, there may be exceptions.

Any injury that arises out of an activity that was reasonably contemplated by the employment relationship is covered. This includes any acts that may occur incidental to or reasonably close in time and space to your duties contemplated by your employment. Coverage may also be available in any number of instances where the employee is injured while engaging in some activity that related to the personal comfort of the employee. This is known as the "personal comfort' doctrine. Generally, "personal comfort" injuries are covered.

Although crimes may not be reasonably contemplated as part of the employment relationship, if you are injured as a result of a crime occurring at your place of employment, you are entitled to receive workers' compensation benefits. In addition, your employer is obligated to inform you in writing of your right to workers' compensation benefits under these circumstances.

If there are any doubts as to whether the injury arose within the context of the employment relationship, the courts decide in favor of coverage. Therefore, never assume that your injury will not be covered until you have spoken to an attorney who is knowledgeable about workers' compensation law.

You should also understand that there may be occasions when your employer acts against you because of an injury that you suffered on the job. Should something like this happen, you should consult an attorney expert in civil employment law, not necessarily, workers' compensation law, although a good workers' compensation attorney should be familiar with both fields. Be aware that this area of the law is very complex, and it is almost impossible not to goof up acting on your own behalf.

Because the workers' compensation prevents you from suing your employer in civil court for certain types of injuries I will mention several areas that are not pre-empted by workers' compensation. This means that you are entitled to sue your employer for the following types of behavior:

If your employer discriminates against you on the basis of your race, sex, age, religion, in violation of California law (FEHA); If your employer breaks an employment agreement or contract; If your employer breaks an implied promise not to terminate (or possibly demote) you except for good cause. Can you sue your employer for discriminating against you on the basis of your disability? It depends. If you are suing under the ADA, you are permitted to sue your employer for failing to provide you with a reasonable accommodation to your disability. The ADA is not pre-empted by workers' compensation. If you are suing under the state law (FEHA), the courts are still undecided. Consult an employment attorney.

TYPES OF INJURIES

There are three types of injuries for which benefits are paid. These are;

1) Specific injuries,
2) Cumulative trauma injuries,
3) Death.

Specific injuries are those that happen as the result of a sudden event such as a traffic accident. A very common specific injury is lifting something heavy and feeling a pain in your back.

Cumulative trauma injuries are those that occur over a period of time and are not the result of one incident. One example of this would be hand injuries from using a computer or typewriter over a period of months or years. Another cumulative trauma injury would be lung disease as the result of inhaling fumes or chemicals at work over a period of time. Back injuries can also occur over a period of time until your back is so painful that any more lifting becomes impossible.

Injuries also include diseases that you contract from your employment.

Injuries include disabling emotional problems that result from your employment. Certain psychiatric injuries are also covered. Under the new law the employee has the burden of showing that more than 50% of the psychological injury resulted from job-related causes. In addition, no coverage is permitted for psychological injuries that were substantially caused by lawful, nondiscriminatory, personnel actions. In other words, you can no longer receive coverage for psychological injuries caused by employer personnel actions if you cannot prove that the actions were done in bad faith.

The only exception to the rule that more than 50% of the employee's psychological injury must be caused by work is if the employee suffers psychological injury as a result of being a victim of a violent act, or is exposed to a violent act. Under those circumstances the employee need show that only 35% to 40% of the mental injury is due to the violent act.

If you suffer emotional injury solely as a result of being fired or laid-off, you cannot receive workers' compensation benefits.

You cannot file a psychological injury claim after you have been terminated unless you can prove that your job was the major cause of your injury and one or more of five additional requirements are met. In this type of situation, consult an attorney.

The third type of injury for which benefits are paid is the death of the employee. Death benefits are payable whether or not the employee died immediately after the accident, or many months later.

You may be entitled to workers' compensation benefits if you are re-injured during physical rehabilitation for first injury that you suffered on the job. If the second injury is a direct consequence of the first injury, you can receive compensation even if the second injury is a new and distinct injury.

Under the new law the maximum death benefits available to a single surviving dependent are $115,000, $135,000 for two dependents, and $150,000 for three or more dependents. After July 1, 1995, it rose to $125,000 for one dependent, $145,000 for two dependents, and $160,000 for three or more dependents.

Once an employee becomes aware that he or she has been injured, he should inform the employer by telling his supervisor or other person in management. Once you have informed your employer, or employer representative, it becomes the employer's obligation to provide the employee with an injury claim form. The form is filled out by the injured worker and is very simple to do (see the sample form of page 338). The form should then be given back to the employer, along with a verbal request for medical treatment, if that is desired by the worker. The employer is obligated to provide medical treatment to an injured worker unless the employer is denying that they have any responsibility under the workers' compensation laws. If the employer does not reject liability within 90 days after the date of the written injury claim, the claim is presumed payable.

What happens if you are injured? Normally, the injured worker is sent to a physician immediately and treatment is paid for by the employer or the employer's insurance carrier. The treating physician then makes a decision as to whether or not the injured worker can return to work, or if he or she should remain off work for awhile to recover from the injury. If the worker is told to stay home, then he or she is entitled to temporary disability benefits during the time he or she is off.

The injured worker is required to inform the employer of the injury within 30 days of the occurrence of the injury. Failure to inform the employer may result in a loss of benefits.

If the employee obtains medical care prior to informing the employer of the injury the employer will not be liable for payment unless there was a medical emergency or attempts to contact the employer would be futile.

The injured employee is entitled to be treated by the physician or facility of his or her choice beginning 30 days after reporting the injury to the employer. If the employee provides written notice to the employer in advance of an injury that the employee has a personal physician, the injured employee is entitled to go to that physician. Your personal physician includes health organizations and clinics.

If the employer chooses the physician the employee is entitled to change the physician to one of his or her choice. The employee can make this change only one time but the employee can make the request at any time and the employer must accommodate the change within five days after the request is made.

**In July 1, 1996 the maximum benefit for
temporary and permanent total disability
increased to $490 per week.**

There are two classes of temporary disability, temporary total and temporary partial. How much money can you receive under temporary total disability? Temporary total disability is paid at a maximum rate of $406 a week. The maximum amount varies depending on the year in which the injury occurred. The above figure is for injuries which occur after July 1, 1994. This is because the laws have changed over the last several years and the rates have been changed based upon the date of the injury. This amount is going to increase each year under a new law which went into effect January 1, 1994. The maximum rate rises to $448 a week for injuries occurring after July 1, 1995, and $490 a week for injuries occurring after July 1, 1996. This rate is calculated based upon two-thirds of the worker's gross pay per week (before taxes and other deductions are taken out). Therefore, to calculate your temporary disability rate, take (⅔) two-thirds of your pay and that is what you will be paid each week. The minimum that you must be paid is $98 a week. The minimum payment of $98 per week applies to part-time workers as well.

How much money can you receive under temporary partial disability? You are entitled to receive payments at a rate of ⅔rds of your weekly **loss** in wages for the period that you are partially disabled. Temporary total disability is computed on ⅔rds of your total wages, temporary partial disability is computed on ⅔rds of your loss in wages arising from the disability.

Is there a limit to how long an injured worker can collect temporary total disability payments? There is no limit to the number of days a person can collect temporary total disability benefits. After the injured worker is determined to be able to return to work the temporary total disability benefit ceases unless he or she becomes disabled again.

Temporary partial disability benefits cannot be paid longer than 240 weeks within five years of the injury that caused the disability.

If I receive workers' compensation money, can I still collect unemployment benefits? You are eligible to receive unemployment benefits if you are receiving compensation for a temporary partial disability and you are still available for work.

You are not eligible to receive unemployment benefits if you are receiving compensation for a temporary total disability and those payments are greater than what you would have received from unemployment. If your workers' compensation monies received are less than what you would have received on unemployment, then you are eligible to receive only enough unemployment benefits to make up the difference between the two. In other words, you are not entitled to receive full payments both for unemployment and workers' compensation.

Disability benefits must be paid within 14 days of the employer's knowledge of the injury and disability. If the employer is late in paying, a 10% penalty is added to the payment. There is no late payment penalty if the employer continues paying the employee's wages and the payment is at least equal to what the employee would otherwise receive in disability payments. There is no late penalty if the following four conditions are met.

1) The employer is unable to determine within the 14 days, whether any disability is owed.

2) The employer tells the employee why payment cannot be made within the 14 days.

3) The employer must state what additional information is needed in order to make a determination regarding the employer's liability.

4) The employer must state when he or she expects to have the needed information.

What happens if my employer refuses to pay my benefits?

If an employer refuses to pay benefits, the injured worker may be entitled to collect State Disability Benefits from the Employment Development Department. The state will pay injured workers benefits if a physician states that they are temporarily disabled. This should be the first place an injured worker goes to if they do not receive temporary disability benefits from the employer. The employer or insurance carrier will reimburse the State of California at a later time if it is later determined that the employer or insurance carrier should have been paying temporary disability payments to the injured worker.

Permanently disabled employees are entitled to receive benefits even if they are able to return to work at a higher rate of pay than before the injury!

PERMANENT DISABILITY BENEFITS

Even if the injured worker is able to return to his or her job and perform the duties of that job, he or she may still be entitled to collect a permanent disability benefit. This money is paid either in a lump sum or in a weekly payment over a period of months or years, depending on the severity of the disability.

A permanent disability is any injury that is expected to remain substantially the same for the rest of the injured person's life.

The purpose of the permanent disability payments is to compensate an injured person for his or her inability to obtain jobs which would require him or her to perform lifting, bending, standing, or other types of physical activity which he or she is now restricted from doing as a result of the damage done to the employee's body by the injury. It does not matter that you would not have wanted to do other types of work involving these activities, or that you have ever done the type of work that would involve these activities.

An example of this would be a secretary who trips on an electrical cord at work and injures her back. This back injury may prevent her from becoming a dock worker who would load and unload merchandise weighing 100 lbs or more. Even if the secretary would never have applied for a job like that, or even if she only weighed 100 lbs herself makes no difference. It simply doesn't matter. The fact that a physician states that she should not now to that type of work, due in part to her back injury, is enough to obtain a permanent disability award. She is now entitled to permanent money payments even if she returned to her old position at a higher rate of pay!

This may sound very illogical (possibly unbelievable!) and most workers' compensation attorneys would not disagree with you. But because the workers' compensation laws are sometimes illogical, complex, and may involve potentially significant sums of money,

"Well, the injury to your wrist won't affect your current job, but you won't ever be able to get a job loading steel bars. I'll recommend you for a permanent disability benefit."

I recommend hiring an attorney to represent you should you get injured at work. Do not attempt to handle the matter yourself! This is especially true if the employer or insurance company denies your claim. Due to complex procedural requirements it is very difficult to represent yourself and expect to obtain the same results that an attorney could obtain for you.

How much should you expect to pay an attorney?

Attorneys generally receive 12% of your permanent disability award or settlement. This is paid to the attorney only when you settle your case or after your case goes to trial. This means that if you settled your case for $10,000 your attorney would receive $1,200, leaving you with $8,800. This fee is set by the Workers' Compensation Appeals Board and it is up to the individual judge to determine the appropriate fee. Normally an attorney will receive 12% and possibly up to 15% if the judge believes that the case was an exceptionally complex one which would justify an increased award. Attorneys do not receive any portion of your temporary disability money and therefore you are really paying much less than 12% of your total benefits.

REHABILITATION BENEFITS

In addition to temporary disability and permanent disability there is also a rehabilitation benefit that you may receive. This becomes available to a worker when there is a determination made by a physician that the worker is unable to return to his or her usual and customary occupation as a result of the injury. Generally, this is the occupation in which the worker was working at the time he or she was injured. This means that if the injured worker is unable to perform one or more of the functions of his or her current job and no other job is found for them with their current employer, then he or she is entitled to retraining into a new field of work!

The rehabilitation benefit is probably one of the best benefits in the workers' compensation system and has become very expensive for the insurance carriers and employers. This is due to the fact that a person who is being retrained into another type of work is entitled to a rehabilitation maintenance payment of up to a maximum of $246 a week during the entire time that retraining and job placement take place. A rehabilitation counselor is also hired by the insurance carrier or employer and is assigned to work with the injured worker until the training and job search are completed. Additionally, all tuition, books, and other necessities for job retraining are paid by the employer or insurance carrier.

Due to the great expense in rehabilitation, a law was recently enacted limiting the total expense paid by an employer or insurance carrier for this benefit. An injured worker in now limited to a total of $16,000 for job rehabilitation, including the cost of the rehabilitation counselor and the rehabilitation maintenance benefit payments. The law went into effect on January 1, 1994 but there are some exceptions to it and again, it pays to have an attorney who is experienced in workers' compensation. You may be entitled to more than the $16,000 limit under certain circumstances. A good attorney will help you get all that you are entitled to.

Prior to the new legislation of January 1994, a person was entitled to rehabilitation outside of California if they decided to leave the state. However, under the new law an injured employee is only entitled to be rehabilitated out of state if there is a very good reason to do so. Otherwise, if the injured employee moves out of state after being injured in California, they will lose their rehabilitation benefits.

One example of rehabilitation would be a factory worker who injured his or her back and was no longer able to do the heavy lifting and bending required by the job. If no other job which they could perform was offered to them by their employer then they would be eligible for rehabilitation. They would be given an aptitude test and other tests by the rehabilitation counselor to determine their abilities. The counselor and the injured worker would select an appropriate job retraining program which could be one of many occupations. These occupations could include such things as a construction estimator, private investigator, security guard, claims adjustor, paralegal, or one of hundreds of other occupations which would not involve heavy lifting or bending.

The worker would then enroll in whatever training course he or she and the counselor decided upon and the injured worker would receive up to $246 per week while being retrained. All of this would have to be approved by the insurance carrier or employer if the employer were self insured. This is where an attorney can be helpful to try to get you the type of retraining that you would prefer, assuming that it is within reason.

If the parties are unable to agree on a retraining program then a rehabilitation consultant from the Workers' Compensation Appeals Board will assist the parties and make a final decision if the parties still cannot come to an agreement.

As a word of caution to those of you who have been injured on the job and qualify for the retraining program. It is not uncommon for the employer's insurance company to agree to permit you retraining without your need to obtain a lawyer to represent you in advance. Beware! You are untrained and a perfect candidate for being further victimized by the system.

You are entitled to up to $16,000 in rehabilitation benefits, however, understand that this total includes all maintenance payments to you, plus all fees for the (employer's) insurance company's "counselor," as well as all educational tuition and book costs. In addition, the payments to you for rehabilitation cannot extend beyond 12 months, This means that, at best, your educational training program cannot extend beyond one year.

Beware of the "counselor" who is appointed to guide you through this process. He or she may be primarily interested in obtaining their maximum fees of $4,600 off the top of the $16,000, leaving you with only $11,400 to work with. My advise? Remember that the insurance company does not love you. Protect yourself. Hire a workers compensation lawyer experienced in the field, and do so before you are examined by a doctor, Do not delay, as a delay may result in irreversible losses. You will be money ahead, even after you pay the fees for your attorney. That's my experience.

SETTLING A WORKERS' COMPENSATION CLAIM

When the injured worker finally recovers as well as can be

expected from the job-related injury, it is then time to settle the permanent disability benefit. This can be done in one of three ways. One of these ways is by taking the case to trial and letting the judge decide. This is done in less than 10% of the cases. Nine out of ten cases are settled through a settlement agreement, rather than by going to trial.

If you decide to settle your case by agreeing to a settlement agreement, rather than by going to trial, there are two types of non-trial settlements.

The first is by way of a stipulation. The second is through a compromise and release. What do these phrases mean?

A stipulation is a document which indicates that you have been injured and are entitled to a specific amount of money made to you in payments over a certain period of time. The amount of money is based upon the medical reports which are obtained by you and the insurance carrier or employer. It is an agreement by both parties based upon these reports. Normally, it will also provide for future medical care for life for the part or parts of your body which were injured. The judge signs this agreement (stipulation) and it becomes an order of the court, the same as if the judge made the decision himself in the first place.

The stipulation allows the parties to make their own judgement instead of taking their chances with the judge. Both parties know in advance through their agreement what the outcome will be.

It may be possible to modify a stipulation at a later date should the injured workers condition worsen. This means that you can come back and change the terms of the stipulation to require payment of a larger sum of money every week, should that become necessary. This can be done up to five years after the date of the injury.

It does not matter when the stipulation was entered into when you are determining how much time you have to modify a stipulation. For example, if the injury occurred on February 1, 1985, and the stipulation was made on March 1, 1990, your stipulation cannot be modified. Why? Because you only have five years after the date of the **injury** to modify a stipulation. In this case the stipulation was entered into more than five years after the injury, and therefore no modifications of that agreement are permitted. If your injury occurs in 1994 you will have until sometime in 1999 to modify any stipulations that you may have entered into as a result of your injury.

The second method of settling a case without going to trial is known as a compromise and release. A compromise and release is a full, complete, and final settlement of all the issues arising out of your injury. A compromise and release is an agreement that the insurance company or the employer will pay you a single lump sum of money for your injuries. You will not be entitled to anything else in the future, including future medical treatment should that become necessary. You are not permitted to come back at a later date and modify this agreement based on changed circumstances as you could with a stipulation. This type of settlement can include rehabilitation benefits in some limited circumstances, but normally they do not.

The advantage of the compromise and release is that you receive a lump sum payment of money as opposed to a weekly payment of up to $148 a week, as in a stipulation. The amount of money you receive is usually larger than what you would have received in total in periodic payments under a stipulation. The reason the lump sum payment is generally larger than what you would receive in payments over time is because you are being paid for your right to future medical care, which can be costly. Most injured workers settle this way because of the lure of a large sum of money at one time. In addition, injured workers often believe that they can obtain future health coverage from the next employer. The obvious risk to the injured worker is in spending the money and having nothing left to pay future medical bills, should additional medical care become necessary.

Is my employer liable to me for additional monies if he or she caused my injuries? This is a common question. Workers' compensation, unlike personal injury (tort) law, is a no-fault system. Therefore, it is not relevant who caused your injuries. The injured worker is entitled to benefits no matter who caused the injuries. This also means that the injured worker is prevented from suing the employer for negligence for any injuries suffered by the worker and caused by the employer's negligence. As you might have anticipated, there are some exceptions to this rule. For example, if the injured worker injured himself or herself intentionally, or was injured while intoxicated the employee will not be entitled to benefits. Nor will the injured worker be entitled to benefits if the injury resulted from a fight that the injured worker started.

If the injuries are the result of the injured worker's negligence, the worker will still be entitled to benefits. Negligent self-injury is covered.

There are different coverages for injuries caused by either serious and willful misconduct of the employer or injured employee. If the employee is injured by serious and willful misconduct of the employer or his representative, the injured employee's benefits are increased by one-half (+50%). The employee is also entitled to costs and expenses of $250. Serious misconduct normally involves some element of deliberate and knowing disregard for the safety of the employee.

If the employee is under the age of 16 and is employed illegally at the time of injury, the compensation is increased by one-half.

If the injury is caused by the serious and willful misconduct of the injured employee, the compensation that is normally recoverable is reduced by one-half. There is no reduction if any one of the three following conditions are present;

1) The injury results in death or at least 70% permanent disability.

2) The injured employee is under 16 years old at the time of injury.

3) The injury is caused by the employer's failure to comply with work safety rules or orders.

Injured workers are not entitled to coverage for injuries suffered while engaging in recreational activities off-duty. There would be coverage if the recreational activities were expressly or impliedly required as part of the job.

Every employer is required to post a conspicuous notice that injuries suffered in voluntary off-duty activities are not covered by workers' compensation.

If an employee is injured on the job and suffers a disability as a result of the injury, may the employee sue the employer for discrimination if the employer discriminates against the employee based on the employee's disability? No. If the employer discriminates against the employee based on a disability that resulted from an injury on the job, the employee must seek compensation through the workers' compensation process, not through a civil lawsuit. In other words, you cannot sue your employer for physical disability discrimination.

EMPLOYEES COVERED

All employees are covered under the workers' compensation. This includes part-time employees, residential and child care employees, and employees of unlicensed construction contractors. An employee who is hired in California to perform work outside of California and is injured outside of California, is covered. An employee who regularly works in California but is injured outside of California is covered, even though the immediate hiring may have occurred out of state.

Are undocumented or illegal workers entitled to coverage? Yes. Illegal aliens are entitled to workers' compensation benefits if they are injured on the job. Illegal aliens are entitled to all benefits, including rehabilitation. However, illegal aliens are not entitled to job placement since they cannot be legally employed.

Independent contractors are not employees and are therefore not covered under workers' compensation.

There are numerous exceptions to coverage for certain volunteer employees.

A person working for food or aid for a religious or charitable organization is not covered.

Voluntary ski patrolmen are not covered.

Amateur athletes or voluntary officials of amateur athletic competitions are not covered.

Ski lift employees employed to work at a ski resort who are injured while skiing or engaging in other recreational activities while off-duty are not covered.

Volunteers for non-profit companies or public agencies are not covered.

EMPLOYERS COVERED

All employers in California are required to either have workers' compensation insurance or receive permission from the State of California to be self insured. If you are injured while working for an employer that is uninsured or not permissibly self insured this usually becomes apparent when the employer is notified of the injury. They will sometimes admit that they do not have insurance, or will try to settle the case with you on the spot.

No workers' compensation case can be settled without the approval of the Workers' Compensation Appeals Board.

The Workers' Compensation Appeals Board must review every settlement to determine if it is adequate enough for the injured worker in light of the medical evidence. Therefore, if an employer offers to settle a case without sending the settlement documents to the Workers' Compensation Appeals Board then you should notify the Information and Assistance Officer at the Workers' Compensation Appeals Board nearest you. The Information and Assistance Officers are there to assist the public and there is an officer assigned to almost every Workers' Compensation Board. The Boards are located all over the State of California and can be found in the white pages of most telephone directories under "state government."

HOW MUCH IS YOUR CASE WORTH?

Determining the value of your case is, of course, very important but very difficult to answer. The only way to determine the value of your case is to review the medical reports and determine the level of permanent disability and the cost of future medical care. This will give you some idea of the value of the case. However, only an experienced workers' compensation attorney can "rate" the medical report. "Rating" a medical report translates the doctor's comments regarding the level of disability into a percentage of disability. Rating a medical report is a very complicated procedure which can also be done by the Workers' Compensation Appeals Board Rating Specialist. The appeals board specialists do not charge for this service and there is a procedure by which they will evaluate the medical reports.

Once the rating of the medical reports is completed the percentage of disability is converted into a dollar amount through the use of a permanent disability table. The table assigns a dollar figure to each percentage of permanent disability.

There are additional reasons that experts should be consulted to determine the overall value of your case. You may need to place a value on such items as future medical care or any temporary disability benefits that you may not have been paid.

Workers' compensation benefits do not include payment for pain and suffering.

You should know that the workers' compensation laws are not designed to fully compensate an injured employee. The benefits are not enough to allow an injured employee retire or become wealthy, even though the injured employee may have difficulty finding work in the future. The benefits do not include payment for pain and suffering. This is frequently misunderstood by injured workers and is just the opposite of personal injury (tort) law, which provides for money damages for pain and suffering. One example of this would be the bus driver who is injured in an auto accident. Under workers' compensation the bus driver would not be able to recover for pain and suffering. However, if the bus driver could prove that the driver of the car was negligent then he would be able to collect money for pain and suffering from the driver of the car!

Due to the complexity of the laws it is important to get legal advice as quickly as you can after an injury. If you delay you may be prevented from being compensated for your injuries.

If you are injured and thereafter are discriminated against by your employer, or suffer any other type of adverse, or negative employment change, you need to consult with an employment attorney. This will be in addition to your workers' compensation attorney. I recommend that you do so promptly, before your workers' compensation case proceeds very far. Just do it. Trust me.

Chapter Seven
MINORS

A minor is someone who is under 18 years old. Minors are generally required to attend school. A person under the age of 18 who is not required to attend school just because that person is a nonresident of California is still a minor. Children between the ages of 6 and 16 must attend school full-time, unless the child is receiving continuing education or tutoring from a licensed tutor. A child with a full-time work permit may attend classes part-time.

Generally, minors may not work more than four hours on school days.

If you are under 18 years of age your employer may be permitted to pay you less than the regular minimum wage. Under certain conditions your employer can pay you $4.90 per hour, which is 85% of the adult minimum wage.

When can your employer legally pay you less than the adult minimum wage?

DURING THE SCHOOL YEAR

If you work for a company that employs ten people or more, your employer can pay minors $4.90 an hour so long as the lower rate only applies to, at most, one out of four workers. In other words, no more than 25% (one out of four) of the employees at the company can be paid at the lesser rate. For example, lets say that there are twenty employees and all the employees are under 18 years old. The rule says that during the school year, your employer can pay five of you (one out of four) $4.90 an hour, and the rest must be paid $5.75 an hour. If there were twenty employees and fifteen were over the age of 18, and only five were younger, then the employer would be able to pay all five at the lower rate, since that is still one out of four total employees.

If there are less than ten employees at your company, your employer can pay three people under the age of 18 the lower rate of $4.90 an hour. For example, if your company only had four people working and all four were minors, your employer could pay three of them at the lesser rate of $4.90 an hour. The fourth minor would have to be paid $5.75 an hour.

DURING VACATION

Your employer can legally pay all employees under 18 years old the lower rate of $4.90 an hour. In other words, your employer is not limited to paying the lower wage to no more than one out of four of the total number of employees.

UNDER AGE 12

Generally minors under age 12 must attend school full time.

They are only permitted to work in the entertainment industry on permits issued by the Labor Commissioner. Minors under the age of 12 are not permitted to work in any other occupations that require a work permit. Minors under age 12 may work in occasional private household jobs, such as baby-sitting.

12 AND 13 YEARS OLD

Generally minors, 12 and 13 years old must attend school full time, unless they are a high school graduate. (geniuses?) They may be employed only on non-school days.

Minors 12 or 13 years old may work a maximum of eight hours a day and forty hours a week.

They may only work between the hours of 7 a.m. and 7 P.M., except from June 1 to Labor Day (the first Monday in

September). During that time they may work until 9 P.M.

14 AND 15 YEARS OLD

In most businesses, minors 14 or 15 years old may work a maximum of eight hours a day and forty hours a week. When school is in session they may work a maximum of three hours a day and eighteen hours a week. They may only work between the hours of 7 a.m. and 7 P.M., except from June 1 to Labor Day (the first Monday in September). During that time they may work until 9 P.M. During a school day, all hours of work, up to the maximum of three, must be outside normal school hours. In other words, a 14 or 15 year old minor cannot work during the time the normal school day is in session.

Minors under the age of 16 are prohibited from working in certain occupations. Minors under 16 years of age cannot work in occupations that are dangerous to lives, limbs, health, or morals. Minors under the age of 16 cannot work on a railroad, vessel, aircraft, or operate a car on a job. They are prohibited from working in places where acids, dyes, gases, or dangerous chemicals are used. They cannot work in the production of tobacco, or close to moving machinery, or with various tools or machines. They cannot work in poolrooms, or gas stations, or bars. They are not permitted to work in delivery jobs, or as messengers in any telegraph, telephone, or messenger company.

There are restrictions in their right to sell door-to-door. They are permitted to sell door-to-door for the purposes of selling newspaper and magazine subscriptions, or of candy, cookies, flowers, or other merchandise or commodities, if they are within fifty miles of their home. They must also be required to work in pairs as a team. There must be at least one adult supervisor for 10 or fewer minors, and they must be within sight or sound of the supervisor once every 15 minutes.

Parent employers are subject to the same occupational limitations as other employers when employing their own minor children.

16 TO 18 YEARS OLD

Minors who are at least 16 years old may work up to eight hours on a school day preceding a non-school day. A minor 16 years old may work in agriculture for six hours a day on school days, otherwise a 16 year old may only work a maximum of 4 hours a day. A minor 16 to 18 years old may not work more than forty-eight hours a week, nor before 5 A.M., nor after 10 P.M..

A minor may work until 12:30 A.M. when the following day is not a school day, normally Friday and Saturday nights. If the school year is in session and the 16 to 18 year old is required to attend, he or she shall not work more than six hours a day, nor more than twenty hours a week.

A minor who is enrolled in Work Experience Education must be paid at least the adult minimum wage for any work performed between 10 p.m. and 12:30 a.m.

A minor that has graduated from high school, or has passed the G.E.D., may work the same schedule as an adult. If the minor works a schedule otherwise permissible only to adults, the minor must be paid the same as an adult. This does not mean that the employer need only pay the minor $5.75 an hour. The law is an equal pay law for minors, which means that the minor is entitled to be paid at the same rate that the adults are being paid. For example, if the adults are being paid $6.50 an hour, the minor is entitled to the same amount.

Minors that have legally been declared free from the control of their parents (emancipated minors) are not exempt from the hour and occupational limitations of the educational and labor codes.

OCCUPATIONS NOT PERMITTED FOR MINORS

Minors are prohibited under the federal laws from working in any hazardous occupation. Prohibited occupations include; Manufacturing and storing explosives (including small arms ammunition); motor vehicle driving and outside helper; logging and sawmilling; power-driven woodworking machines; power-driven circular saws, band saws, and guillotine shears; power-driven hoisting apparatuses (including forklifts); roofing, excavation; wrecking, demolition, and shipbreaking operations; power-driven metal-forming, punching, and shearing machines; slaughtering, or meat-packing, processing or rendering; power-driven bakery machines; power-driven paper-products machines; manufacturing brick, tile, and kindred products; coal mining; mining other than coal mining; and exposure to radioactive substances.

If a person under 18 years old is a high school graduate and has completed a training program in a hazardous occupation, that person may be employed in that occupation.

Students or apprentices who are at least 16 years old, may be trained and employed under limited circumstances in; slaughtering or meat-packing and processing; power-driven paper products machines; power-driven circular saws, band saws, and guillotine shears; roofing; and evacuation.

Under California law a minor may not be employed: In gas stations, in any work using pits, racks, lifting apparatuses, or inflating any tire mounted on a rim with a removable retaining ring. A minor cannot work in or on that portion of an establishment primarily designed for on-site consumption of alcohol; A minor cannot sell alcoholic beverages for off-site consumption unless constantly supervised by a person 21 or older; A minor cannot sell lottery tickets unless constantly supervised by a person 21 or older.

EXCLUSIONS TO THE 8 HOUR AND 48 HOUR LIMITS

Minors employed in the following industries are exempt from the working hour limits:

1) Minors 16 to 18 years old that are employed in agriculture, horticulture, viticulture, or as domestic laborers.
2) Minors 16 to 18 years old that work in the preparing of agricultural products.

If the minor is employed in the above-listed occupations beyond the hour limits generally applicable to minors, then the minor must be paid, as a minimum, the adult minimum wage for all hours worked, not just the hours in excess of the maximums.

WORK PERMITS FOR MINORS

An employer must obtain a work permit in order to employ a minor. The permit must be kept on file by the employer during the term of the employment. If the minor is not required to attend school but is otherwise required to obtain a work permit, a certificate of age will suffice instead of the permit. A certificate of age is issued in person to the parent or guardian of the minor.

Work permits may be issued to persons between the age of 12 and 18 years old. An emancipated minor may apply for a work permit by himself. Otherwise, a minor's parent or guardian must file a written request before a work permit can be issued. To obtain a work permit to work on school days, the minor must be 14 years old and have completed the seventh grade. Full-time work permits can be issued to minors 14, 15, or 16 years old, only on a showing of successful completion of an elementary school course, and no sufficient financial support.

No work permit is required if the minor is employed by his parents or guardian, or if the minor performs such common employment as baby-sitting, newspaper delivery, or yard work.

See the chapter on workers' compensation for issues relating to the injury of a minor.

PARENTAL ENTITLEMENT TO MINOR'S WAGES

Parents are entitled to receive the earnings and worker's compensation payments of their minor children. Each parent is equally entitled to their children's earnings. If the parents are living separately, the child's earnings are the separate property of the custodial parent, meaning that the child's earnings need not be shared with, or cannot be claimed by, the parent who does not have custody of the child.

The employer may pay the minor's earnings directly to the minor child until such time as the parent or guardian gives notice that he or she is entitled to them.

Other rules apply to a minor's earnings from professional entertainment and sports contracts. In brief, the parents are entitled to one-half of the minor's earnings, the balance is placed in trust for the minor until such time as the minor comes of age.

Chapter Eight

UNIONS

CONCERTED ACTIVITIES

An intriguing protection for employees is that offered by concerted labor activity laws. Employees are protected under federal laws from interference, restraint, or coercion from employers in engaging in concerted activities for mutual aid or protection. For example, suppose you have a complaint against management for some rule or policy. If you state your complaint alone you may be regarded as a malcontent or a disrupter of the workplace. The next thing you know you have been demoted or fired. However, if you share your complaint with another employee, and afterwards you both file the complaint, your concerted activity (the complaint) is protected under the laws protecting concerted labor activities and neither one of you can be retaliated against. If your employer punishes you it is a federal labor violation.

If you are illegally terminated or retaliated against you must file your claim with the National Labor Relations Board.

UNIONS

Labor unions are employee organizations created to obtain better working conditions and benefits for their members. Labor unions were granted legal protection with the passage of the National Labor Relations Act (NLRA) in 1935. The NLRA made it illegal for employers to retaliate against, or otherwise obstruct employees, in their efforts to participate in labor organizations. Enforcement of the NLRA is conducted through the National Labor Relations Board (NLRB). Today only about 12% of all private employees are members of unions.

The Agricultural Labor Relations Act established the right of agricultural workers to organize unions and bargain collectively.

California favors employee organizations. Consequently, any agreements between employers and employees that attempt to prevent employees from being able to unionize, are illegal.
Such illegal anti-union contracts in which the employees promise not to organize or join a union are called "yellow dog" agreements. It is also illegal in California for an employer to form an employer-controlled union.

California permits, but does not compel, unionization among private employees. California does not have "right to work" laws, which are laws that make it illegal for unions to require either membership, or payment of dues, as a condition of employment.

"Union shops" are permitted in California. A "union shop" agreement is one in which the employer agrees to condition employment upon the employee agreeing to join the union within a given period of time (usually 30 days after commencing work). "Union shop" agreements are regarded as private contracts and not state action, and therefore do not violate non-members fourteenth amendment rights. In a related issue, employers and unions often agree to deduct union dues directly from the member employee's paycheck. Such practices are regarded as voluntarily entered into by the employee and are legal.

If you are a member of a union and you are subject to a collective bargaining agreement that requires you to accept arbitration of any dispute, you are still entitled to pursue wage claims through the Labor Commissioner. You may go to the Labor Commissioner even if your collective bargaining agreement says you cannot.

The State of California will not resolve labor disputes that require the state to interpret a union collective bargaining agreement. If the state has passed a law that provides for rights not provided for in the collective bargaining agreement, the employee can proceed with a claim under the state law, so long as it does not require the state to interpret the terms of the agreement.

STRIKES

A strike is a temporary refusal to work by an employee, or group of employees, conducted to force the employer to comply with the employees' demands. Employees have the right to strike. On the other hand, sit-down strikes in which the strikers seize the employer's property, refuse to leave the premises, or prohibit others from entering or exiting the premises, are illegal. Seizing control of the employer's personal property such as trucks or equipment, is also illegal.

It is illegal for an employer to use a professional strikebreaker to replace any employee involved in a strike or lockout.

BOYCOTTS

A primary boycott is a collective refusal to patronize, or buy from, an employer, distributor, retailer, or other party. A secondary boycott is a collective effort to convince other people not to patronize an employer, distributor, etc. The most famous secondary boycott was the boycott against grapes conducted by Caesar Chavez. The farm workers union attempted to persuade the public not to buy grapes in order to force the growers to agree to better working conditions for the field laborers.

Secondary boycotts are legal in California, but the means by which they are conducted may make any particular secondary boycott illegal. If the secondary boycott utilizes means of intimidation, threats of violence, or actual violence, then, of course, the secondary boycott would be illegal.

PICKETING

Peaceful picketing, not accompanied by violence, threats of violence, or fraud is legal. The state has the right to regulate and set limits on the activity. Like strikes, if the participants combine their constitutional right to express themselves with unprotected violence or other illegal behavior, then picketing can be properly restrained.

The court has the right to prohibit peaceful picketing if the labor dispute has been violent in the past, and the prospect of picketing would have an intimidating effect on the general public. Mass picketing that prevents access to the picketed premises is illegal. Picketers are not permitted to sit down in front of the picketed place of business. You must keep moving to avoid being cited by the police for obstructing access to the business.

The information displayed to the public by pickets must be truthful. Untruthful picketing is unlawful picketing. It is not untruthful or fraudulent picketing to describe an employer as "unfair" or "destructive."

You cannot sit down in front of the business that you are picketing. You must keep moving, or you face arrest by the police.

LEAFLETING

The distribution of truthful leaflets, which describe certain products as nonunion-made, and which ask the public not to purchase products that are nonunion-made, is legal. Note that the leaflets have to tell the truth. If the statements are misleading, false, or half-truths, then the leafleting is illegal.

EMPLOYER'S PROPERTY

There is no right to picket on the employer's private property, such as on his or her front yard or on his or her private sidewalk. However, there may be certain limited situations in which the employees are entitled to picket the employer's private residence.

On one hand, the employer has a right to privacy, and a right to be free from intrusion. On the other hand, the picketers have a right to freedom of expression and assembly. Permitting the picketing might invade the employer's privacy. Prohibiting the picketing might violate the right to freedom of speech. By placing limitations on the time, space, and manner of the picketing, the authorities might affect a minimal intrusion on the first amendment privileges of the people who wish to picket. At the same time, the limitations would protect the privacy rights of the employer.

Another exception to the prohibition on trespassing onto the employer's property is that farm worker representatives are permitted to go onto the employer's private property to access farm labor camps for the purposes of conducting lawful union activities. However, recent cases have held that employers can place "reasonable time, place, and manner" restrictions on access to the property.

SHOPPING CENTERS

Although shopping centers are private, you have the right to picket in areas of normal public access.

PARKING LOTS

You are also entitled to picket in parking lots open to the public. The Courts have theorized that the public is entitled to exercise first amendment privileges in areas that they have been invited to make use of. If the public is invited to use the area, even though it is private, the public can also picket there.

RELATED RIGHTS

You have the right in a labor dispute to publicize the existence of the labor dispute or the facts relating to any labor dispute by:

1) advertising
2) speaking
3) patrolling any public street or any place where people may lawfully be, or by any other lawful method— peaceful picketing or assemblage.

THE END

Labor Commission District Offices

Department of Labor Standards Enforcement (DLSE).
District Offices (D)
Bureau of Field Enforcement Offices (BOFE)
Public Works Units (PWU)

DLSE
Discrimination Complaint
Investigative Unit
P.O. Box 420603
San Francisco, CA 94142

HEADQUARTERS
30 Van Ness Avenue, Suite 3400
San Francisco, CA 94102
or
P.O. Box 420603
San Francisco, CA 94142
(415) 557 7878

Bakersfield
5555 California Avenue
Suite 200 93309
(805) 395-2710 (D)
(805) 395-2582 (BOFE)

Eureka
619 Second Street
Room 109 95501
(707) 445-6613 (D)

Fresno
770 East Shaw Avenue
Suite 315 93710
(209) 248-8400 (D)
(209) 248-8411 (BOFE)

Long Beach
245 West Broadway
Room 450 90802
(562) 590-4843 (D)
(562) 590-5466 (BOFE)

Los Angeles
107 South Broadway
Room 5015, 5029 90012
(213) 897-4037 (D)
(213) 897-2905 (BOFE)

Marysville
922 "G" Street 95901
(530) 741-4062 (D)

Oakland
360 22nd Street
Room 500 94612
(415) 557-7878 (D)
(415) 557-7878 (BOFE)

Redding
2115 Akard Avenue
Room 17 96001
(530) 225-2655 (D)
(530) 225-2653 (BOFE)

Sacramento
2424 Arden Way
Suite 340, 360 95825
(916) 263-2840 (D)
(916) 263-2890 (BOFE)

Salinas
21 West Laural Drive
Suite 69 93906
(415) 557-7878 (D)
(415) 557-7878 (BOFE)

San Bernardino
303 West Third Street
Room 140 92401
(909) 383-4333 (D)
(909) 383-4336 (BOFE)

San Diego
8765 Aero Drive
Suite 120 92123
(619) 637-5500 (D)
(619) 637-5520 (BOFE)

San Francisco
30 Van Ness Avenue
Room 3400, 4400 95113
(415) 557-7878 (D)
(415) 557-7878 (BOFE)

San Jose
100 Paseo de San Antonio
Room 120, 126 95113
(415) 557-7878 (D)
(415) 557-7878 (BOFE)

Santa Ana
28 Civic Center Plaza
Room 625 92701
(714) 558-4111 (D)
(714) 558-4114 (BOFE)

Santa Barbara
411 East Canon Perdido Street
Room 3 93101
(805) 568-1222 (D)

Santa Rosa
50 "D" Street
Suite 360 95404
(707) 576-2362 (D)

Stockton
31 East Channel Street
Room 317 95202
(209) 948-7770 (D)
(209) 948-3616 (BOFE)

Van Nuys
6150 Van Nuys Boulevard
Room 200 91401
(818) 901-5312 (D)

DLSE Claim Form (English)

STATE OF CALIFORNIA — DEPARTMENT OF INDUSTRIAL RELATIONS
DIVISION OF LABOR STANDARDS ENFORCEMENT
STATE LABOR COMMISSIONER

INITIAL REPORT OR CLAIM

FOR OFFICE USE ONLY		
TAKEN BY	PROCEEDING NUMBER	ACTION
DATE TAKEN	PROGRAM	SOURCE	IND. CODE
	DO	BOFE	1 2 3	
FIELD INVESTIGATION REFERRAL		
REFERRING OFFICE		DATE

PLEASE PRINT ALL INFORMATION

YOUR NAME	SOCIAL SECURITY NO.	NO. TAX EXEMPTIONS
YOUR ADDRESS — NUMBER AND STREET, APARTMENT OR SPACE NO., CITY, ZIP CODE	HOME PHONE NO. ( )	WORK PHONE NO. ( )
KIND OF WORK DONE (OCCUPATION)	DATE OF HIRE	CALIFORNIA DRIVER'S LICENSE NO.	DATE OF BIRTH
WORK DONE AT — NUMBER AND STREET, CITY, COUNTY, ZIP CODE	PUBLIC WORKS PROJECT? ☐ YES ☐ NO	WAS YOUR JOB UNION? ☐ YES ☐ NO

AGAINST

NAME OF BUSINESS	EMPLOYER'S NAME	☐ BANKRUPTCY ☐ BUSINESS SOLD ☐ INSOLVENCY
ADDRESS OF BUSINESS (INCLUDE ZIP CODE)		TELEPHONE NUMBER ( )
NAME OF PERSON IN CHARGE	TYPE OF BUSINESS	ESTIMATED NO. OF EMPLOYEES:	MINORS EMPLOYED? ☐ YES ☐ NO

WAGES — CONDITIONS OF EMPLOYMENT

RATE OF PAY — PER HOUR, DAY, WEEK OR MONTH (SPECIFY) $	PAID BY PIECE RATE? ☐ YES ☐ NO	DID YOU WORK SPLIT SHIFTS? ☐ YES ☐ NO
TOTAL HOURS WORKED PER DAY: PER WEEK:	PAID OVERTIME? ☐ YES ☐ NO	4 DAY / 10 HOUR WORKWEEK? ☐ YES ☐ NO	IF YES, WRITTEN AGREEMENT? ☐ YES ☐ NO
ARE YOU STILL WORKING FOR THIS EMPLOYER? ☐ YES ☐ NO	QUIT ☐ DISCHARGED ☐ ON WHAT DATE?	IF QUIT, DID YOU GIVE 72 HOURS NOTICE? ☐ YES ☐ NO	WERE YOU PAID AT TIME OF DISCHARGE? ☐ YES ☐ NO
HAVE YOU ASKED FOR YOUR WAGES? ☐ YES ☐ NO	IF YES, ON WHAT DATE?	CHARGED FOR SHORTAGES? ☐ YES ☐ NO	RECORD OF HOURS WORKED KEPT? ☐ YES ☐ NO
HOW WERE YOU PAID? ☐ BY CHECK ☐ IN CASH	GIVEN A DEDUCTION STATEMENT? ☐ YES ☐ NO	UNIFORM / TOOLS REQUIRED? ☐ YES ☐ NO	IF YES, FURNISHED BY EMPLOYER? ☐ YES ☐ NO
MEAL PERIOD: ☐ ON DUTY ☐ OFF DUTY	MEALS FURNISHED? ☐ YES ☐ NO	IF YES, WRITTEN AGREEMENT? ☐ YES ☐ NO	MEALS FURNISHED: ☐ BREAKFAST ☐ LUNCH ☐ DINNER
LODGING FURNISHED: ☐ INDIVIDUAL ROOM ☐ SHARED ROOM ☐ APARTMENT	RENTAL VALUE OF APT. TO PUBLIC $	CASH ADVANCES (IF ANY) $

GROSS WAGES CLAIMED (Do Not Deduct Payroll Taxes)

FROM (DATE) 19	TO (DATE) 19	NUMBER OF HOURS, DAYS, WEEKS OR MONTHS CLAIMED (SPECIFY)	
AT THE RATE OF — PER HOUR, DAY, WEEK OR MONTH (SPECIFY) $		SUB—TOTAL ➝	$

BRIEF EXPLANATION OF ISSUES (Use Additional Sheet If Necessary)

SUB—TOTAL ➝	$
MINUS TOTAL OF CASH OR CREDITS RECEIVED ➝	$
AMOUNT DUE OR BALANCE CLAIMED ➝	$

. . . .
. . . .
. . . .
. . . .
. . . .

I HEREBY CERTIFY that this is a true statement to the best of my knowledge and belief.

MY NAME MAY BE USED IN ANY INVESTIGATION. ☐ YES ☐ NO

(Signed) . . . . Date . . . .

Address: . . . .

DLSE 1 (REV. 1/91)   **INITIAL REPORT OR CLAIM**   91 61155

DLSE Claim Form (Spanish)

ESTADO DE CALIFORNIA—DEPARTAMENTO DE RELACIONES INDUSTRIALES
DIVISION DE ENFORZAMIENTO DE NORMAS LABORALES
COMISARIO DE LABOR DEL ESTADO

**REPORTE INICIAL
O RECLAMO**

PARA USO DE OFICINA SOLAMENTE		
TAKEN BY	PROCCEDING NUMBER	ACTION
DATE TAKEN	PROGRAM	SOURCE	IND. CODE
	DO BOFE 1 2 3	
FIELD INVESTIGATION REFERRAL		
REFERRING OFFICE	DATE	

PORFAVOR ESCRIBA A MOLDE TODA INFORMACION

SU NOMBRE | NO. DE SEGURO SOCIAL | NO. DE EXONERADOS DE IMPUESTOS:

SU DIRECCION — NO. Y CALLE, APARTAMENTO O NO. DE ESPACIO, CIUDAD, ZONA POSTAL | TELEFONO — CASA | TELEFONO — TRABAJO

CLASE DE TRABAJO QUE HACE (OFICIO) | FECHA DE EMPLEO | NO. DE SU LICENCIA DE MANEJAR DE CALIF. | FECHA DE NACIMIENTO

TRABAJO HECHO EN — NO. Y CALLE, CIUDAD, CONDADO, ZONA POSTAL | PROYECTO DE OBRAS PUBLICAS? ☐ SI ☐ NO | SU EMPLEO ERA DE UNION? ☐ SI ☐ NO

EN CONTRA

NOMBRE DEL NEGOCIO | NOMBRE DEL PATRON | ☐ BANCARROTA ☐ VENDIO EL NEGOCIO ☐ INSOLVENTE

DIRECCION DEL NEGOCIO (Incluye Postal Zona) | TELEFONO

NOMBRE DE PERSONA A CARGO | TIPO DE NEGOCIO | APROX. NO. DE EMPLEADOS: | MENORES EMPLEADOS? ☐ SI ☐ NO

SUELDO — CONDICIONES DE EMPLEO

TASA DE PAGO — POR HORA, DIA, SEMANA O MES (ESPECIFIQUE) $ | PAGADO POR PIEZA? ☐ SI ☐ NO | TRABAJA JORNADAS DE TRABAJO DIVIDIDA EN DOS TURNOS? ☐ SI ☐ NO

TOTAL DE HORAS TRABAJADAS POR DIA: POR SEMANA: | LE PAGABAN TIEMPO SUPLEMENTARIO? ☐ SI ☐ NO | 4 DIAS / 10 HORAS A LA SEMANA? ☐ SI ☐ NO | SI ES QUE SI, ACUERDO POR ESCRITO? ☐ SI ☐ NO

AUN SIGUE TRABAJANDO POR ESTE PATRON? ☐ SI ☐ NO | ☐ ABANDONO ☐ DESPIDIERON EN QUE FECHA? | SI LO ABANDONO, DIO UD. 72 HORAS DE AVISO? ☐ SI ☐ NO | LE PAGARON CUANDO SE LE DESPIDIO? ☐ SI / ☐ NO

HA SOLICITADO SU SUELDO? ☐ SI ☐ NO | SI ES QUE SI, EN QUE FECHA? | LE COBRARON POR DEFICITS? ☐ SI ☐ NO | REGISTRO DE HORAS TRABAJADAS QUE TENGA CONSERVADAS? ☐ SI ☐ NO

COMO LE PAGABAN? ☐ CON CHEQUE ☐ EN EFECTIVO | LE DIERON UN INFORME DE DEDUCCION? ☐ SI ☐ NO | UNIFORME / HERRAMIENTA REQUERIDA? ☐ SI ☐ NO | SI ES QUE SI, PROPORCIONADA POR EL PATRON? ☐ SI ☐ NO

PERIODO DE COMIDA: ☐ MIENTRAS TRABAJA ☐ FUERA DE TRABAJO | COMIDAS PROPORCIONADAS? ☐ SI ☐ NO | SI ES QUE SI, ACUERDO POR ESCRITO? ☐ SI ☐ NO | COMIDAS PROPORCIONADAS: ☐ DESAYUNO ☐ ALMUERZO ☐ COMIDA

ALOJAMIENTO PROPORCIONADO: ☐ HABITACION INDIVIDUAL ☐ HABITACION COMPARTIDA ☐ APARTAMENTO | VALOR DE RENTA DEL APT. AL PUBLICO $ | ADELANTOS EN EFECTIVO (SI ALGUNO) $

GANANCIAS EN BRUTO RECLAMADAS (No Descuente Impuestos De Nomina De Pago)

DE (FECHA) 19 | A (FECHA) 19 | NUMERO DE HORAS, DIAS, SEMANAS O MESES RECLAMADOS (ESPECIFIQUE)

AL PAGO DE — POR HORA, DIA, SEMANA O MES (ESPECIFIQUE) $ | SUB-TOTAL ➔ $

BREVE EXPLICACION DE LOS ASUNTOS (Use Papel Adicional Si Es Necesario) | MENOS EL TOTAL DE DINERO EN EFECTIVO O CREDITOS RECIBIDOS ➔ $

| CANTIDAD PAGADERA O BALANCE RECLAMADO ➔ $

....

....

....

....

....

YO POR LA PRESENTE CERTIFICO, Que esta es una declarcion verdadera segun mi concocimiento y creencia.

MI NOMBRE SE PUEDE USAR EN CUALQUIER INVESTIGACION. ☐ SI ☐ NO

(Firma) ....

Direccion .... Fecha ....

DLSE 1-S (REV. 2/91) INITIAL REPORT OR CLAIM (SPANISH)

I-9 Form (INS)

U.S. Department of Justice
Immigration and Naturalization Service

OMB No. 1115-0136
Employment Eligibility Verification

Please read instructions carefully before completing this form. The instructions must be available during completion of this form. **ANTI-DISCRIMINATION NOTICE. It is illegal to discriminate against work eligible individuals. Employers CANNOT specify which document(s) they will accept from an employee. The refusal to hire an individual because of a future expiration date may also constitute illegal discrimination.**

Section 1. Employee Information and Verification. To be completed and signed by employee at the time employment begins

Print Name: Last	First	Middle Initial	Maiden Name

Address (Street Name and Number)	Apt. #	Date of Birth (month/day/year)

City	State	Zip Code	Social Security #

I am aware that federal law provides for imprisonment and/or fines for false statements or use of false documents in connection with the completion of this form.

I attest, under penalty of perjury, that I am (check one of the following):
- [ ] A citizen or national of the United States
- [ ] A Lawful Permanent Resident (Alien # A _____)
- [ ] An alien authorized to work until ___/___/___ (Alien # or Admission #

Employee's Signature	Date (month/day/year)

Preparer and/or Translator Certification. (To be completed and signed if Section 1 is prepared by a person other than the employee.) I attest, under penalty of perjury, that I have assisted in the completion of this form and that to the best of my knowledge the information is true and correct.

Preparer's/Translator's Signature	Print Name

Address (Street Name and Number, City, State, Zip Code)	Date (month/day/year)

Section 2. Employer Review and Verification. To be completed and signed by employer. Examine one document from List A OR examine one document from List B **and** one from List C as listed on the reverse of this form and record the title, number and expiration date, if any, of the document(s)

List A	OR	List B	AND	List C
Document title:				
Issuing authority:				
Document #:				
Expiration Date (if any): ___/___/___		___/___/___		___/___/___
Document #:				
Expiration Date (if any): ___/___/___				

CERTIFICATION - I attest, under penalty of perjury, that I have examined the document(s) presented by the above-named employee, that the above-listed document(s) appear to be genuine and to relate to the employee named, that the employee began employment on (month/day/year) ___/___/___ **and that to the best of my knowledge the employee is eligible to work in the United States. (State employment agencies may omit the date the employee began employment).**

Signature of Employer or Authorized Representative	Print Name	Title

Business or Organization Name	Address (Street Name and Number, City, State, Zip Code)	Date (month/day/year)

Section 3. Updating and Reverification. To be completed and signed by employer

A. New Name (if applicable)	B. Date of rehire (month/day/year) (if applicable)

C. If employee's previous grant of work authorization has expired, provide the information below for the document that establishes current employment eligibility.

Document Title: _____ Document #: _____ Expiration Date (if any): ___/___/___

I attest, under penalty of perjury, that to the best of my knowledge, this employee is eligible to work in the United States, and if the employee presented document(s), the document(s) I have examined appear to be genuine and to relate to the individual.

Signature of Employer or Authorized Representative	Date (month/day/year)

Form I-9 (Rev. 11-21-91) N

Workers' Compensation Claim Form

State of California
Department of Industrial Relations
DIVISION OF WORKERS' COMPENSATION

Estado de California
Departamento de Relaciones Industriales
DIVISION DE COMPENSACIÓN AL TRABAJADOR

EMPLOYEE'S CLAIM FOR WORKERS' COMPENSATION BENEFITS

PETICION DEL EMPLEADO PARA BENEFICIOS DE COMPENSACIÓN DEL TRABAJADOR

If you are injured or become ill because of your job, you may be entitled to workers' compensation benefits.

Complete the "**Employee**" section and give the form to your employer. Keep the copy marked "**Employee's Temporary Receipt**" until you receive the dated copy from your employer. You may call the Division of Workers' Compensation at **1-800-736-7401** if you need help in filling out this form or in obtaining your benefits. An explanation of workers' compensation benefits is included on the back of this form.

You should also have received a pamphlet from your employer describing workers' compensation benefits and the procedures to obtain them.

Si Ud. se ha lesionado o se ha enfermado a causa de su trabajo, Ud. tiene derecho a recibir beneficios de compensación al trabajador.

Complete la sección "Empleado" y entregue la forma a su empleador. Quédese con la copia designada "Recibo Temporal del Empleado" hasta que Ud. reciba la copia fechada de su empleador. Si Ud. necesita ayuda para completar esta forma o para obtener sus beneficios, Ud. puede hablar con la Division de Compensación al Trabajador llamando al 1-800-736-7401. En la parte de atrás de esta forma se encuentra una explicación de los beneficios de compensación al trabajador.

Ud. también debería haber recibido de su empleador un folleto describiendo los beneficios de compensación al trabajador lesionado y los procedimientos para obtenerlos.

Any person who makes or causes to be made any knowingly false or fraudulent material statement or material representation for the purpose of obtaining or denying workers' compensation benefits or payments is guilty of a felony.

Toda aquella persona que a proposito haga o cause que se produzca cualquier declaracion o representación material falsa o fraudulenta con el fin de obtener o negar beneficios o pagos de compensación a trabajadores lesionados es culpable de un crimen mayor "felonia".

Employee: *Empleado:*

1. Name. *Nombre.* _____   Today's Date. *Fecha de Hoy.* _____

2. Home Address. *Dirección Residencial.* _____

3. City. *Ciudad.* _____   State. *Estado.* _____   Zip. *Código Postal.* _____

4. Date of Injury. *Fecha de la lesión(accidente).* _____   Time of Injury. *Hora en que ocurrió.* _____a.m._____p.m.

5. Address and description of where injury happened. *Dirección/lugar dónde occurió el accidente.* _____

6. Describe injury and part of body affected. *Describa la lesión y parte del cuerpo afectada.* _____

7. Social Security Number. *Número de Seguro Social del Empleado.* _____

8. Signature of employee. *Firma del empleado.* _____

Employer—complete this section and give the employee a copy immediately as a receipt.
Empleador—complete esta sección y déle inmediatamente una copia al empleado como recibo.

9. Name of employer. *Nombre del empleador.* _____

10. Address. *Dirección.* _____

11. Date employer first knew of injury. *Fecha en que el empleador supo por primera vez de la lesión o accidente.* _____

12. Date claim form was provided to employee. *Fecha en que se le entregó al empleado la petición.* _____

13. Date employer received claim form. *Fecha en que el empleado devolvió la petición al empleador.* _____

14. Name and address of insurance carrier or adjusting agency. *Nombre y dirección de la compañía de seguros o agencia administradora de seguros.* _____

15. Insurance Policy Number. *El número de la póliza del Seguro.* _____

16. Signature of employer representative. *Firma del representante del empleador.* _____

17. Title. *Título.* _____   18. Telephone. *Teléfono.* _____

Employer: You are required to date this form and provide copies to your insurer or claims administrator and to the employee, dependent or representative who filed the claim within **one working day** of receipt of the form from the employee.

SIGNING THIS FORM IS NOT AN ADMISSION OF LIABILITY

Empleador: Se requiere que Ud. feche esta forma y que provéa copias a su compañía de seguros, administrador de reclamos, o dependiente/representante de reclamos y al empleado que hayan presentado esta petición dentro del plazo de un día hábil desde el momento de haber sido recibida la forma del empleado.

EL FIRMAR ESTA FORMA NO SIGNIFICA ADMISION DE RESPONSABILIDAD

Original (Employer's Copy)
DWC Form 1 (REV. 1/94)

ORIGINAL (Copia del Empleador)
DWC Forma 1 (REV. 1/94)

Index

David Hurd
Attorney at Law
3172 Airport Road
Placerville, CA 95667
Tel: (530) 626 9518
Fax: (530) 626 6727

EMPLOYMENT QUESTIONNAIRE (Please Print)
Do not fill out those items that are not relevant to your particular situation. This questionnaire is designed to obtain preliminary information regarding a variety of situations.

1.   Name_____Date _ / _ /
2.   Address_____
3.   City _____State_____Zip Code___
4.   Home Phone ( )   _
        Work Phone ( )   -
5.   Person to contact if you cannot be reached:
        Name_____   Phone ( ) _____
6.   Name of former employer_____
7.   Type of Business_____
8.   Date started (/   /   /)
        Last Position_____
        Salary $_____ per _____
9.   Name of Employer_____
10.   Address_____
12.   City_____Zip Code_____
13.   What kind of business is this employer in?_____
        _____
14.   How many employees work in the company? (include part-
        time) _____
15.   What date did you begin employment there?_____
16.   What date did you stop working at this job? _____
17.   When did you first learn your employment would be
        terminated?_____

18. What was the last position you held with this company?___
_____

19. What was your last salary or wage? $_____per_____

20. Name and job title of your last supervisor_____
_____

21. Does this employer have written personnel policies or
procedures or employment rules and regulations?_____
Do you have copies?_____

22. Does this employer have an Employee Handbook?_____
Do you have a copy?_____

23. Does this employer provide written performance evalua
tions?_____
Do you have copies of evaluations? _____

24. Did you ever receive any commendations or letters or
memos telling you that you are doing a good job? _____
_____

25. Did you ever receive raises and/or promotions from
this employer?_____If so, briefly describe:_____
_____
_____

26. Did you ever received disciplinary action(s),___
suspension(s)__, or warning(s)___ of poor performance?
-If yes to any of the above, explain, giving dates:_____
_____
_____
_____
_____

27. What is your complaint:_____
Termination?_____; Forced resignation?_____
Harassment? _____; Demotion?_____
Denial of Pay/Benefits?_____; Other? _____
_____

28. What reason was given by the employer for its action(s)?__
_____
_____

29. What do you think was the real reason?_____

_____

_____

30. Do you feel that the treatment you received was due to discrimination?_____; Race or Origin?__ Age? _____; Sex?_____ ; Religion?_____; Physical Handicap?_____; Marital Status?_____; Medical Condition?_; Other?_____

31. Do you feel that the treatment you received was due to your reporting misconduct or illegal conduct to either manage ment or public authorities? - If so, what did you report and to whom?_____

_____

_____

32. Do you feel the treatment you received was due to some other reason?_____ If so, what was the reason?__

_____

_____

33. Were you given any warnings before you were terminated? _____If so, when, by whom and what about?_____

_____

_____

34. Do you have any evidence, or have you heard any conversa tions from anyone that would indicate that a manager, or person of authority, or another employee at your place of employment said anything bad about you? In other words, anything defamatory or slanderous? Any comments that you are not a company person, that you are untrustworthy, that you did something wrong, etc. Person's name? Phone number?_____

_____

_____

_____

ADMINISTRATIVE PROCEDURES

35. Did you inform anyone in management of your problems? If so, what is the name and title of the person(s) informed?

_____

_____

_____

36. Does the company have a grievance or complaint proce dure?_____If so, did you file a complaint?_____ When?_____With whom?_____ What happened?_____

_____

_____

37. Were you a member of a union? _____If so, what is the name of the union and the local?_____

38. Have you filed a charge with EEOC?_____ When?_____

39. Have you filed a charge with DFEH? _____When?

_____

40. Do you have a copy of your charge?_____(If so please enclose)_____

41. What is the status of your charge?_____

_____

42. Have you received a Right to Sue letter from either the EEOC or the DFEH? _____When is the letter dated?_____

43. Have you applied for unemployment benefits?_____ When?_____

44. Did your employer oppose your application for benefits?

_____

45. Did anyone appeal the initial decision of the unemployment office?_____If so, who_____

46. Was a hearing held before a Judge?_____When?_____

47. Has there been a decision?_____(If so, please enclose).

48. Have you sought any treatment or counseling as a result of your employment problems?_____If so, provide names, addresses and telephone numbers of persons consulted and

the dates of treatment:_____

_____

_____

_____

_____

_____

49.   If we accept a case for you, what do you hope to accomplish?_____

_____

50.   Do you have any witnesses who will help you?_____List the names, addresses and telephone numbers:

_____

_____

_____

_____

_____

_____

51.   Summarize the facts surrounding your complaint. (Add any other information you think is pertinent).

For Example:

        Jan 1, 1989– I am hired at Acme Co.

        Mar 13, 1991– I get into an argument with my manager Joe Smith

        July 2, 1992- I transfer out of Smiths work group

        Nov 30, 1993- I am promoted to first level sales group

        Sept 10, 1995- Smith is transferred to be my new manager once again

        Oct 3, 1995- I receive my first bad review

        Oct 7, 1995- I complain about Smith to Human Resources

        Dec 1, 1995- Company is cutting back. I am laid off by

Order Form

To Order:

Make your check or money order payable to:

Pro Per Publications

Mail your check or money order to:

Pro Per Publications
3172 Airport Rd
Placerville, CA 95667

Company Name:_____

Your Name:_____

Address:_____

_____

City:_____

State:_____Zip:_____

No. of Copies desired:_____

Payment:

Price per copy---------------------$17.95 $_____

Sales Tax per copy for books ----$1.30 $_____

Postage----------------------------$1.75 $_____

Total (per book)-------------------$21.00 $_____

For priority U.S. Mailing, add---$1.50 $_____

Please ship me **The California Employee Survival Handbook.** I understand that if I am dissatisfied for any reason, I may return the book(s) for a complete refund.